D1253761

AMERICAN EDUCATION

Its Men,

Ideas

and

Institutions

Advisory Editor

Lawrence A. Cremin
Frederick A. P. Barnard Professor of Education
Teachers College, Columbia University

The
Educational Frontier

William H. Kilpatrick and Others

ARNO PRESS & THE NEW YORK TIMES
*New York * 1969*

Reprint edition 1969 by Arno Press, Inc.

*

Library of Congress Catalog Card No. 70-89194

*

Manufactured in the United States of America

Editorial Note

A MERICAN EDUCATION: *Its Men, Ideas and Institutions*
presents selected works of thought and scholarship that have
long been out of print or otherwise unavailable. Inevitably, such
works will include particular ideas and doctrines that have been
outmoded or superseded by more recent research. Nevertheless,
all retain their place in the literature, having influenced educational thought and practice in their own time and having provided
the basis for subsequent scholarship.

Lawrence A. Cremin
Teachers College

The
Educational Frontier

THE EDUCATIONAL FRONTIER

WRITTEN IN COLLABORATION

BY

WILLIAM H. KILPATRICK (*Editor*)
Professor of Education, Teachers College, Columbia University

BOYD H. BODE
Professor of Education
Ohio State University

JOHN DEWEY
Professor Emeritus of Philosophy
Columbia University

JOHN L. CHILDS
Assistant Professor of Education
Teachers College, Columbia University

R. B. RAUP
Associate Professor of Education
Teachers College, Columbia University

H. GORDON HULLFISH
Professor of Education
Ohio State University

V. T. THAYER
Educational Director
Ethical Culture Schools

D. APPLETON-CENTURY COMPANY

INCORPORATED

NEW YORK   LONDON

PRINTED IN U. S. A.

FOREWORD

This book results from the union of two lines of events. On the one hand, the authors in relative independence had individually concluded that the social-economic situation now makes the outstanding demand on education. On the other, the National Society of College Teachers of Education requested of them a yearbook in the philosophy of education.

The initial decision was to deal directly with the social-economic situation and its interaction with education, and in this way to show the philosophy of education properly at work. It was further agreed to present as far as possible one unified treatment rather than a collection of separately written essays. What here appears is the result of these decisions. Extended conferences have sought through earnest discussion to effect a single outlook and a consistent argument. The actual writing, however, has perforce been apportioned, with no effort to "iron out" individuality. The observant eye will accordingly discern amid obvious differences of style some remaining differences of emphasis.

In the sense thus explained, the several chapters may be assigned as follows: Chapter I to Professor Bode; Chapter II to Professors Dewey and Childs, a joint product of thought written out by Professor Dewey; Chapter III to Professor Raup; Chapter IV to Professor Kilpatrick; Chapter V to Professor Hullfish; Chapter VI to Professor Hullfish and Dr. Thayer, the former doing the writing; Chapter VII to Dr. Thayer; Chapter VIII to Professor Kilpatrick; Chapter IX to Professors Dewey and Childs, again as before. Professor

Kilpatrick has served as editor with the help of Professors
Raup, Childs, and Hullfish.

The hearty thanks of the authors are hereby tendered to
Miss Marion Y. Ostrander, Secretary of the Committee, for
her generous and helpful contribution to the making of the
book.

The authors offer this book to their fellow members of the
profession and to all thoughtful citizens with the most earnest
hope that it may serve to foster thinking in what seems surely
to be the chief problem of our times.

TABLE OF CONTENTS

THE EDUCATIONAL FRONTIER

Chapter I

THE CONFUSION IN PRESENT-DAY EDUCATION

IT is a favorite pastime among educators to discourse on the progress of education in the United States. This amiable indulgence is entirely natural. The mounting figures on enrollments and on expenditures would have seemed wholly incredible if they had been predicted a few short decades ago; they are scarcely credible even now when we view them as accomplished facts. Along with this expansion there has come an expansion in the curriculum that is equally overwhelming. From the first grade to the graduate school our educational system exhibits a hospitality to every form of human interest that is as broad as the Christian principle of charity. Our faith in education has become a faith akin to the faith of religion.

The major causes that have contributed to this phenomenal development lie close at hand. Technological progress has put new premiums on education. The urbanization of the population has created demands on the school that were formerly met in the home. The economic, political, and social problems arising out of present-day conditions require a kind of insight and disposition which we expect to come in large part from the schools. Discussions ranging all the way from the observance of traffic regulations to world peace have a way of terminating in the conclusion that the problem in hand is, in the final analysis, a problem of education, and, more specifically, a problem of the schools.

If we note next how the schools adapted themselves to this rising tide of demands, we are in a position to see both how our

3

educational system has become needlessly cumbersome and how it has become involved in a sorry confusion of purposes or aims. The cumbersomeness is a natural result of the tendency to meet new demands by the simple process of adding new courses without engaging in any basic reconstruction of the curriculum. If, for example, the pressure for a new subject, like music or art or commercial geography, became sufficiently strong, the situation was met by the expedient of adding new courses and special teachers. If children were found to have no proper sense of the value of money, school banks and lessons in thrift were provided. If patriotism became a matter of concern, flag drills and the like were made part of the program. If business men complained too vigorously that the graduates of the schools were deficient in the three R's, the subject-matter was carefully combed so as to eliminate useless material, and more attention was given to drill. If a health movement got under way in the community, a course in this subject was placed on the books. Whenever something is found to be lacking, the favorite remedy is to start an agitation for an extension of the curriculum. The following passage from a newspaper article is an illustration:

"What practical courses in social life and citizenship has a State Department of Education prescribed for the public schools of its state? What Board of Education has made any provision during the past year for teaching the practical duties of good citizenship, for the formation of right character? They have appointed special teachers for athletic training, for music, art, dramatics,—but who takes classes once a week to discuss with the boys and girls the ways and art of living with others in school and out? What principal has any plan for his teachers doing it?"

The result of this general tendency has naturally been to produce a curriculum containing a bewildering variety of more or less unrelated "subjects." New subjects were added as occasion arose, without disturbing those which were already in the curriculum, except to require them to move up so that the new-comer might have a seat along with the rest.

By and large, then, the general trend of this development as it proceeded was to make the curriculum a reflection of various specific and correspondingly unrelated interests exist-ing outside of the school. In terms of schoolroom procedures, this tended toward a segregation of aims or objectives. The three R's were classed as tool subjects, with the main emphasis on skill. Physiology was perhaps dominated by the idea of health. In history the emphasis shifted toward the acquisition of a certain body of information; in civics the idea of citizen-ship was uppermost. In vocational courses the guiding idea was occupational efficiency; in literature it was appreciation; in science it was method, and so on along the line.

This natural tendency was reinforced by the protective atti-tude of the interests outside the school. Patriotism, for ex-ample, in the sense of loyalty to our existing institutions, must be kept separate from sentiments of pacifism or interna-tionalism. Moral and religious standards must be protected against the apparent implications of the natural sciences or psychology. Our economic order must be kept inviolate from criticisms emanating from political or economic history. In a word, this pressure from outside vested interests, being all in the direction of keeping the aims or values represented in the curriculum segregated or compartmentalized, became a source of intellectual confusion and insincerity. Conflicts could be avoided most easily by maintaining this compart-mentalization, in much the same way that a clergyman can avoid trouble by confining himself to "preaching the gospel" and staying away from business and politics. Plain sincerity, as expressed in clear thinking, was sacrificed to expediency.

In the days of our prosperity this device of compartmental-ization was like the answer to a maiden's prayer. The Ameri-can people, on the whole, were too well satisfied with their institutions and with themselves to find any serious fault. Hence compartmentalization was suited admirably to the circumstances. It was a device which made it possible to accommodate every new interest that seemed entitled to serious consideration, without disturbing the arrangements that were already in operation. We were too fatly prosperous to have any yearnings for reform. In other words, we had no desire to discover the confusion in our aims and purposes. More recently, however, we have been assailed with misgivings. A civilization that shows so many major maladjustments must have something seriously the matter with it. There probably never was a time during the past century when the American people were less sure of the essential finality of their institutions than they are at the present moment. But what is it that is wrong? On this point we seem to be pretty much at sea. For this situation education, owing to its own inherent confusion, must accept a large measure of responsibility.

If we take another look at our educational system, we can discover at least a partial reason for our confusion and apparent helplessness. Our educational practice of compartmentalization not only keeps basic problems out of sight, but adds to the difficulty of locating them. At present, for example, our millions of unemployed are curiously disposed to take their misfortune as merely "hard luck," to be endured as best they can. Since history shows that depressions are bound to occur periodically, there seems to be nothing that can be done about it. Depressions are part of the cosmic weather. They classify along with droughts and floods and earthquakes and all those occurrences which lawyers call "acts of God." That such views should prevail when we are dealing with a phenomenon which is so obviously a matter of social organization, pure and simple, is passing strange. It betokens a complete inability to conceive of an industrial system except as based on competition and motivated by the desire for personal profit.

This obtuseness is too complete to be dismissed offhand as the product of human stupidity. Education, in this instance, must have come to the assistance of nature. Our practice of compartmentalizing different values, both in school and out, has not merely fostered the habit of thinking in terms of fixed patterns, but has provided inhibitions, in case there is any tendency to depart from these patterns. We are willing, for example, to devote much effort and money to the relief of unemployment, but we seem incapable of dealing with the causes of unemployment, because, forsooth, this would involve a departure from our tradition of economic individualism, which we are called upon to maintain in the interests, not of business, but of loyalty to our ideals of citizenship, and perhaps loyalty to our ideals of morality and religion.

The consequence of such education is that we acquire an insensitiveness to contradictions in beliefs and practices which would otherwise be quite unintelligible. A business man, for example, who has become thoroughly grounded in the notion of business as based on competition and as being incompatible with sentiment, joins the Rotary Club, where he absorbs the idea that business should be conducted in the spirit of service. How these different conceptions harmonize with one another is not immediately apparent to the unaided eye, but they seem to dwell together in the same bosom without causing any disturbance. Or a person brought up with traditional religious beliefs may also adopt the scientific belief that even the most trifling details of this universe of ours are determined by natural law; yet he may remain completely untouched by what is commonly called the conflict between science and religion. Or again, we insist that people must regulate their conduct in accordance with their best insight and conscience, but we grow indignant when pacifists undertake to put our teachings into practice. The belief in anything is apparently not regarded as a bar to the belief in its opposite.

This state of affairs is astonishing evidence of the adaptability of the human mind. Logically it is impossible to believe that a thing is round and also to believe that it is square, but psychologically there does not seem to be any particular difficulty about it. All that is needed is to keep these beliefs in separate compartments and to use them in turn, as may be convenient. This gives us a wide range of freedom and protects our self-respect. The beauty of this arrangement is exemplified by the testimony given by a colored man at a prayer meeting, which was to the effect that, while he had robbed henroosts and got drunk and slashed folks with razors, he never, thank God, had lost his religion.

Our national history indicates that as a people we have disposed of public problems in much the same way that the colored man dealt with the problems of his personal life. We adopted at the outset a philosophy of freedom and equality and announced that government must rest upon the consent of the governed. We did not, however, apply this doctrine to the slaves at the time the Constitution was adopted nor to the South at the time of the secession nor to the Philippines when they staged an insurrection. But did we admit at any time that we had lost our religion? Not for a moment! These other matters were treated under different labels. Slavery was a "peculiar institution"; the Civil War was necessary to preserve the Union; in the Philippines we manfully assumed the White Man's Burden. As a people we have made mistakes, of course, but fortunately nothing has happened to disturb our complacent conviction that we have kept the faith delivered unto us by the Fathers.

This complacency is possible only because we do not permit our beliefs to come into collision with one another. If it were not for this precaution, we might not find it so easy to live with ourselves. The business man, for example, is apt to be resentful of governmental interference. He regards this as an

infringement on what we call our rugged American individualism. Yet, as recent writers have pointed out, the government
is constantly under pressure from business interests to make
regulations, and this pressure has been applied so long and so
successfully that the whole notion of rugged American individualism is simply a myth. But if this seems inconsistent,
we need only distinguish between wholesome regulation and
meddlesome interference, which is a distinction that each
man can make for himself and as may suit his convenience.
When we try to protect our rugged individualism, it is of
course only harmful interference that we have in mind.

To add another illustration, we have long prided ourselves
on our standard of living in the United States. In times of
depression, so it is argued, every citizen should try to maintain
his standard of living, not merely as a privilege, but as a
patriotic duty. By spending freely we maintain a market for
our factories and thus contribute to the prosperity of the
community. According to this reasoning, thrift is no longer
a virtue. To save up for a rainy day has become selfish and
out of keeping with the American spirit. Perhaps this has a
certain plausibility, but on the other hand, what is to be
done when people grow old and are compelled to retire from
work, when unemployment befalls them as a result of sick-
ness or business depression or for other reasons? Shall we
provide for such contingencies by unemployment insurance or
old-age pensions? It appears that we cannot go that far, because such measures would be an unreasonable burden on business or would amount to a governmental dole, which is likewise out of keeping with the American spirit. Every person
must expect to take care of himself. Just how these views are
to be reconciled is not entirely clear, but it is reassuring to
know that it is being done. Perhaps the best advice to be given
under such circumstances is the kind which an old lady gave to

a friend who had suffered a serious misfortune: "You must take it philosophically; don't think about it."

Taking things "philosophically" in this sense means that we do not see them in their bearings or implications. We teach the duty of obeying the law, for example, but it does not usually occur to us that the Boston Tea Party or the "Underground Railroad" of ante-bellum days were flagrant instances of flouting the law. What considerations should determine obedience to law? Or, to take one more illustration, we have modeled our conception of democracy after the New England town meetings and so have evolved the absurdity known as the "long ballot." No one would seriously propose, however, that a vote should be taken on every item of a tariff bill, or on the specifications for a new battleship, even if it could be done conveniently. Those are matters for experts. Our notion of democracy is in part a hang-over from the past and in part a product of modern conditions, which means that we have no respectable philosophy of democracy at all. As long as basic confusions of this kind are kept out of the picture, we just muddle along without realization of the damage that is being done and without profiting greatly from experience.

Fortunately there appears to be a growing sense that something is lacking. The average man is more sensitive than before to the need of some kind of chart or compass by which to shape his course. For good or for evil, the power of authority is waning. The home, the church, and the community no longer exercise the influence over men's minds that they did in times past; they do not, to the same extent, furnish ready-made patterns for thought and conduct. The immediate result of this change is confusion and also a greater tendency to look to education for guidance. Our schools, and particularly our institutions of higher learning, are naturally supposed to be the appropriate agencies for clarifying our vision, for pointing the way to a good life. The expectation is reasonable, but unfortunately our schools are in precisely the same fix as our average man. They too have become victims of compartmentalization, the price of which is confusion. They undertake to provide a "good" education, without any clear notion of what such an education would be like if it could be had.

This confusion becomes apparent if we trace the development of our present conception of general or liberal education. For this purpose the middle ages furnish a convenient point of departure. In those distant times, so Huxley tells us, "Culture meant saintliness—after the fashion of those days; the education that led to it was of necessity, theological; and the way to theology lay through Latin." [1] Whatever the limitations of such an educational scheme, it clearly had the merit of definiteness. In its own way it provided a plan for an inclusive and unified way of life.

This intimate concern with a "way of life" continued as a characteristic and differentiating trait of liberal education for a long time to come. The Revival of Learning, with its emphasis on the glories of ancient Greece and Rome, was essentially a change of content rather than a change of type. Here again a way of life was mapped out, with a high degree of simplicity and clarity. The good life was made to center on the appreciation of the languages, the spirit, and the cultural achievements of antiquity. The simplicity of this program was, indeed, somewhat marred by the necessity of harmonizing it with the spirit of otherworldliness embodied in the medieval conception of saintliness. But after a time a reconciliation was somehow achieved, and so the way was prepared for the conception of the Christian gentleman, which became especially popular with denominational colleges and set a new pattern for education.

With the rise of modern science, however, a more serious

[1] Essay on "Science and Culture."

situation presented itself. The advent of science precipitated a prolonged struggle between "humanism" and "naturalism." The cultivation of the physical sciences seemed to have no very direct bearing on one's way of life. Science can indeed make us acquainted with many curious and interesting facts; it can shed light on our origin, on the constitution of the atom or the solar system, or what not. But all this is, in a sense, irrelevant to the business of living. Science as science is just knowledge; it is of no great concern to any one, except the specialist, until it has been made over into a way of life.

This, at any rate, was the position maintained by Matthew Arnold. When it became impossible to deny to science a place in the curriculum, he sought earnestly to lay down certain stipulations regarding the nature of that place. Science was to come in, not on terms of equality, but as handmaiden to the divinity yclept literature. The task of relating science to other interests in such a way as to give it a human meaning was to be reserved for literature and more specifically the classics.

"For the generality of men there will be found, I say, to arise, when they have duly taken in the proposition that their ancestor was 'a hairy quadruped furnished with a tail and pointed ears, probably arboreal in his habits,' there will be found to arise an invincible desire to relate this proposition to the sense in us for conduct and to the sense in us for beauty. But this the men of science will not do for us, and will hardly even profess to do. They will give us other pieces of knowledge, other facts, about other animals and their ancestors, or about plants, or about stones, or about stars; and they may finally bring us to those 'general conceptions of the universe, which are forced upon us all,' says Professor Huxley, 'by the progress of physical science.' But still it will be *knowledge* only which they give us; knowledge not put for us into relation with our sense for conduct, our sense for beauty, and touched with emotion by being so put; not thus put for us, and therefore, to the majority of mankind, after a certain while, unsatisfying, wearying." [2]

[2] Essay on "Literature and Science."

How science has disregarded this apostolic injunction to keep within its proper place is known of all men. Instead of being humbly content with a seat at the foot of the throne, it proceeded forthwith to establish itself as an independent potentate. The ideal of knowledge for its own sake proved to be stronger than the notion of knowledge as a means to a way of life. *Scholarship* and *scientific method* became terms to conjure with, and presently even literature began to pay tribute to the parvenu in the form of doctoral theses on literary topics, produced in a humble and frequently unedifying attempt to conform to the strictest canons of scientific research. Everybody became so thoroughly cowed that scarcely a voice was raised to question the transcendent merit of the passion for Truth. And so another dimension was added to the temple of culture. The god of culture had grown into a trinity— piety, literary appreciation, and knowledge; with a strong hint that the greatest of these is knowledge.

This development, be it noted, marked a definite break with the older ideal. The conception of education as centering on a way of life no longer dominated the situation. Science set its own standard, which was of a very different kind. Having lost this first battle, traditionalism then proceeded to lose another, which completed the rout. In the wake of science came technological and industrial development, bringing with it new demands on education. New courses gradually found their way into the curriculum, ranging all the way from problems of capital and labor to bee-keeping and advertising. By this time the idea of education as a way of life had receded into the background and the defense for these new departures was made chiefly on the ground that they embodied applications of scientific method and had practical utility. In other words, utility, like science, began to insist on its own standard of value. Utility meant pecuniary profit, with no nonsense about it. Teachers nurtured in the older tradition had an uncomfortable feeling that there was something wrong about all this, but they had become so befuddled and demoralized that they were prepared to yield if the pressure was sufficiently strong.

The net result of all this is that our conception of general education has become a collection of odds and ends for which it is impossible to have any profound respect. Instead of recognizing this fact, however, our schools have been dominated largely by a spirit of ancestor-worship. We have tried to be as faithful to the memory of the fathers as circumstances would let us be. Theological matters have lost much of their prominence in the curriculum, but we still accord them a certain measure of benevolent protection. The ancient prestige of the classics has waned, but we have done the next best thing by insisting on extensive requirements in modern languages and by hardening our hearts against the grumblings of this perverse generation. On the other hand, we have made large concessions to science, but in extenuation it may be pleaded that the scientific attitude of devotion to truth holds in common with traditional culture the spirit of detachment from practical affairs. The concessions to the spirit of utility are perhaps harder to defend. The plain fact there is that we have come upon conditions and circumstances of which our ancestors never dreamed, and the pressure has been too much for us. "The woman whom thou gavest to be with me, she gave me of the tree, and I did eat."

In view of this development, it is no wonder that there has been increasing dissatisfaction with the idea of "general" or "liberal" education, as represented, for example, by our colleges of liberal arts. Its original unity of purpose has been completely lost. This fact can scarcely be disguised by vague talk about the "breadth" or "background" to be obtained from a college education. The vaunted "breadth" is not so much breadth as a confusion of breadth with variety. We have incorporated a number of diverse values into the curriculum by a process of compartmentalization. We teach a little of everything, and then we apparently expect the students to achieve out of the total mass of their learnings a synthesis which, up to the present, the college has been quite unable to achieve for itself.

This is bad enough, but it does not tell the whole story. The compartmentalization previously referred to becomes a means for concealing from the student the things that he is most in need of knowing, if he is to lead an intelligent life. The compartmental divisions tend to obscure the fact that these various values or interests are in serious conflict with one another. Traditional religion and traditional culture, for example, have never harmonized very well. The one has its center in a realm beyond the skies; the other in a domain that does not pretend to be anything but a product of the human mind. It is one thing to derive our patterns and our inspiration from the Lord; it is quite another to derive them from the contemplation of the masterpieces of art and literature with which we have landscaped the realm of our imagination. Traditional religion and modern science do not harmonize, despite all the "reconciliations" that have come off the press. Our traditional conceptions of conduct and personal development are hopelessly out of tune with modern industry and business, where the law of the jungle still holds sway. The students, like the college itself, have inherited all these discordant elements, and no concerted effort is made to set them straight. They come in adhering to all these diverse standards, and they go out in essentially the same condition. They have secured no basis for intelligent living. The various elements in their education tend to neutralize one another, and so the final result is apathy or intellectual and emotional paralysis.

In brief, the basic trouble with the modern college is that, like Stephen Leacock's horseman, it rides off in all directions at once. If the college of liberal arts is to survive, it must recognize that it is confronted by a problem that is essentially new. By and large, the educational patterns of earlier times were the outcome of social conditions and were supported by these conditions. At present we have a variety of such patterns, so that no one of them can set itself up as the model for our whole educational program. Neither religion nor literary culture nor science nor "social efficiency," as these patterns have been evolved, is adequate to all our educational needs. Nor can we comfort ourselves with the notion that an eclectic sampling of these various fields constitutes a respectable education. The accumulation of credits may qualify a student for graduation; it does not qualify him for intelligent living. Our college courses need to be so revised that, besides giving competency in their respective subjects, they will also contribute to a more basic reconstruction of thinking. In a word, college education should be concerned primarily with the task of assisting every student to develop an independent philosophy of life.

This statement of purpose or aim has an academic flavor, but its implications reach far beyond the academic domain. The different values or "patterns" maintain their relative isolation side by side in the college program, partly as a result of intellectual inertia, but also because they represent outside vested interests which insist on these separations. In other words, the college duplicates, in its own way, the vices of the social organization and helps to perpetuate them. In everyday life, business and service, patriotism and scientific thinking, unemployment relief and economic individualism, and religion and imperialism get along together pretty well if they are not permitted to mix. As long as they are kept apart, a person can accept them all and be very much at ease in Zion. Perhaps it is not too far-fetched to suggest that the curious lack of significant issues in the recent Presidential campaign, in these momentous times, is due in large part to this practice of compartmentalizing, to which the colleges have contributed their due share. There is no more effective device known to man for keeping troublesome issues out of sight. Conversely, a philosophy of life arrived at in the light of these inherent conflicts must necessarily, if it has any depth or meaning, be a kind of social gospel for the remaking of the world.

It is a hopeful sign that our colleges of liberal arts are beginning to recognize the need of reëxamining the whole concept of general or liberal education. Up to the present the levels of education below the college have been much more sensitive to this need than the college itself, although it must be admitted that they have usually failed to understand the nature of the difficulty. Thus the movement known as "scientific education" has been disposed to criticize traditional education on the ground of abstractness, without pausing to note that the traditional ideal is not only abstract but incoherent. Hence the proposals for reform were directed mainly to the task of transforming the abstract into the concrete or specific. Instead of undertaking a reinterpretation of old values so as to secure a unified way of life, the advocates of scientific education were content to show how each of these old values was to be realized in a concrete way. In other words, they accepted the old compartmentalization and developed it to the limit. Our colleges of liberal arts viewed this development with pious horror, but without the least suspicion that it was a case of chickens coming home to roost.

How are these old values to be stated in concrete terms? The answer to this question, so it was argued (and with considerable plausibility), can be found through a process of analysis. In vocational training, for example, analysis can inform us in great detail what particular items of knowledge and skills are necessary for the performance of specified tasks. In an analogous way it is possible, so it is held, to determine the items of knowledge and the skills, traits, and ideals which are necessary to perform the functions of a professional man, of the citizen, and of the parent. Again, this same procedure can reveal to us the ingredients of what is called culture. In brief, if we start with a compartmentalized value, it is theoretically possible to determine by analysis the equipment, in terms of knowledge, skills, traits, and ideals, that is necessary for its realization.

The logic appears to be sound; the trouble lies in the premises. Since the mind is not built on any such cash-register plan, the scientific investigator was presently led into a fearful bog, where he appears to be still engaged in analyzing his way out again. But he has already rendered education a real service in developing the implications of compartmentalization. To start with a set of separate values is to start with a set of standards that are already fixed, and so it becomes reasonable to argue that education must be based on an analysis of the "needs" of society. By analysis we can determine the nature and variety of the vocational demands that our educational system should keep in view; we can determine the degree and quality of proficiency which pupils should achieve in the various school subjects; we can determine the standards that should govern our judgments of right and wrong or good and bad, in matters of conduct and taste. But if we grant that the social order must be progressively remade to an undetermined degree, then this whole procedure is beside the mark.

It is not intended to imply, of course, that such analyses have no utility. For certain purposes they may be exceedingly useful. This point is simply that our enthusiasm for scientific analysis is converted into an excuse for avoiding the problem of a social philosophy. When our standards have once been determined, then scientific analysis may be an indispensable tool for discovering the conditions that must be met if the standard is to be realized. But when the standards themselves are in question, the situation is different. All that analysis can show is that certain people hold certain standards—in business, in government, in conduct, and in religion. The basic problems of our civilization have to do precisely with the remaking of standards; and if this fact is ignored, education becomes an instrument for maintaining the *status quo*.

That such remaking of standards is intentionally excluded from consideration is indicated in the following statement which is attributed to a prominent advocate of "scientific" education:

"The school is not an agency of social reform. It is not directly concerned with improving society. Its responsibility is to help the growing individual continuously and consistently to hold to the type of human living which is the best practical one for him. This should automatically result in an enormous improvement in society in general. But this improvement is not a thing directly aimed at. It is only a by-product." [3]

If we turn now to the movement known as "progressive education," we seem to come upon a conscious effort to escape from compartmentalization. The central emphasis falls on the "continuous reconstruction of experience," which is opposed to all forms of compartmentalization or regimentation. This reconstruction of experience, if it is to have any significance, must take the form of actual living and doing. Consequently the school must be transformed into a place where pupils go, not primarily to acquire knowledge, but to carry on a way of life. That is, the school is to be regarded as, first of all, an ideal community in which pupils get practice in coöperation, in self-government, and in the application of intelligence to difficulties or problems as they may arise. In such a community there is no antecedent compartmentalization of values. Shopwork, for example, is not dominated by the idea of personal profit, but becomes a medium for the expression of

[3] *Good Housekeeping,* September, 1929, editorial page.

esthetic values and social aims. The quest for knowledge is not ruled by the standards of research, but is brought into immediate relation with human ends. Judgments of conduct are not based on abstract rules, but on considerations of group welfare. Hence it can be maintained with some plausibility that in a school of this kind we are actually engaged in developing a generalized pattern of conduct or a way of life.

Let us grant that the idea is sound as far as it goes. If it is to go the whole way, however, the school environment must be so set up that the way of life cultivated in the school will be maintained and extended when the pupils pass on from the school environment to the larger social environment outside of the school. Here we strike the difficulty that the school environment is, of necessity, more or less isolated from the larger environment. In the life of the school, at least as hitherto conceived, there is not only no place for the struggle to make a living, but none for the basic conflicts of economic, political, social, nationalistic, and religious interests and creeds that harass our present civilization. In fact, one reason why the school is regarded as an ideal environment is precisely that the pupils are protected against these conflicts and struggles. In other words, the environment created by the progressive school does not provide automatically for the reinterpretation or integration of those major values which are kept asunder by the present nature of our social organization. In some cases, at least, our progressive schools seek to escape from compartmentalization, not by a reconstruction of the values concerned, but by taking refuge in an environment in which compartmentalization plays no significant part.

This criticism will perhaps be met with the reply that the habits formed in these progressive schools will carry over into the larger environment and operate so as to promote a reconstruction of the social pattern. The notion, however, that habits of coöperation, consideration of others, recognition of responsibility for group welfare, and the like will spontaneously undo the effects of compartmentalization, that they will automatically bear fruit in the form of insight into the limitations of our economic, religious, and other standards, involves a strain on our credulity. Because a factory owner has the habit of consulting freely with his employees, we can scarcely expect him to challenge the existing economic order. The doctrine of formal discipline, in its palmiest days, never made a larger claim than this for transfer of training. On the other hand, if we say that the situation in the outside world is to be brought into the school through "vicarious experience" and in the form of "description," we are not much better off. In that case the whole process of reasoning by which this type of education is supported comes apart in the middle. It starts with the contention that education must take the form of living and doing, instead of relying on mere information, and it ends with the conclusion that second-hand information will function in the shaping of disposition and the remaking of the social order.

The intent of the foregoing criticism is not in the least to challenge the general point of view embodied in progressive education, nor yet to maintain that progressive education has failed completely to grasp the problem of the relation between school and society. The purpose is rather to envisage this problem more clearly. We seem to be confronted with a dilemma. On the one hand we cannot make the school a complete reproduction in miniature of the social order. To do this would be to remove all justification for having a school at all. On the other hand, we cannot be content with a school that deals with the outside world merely in the form of "description." This would reintroduce all the mechanization and regimentation from which we are trying to escape. Is there a way out?

If we are sufficiently optimistic, we may find that we have not merely one way, but at least two ways, out of the difficulty. At present the school and the social order stand too far apart. They are relatively isolated from each other, because their respective concerns appear to be unrelated. If we could devise a program or kind of activity in which both could join, this separateness would disappear and education would take on a new vitality and a new effectiveness.

For an illustration let us turn for a moment to Russia. From a distance, at any rate, it appears that the gap between school and society has been pretty well bridged over. The outstanding trait of the general situation, for our present purposes, is the fact that the schools and the social organization are engaged in a common program. This program consists in remaking the institutions and the psychological attitudes of a great and tremendously diversified nation in conformity with the pattern of communism. In order to carry through a purpose of this kind, the leaders of the revolution cannot afford to permit any serious criticism of the principle that lies back of their program. As long as this principle is not questioned, discussion and criticism are permitted and even encouraged, but the principle itself, like Cæsar's wife, must remain above suspicion.

Given these conditions, it is possible to evolve a program for making both the collective activities of the nation and the activities of the schools converge upon a common purpose. To make men center their hopes and fears on the here instead of the hereafter, to make the possession of wealth a badge of shame instead of a mark of good fortune, to portray the menace of capitalism, to stimulate morale for the success of the Five-Year Plan—these and other matters are strategic points in the plan of campaign, both inside the school and out. The same atmosphere pervades the schoolroom and the factory. There is no problem of continuity because the social order and the school are both being made over in the same image. Communism is made synonymous with patriotism and religion, and it brings adults and children together in a common enterprise.

There is little cause for wonder that such a situation should appear attractive to the pedagogic mind. Under conditions such as those which prevail in Russia, the teacher may expect to get an abundant measure of satisfaction out of his work, provided, of course, that he is in whole-hearted sympathy with the basic program. He need never have any serious trouble about making his subject-matter "vital" and "concrete"; he will always have a sustaining sense that he is not merely a purveyor of information but a co-worker in a magnificent enterprise. If we could establish a social program, in the manner of Russia, our educational problems would largely disappear. It is true, of course, that there is no immediate prospect of anything like that happening in this country. But should we set before us, as the ultimate goal of our efforts, the establishment of a social program of some kind, which must not be questioned by anybody and which shall direct and shape both our school and our out-of-school activities?

Before we draw any such conclusion, let us glance briefly at certain counter considerations. It seems evident that a program of this kind, if it is to be more than a collection of platitudes, must develop a psychology akin to the psychology of wartime. As in Russia, it must breed a pervasive sense of danger from without and danger from within. This sense of danger undoubtedly develops a fine spirit of solidarity, as well as other admirable qualities, but unfortunately it also develops other qualities that are not so fine, as we know from our experiences in connection with the recent war. A cause that will tolerate no criticism makes it a virtue to trample human values under foot if they get in the way. When the cause of human rights becomes a dogma, it gradually ceases to be humane. Grant if you like that, despite the cost, a new and better Russia will emerge in the end. Grant also that, in view of all the circumstances, Russia has chosen the best road. Even so, we can afford to bear in mind that the new disposition or attitude wrought into the structure of the nation by this ordeal of fire is bound to exhibit a certain lack of sensitiveness to human values for a long time to come. Militant dogmatism may bring blessings, but it is also a scourge. It warps and militarizes at the same time that it achieves its aims. And when the sense of external pressure disappears, together with the need of espionage and similar controls, the program will degenerate into the same kind of fatuous and futile traditionalism that we have to-day.

Educationally speaking, the great danger and weakness in the Russian experiment is that no provision is made for the reconstruction of attitudes or beliefs as a means of progress. When we begin to operate with fixed principles, there is trouble ahead. In this country it has resulted in the spectacle that, in a world of change, any significant departure from familiar principles, such as free competition and private profit, is apt to be regarded not only as incredible but as rank heresy. Loyalty and patriotism are identified with stand-pattism; the Daughters of the American Revolution, as some one has remarked, are not likely to become mothers of a revolution. We talk about a changing civilization, but we have not really grasped the idea of change. The present is not, like the past, regarded as a period of transition; it is the end of the road, the final goal of progress.

As was suggested above, another road is open to us. The lack of an inclusive social policy or program does not automatically preclude the possibility of promoting greater continuity between the school and the outside world than we have at the present time. A certain degree of continuity has, of course, been secured already. When pupils attain insight into the processes by which men are enabled to provide themselves with food, shelter, protection against disease, and the like, they cease, to that extent, to be utter strangers to their surroundings and they are presented with the opportunity to become participants, emotionally, in man's struggle to control his environment and to build himself a better civilization. Participation, as the Russian experiment suggests, means partisanship; it means concern for the success of a common enterprise. If we can extend the range of this partisanship so as to make it result in the destruction of our traditional compartmentalization, then participation will take the form of sharing in the task of improving our social aims. Instead of starting with a fixed standard or creed as a basis for shared activity, we should focus attention on the problem of remaking our standards in order to conserve values which have developed a disagreeable tendency to cut each other's throats.

An illustration of this tendency is furnished by recent writers on American history. As they point out, the fact that, up to a comparatively recent date, this country always had a frontier was a strong influence in shaping our basic attitudes. As long as there was a frontier, it was always possible to identify equality of opportunity with the opportunity to go out and exploit the resources of this hinterland on the same terms as everybody else. In other words, equality of opportunity became linked up with economic individualism, and to this combination we attached a halo by calling it "our American way of life." With economic individualism thus fortified against attack, other things follow as a matter of natural consequence. Economic teachings that do not square with this view are un-American and should be suppressed; depressions must be endured in a spirit of patient resignation; relief for unemployment must not be extended to cures for unemployment. Because equality of opportunity has been merged with economic individualism, there is no realizing sense that equality of opportunity, under present conditions, is progressively fading out of the picture. We have taken so much satisfaction in making the lion and the lamb lie down together that we fail to notice the disappearance of the lamb.

In brief, a survey of our economic development would seem to indicate that equality of opportunity does not mean what it meant a hundred years ago. In those earlier days the argument that free competition among individuals served to develop desirable qualities or traits had some plausibility. But now great industrial and economic units have come upon the scene, and in them the individual tends to become submerged. Our "American way of life" has disappeared or, at any rate, is fast disappearing; and no appeals or sentimental attachment to the past can alter that fact. Genuine loyalty to the past does not mean opposition to change, but an active concern for the kind of change that will reconstruct what is valuable in our tradition so as to suit present conditions.

If equality of opportunity is to be preserved, the purposes or aims of our economic and industrial organizations must be widened so as to include other considerations besides that of pecuniary profit. If, for example, the idea of public interest could become sufficiently powerful to secure action with reference to the elimination of depressions, of economic insecurity, of unemployment, and of undesirable methods of selling and advertising, our whole national psychology would undergo a corresponding change. Since these matters are of direct concern to the average citizen, whether he happens to be an employee under the organizations immediately concerned or a member of the general public, they would be discussed in the newspapers, on the platform, and at the dinner-table; we should gradually acquire the habit of regarding our economic and industrial life from the standpoint of public interest. This wide participation would obviously be analogous to the participation by the Russian people in the Five-Year Plan; and a similar analogy would exist with respect to the relation between our schools and the rest of the social order. Translated into social terms, the escape from compartmentalization would mean an attempt to reconstruct the social pattern, which would then become a matter of common concern to the school and to the public outside the school.

The analogy can be pushed still another step. A democratic procedure, like Russian communism, involves a definite creed or point of view, and, like all creeds, it "loads the dice" in certain respects. It assumes at the outset, for example, that coöperation, sharing, creative activity, are desirable qualities, and so it advocates the type of school organization with which progressive education has made us familiar. Second, it holds that all the values which enter into the process of reconstruction or reinterpretation must stand on their own merits with no special protection from the outside. In other words, it holds that the outcome of the reinterpretation must not be determined in advance so as to ensure special privileges for certain values as against the rest. This too is a definite creed, which could hardly expect to meet with universal acceptance.

This statement, however, of the presuppositions which determine democratic procedure in education also brings to light the distinctive feature that differentiates this procedure from the rest. This distinctive feature consists in the dictum that the individual must be permitted and encouraged to do his own thinking, to formulate his own social philosophy. It concedes in advance the possibility that some individuals will use the intellectual freedom which is accorded them to draw the conclusion that such freedom is reprehensible and a danger to society. Or, to state it differently, the reconstruction of values, without antecedent special privileges to any of them, may lead to the belief that certain values should be protected, that conclusions should be predetermined, that, in short, the democratic procedure is all wrong. Such an outcome might be considered regrettable from the standpoint of the school, but it could not be ruled out in advance without stultifying the whole idea of democratic procedure.

This implication of democratic procedure, it may be noted, has a direct bearing on the idea of "participation." In the Russian scheme, participation in the main means coöperation in the realization of a program that is laid out in advance. In our own schools the terms *participation* and *social* are all too frequently limited in the same way. Pupils are encouraged to participate or to be social by exhibiting a spirit of helpfulness. There is, however, a different and in some ways far deeper meaning of these terms. If we take these terms to refer to the *search* for a program, i. e., if we take them to mean sensitiveness to values and an active concern for the reconciliation and conservation of conflicting values, the individual acquires a certain new distinctiveness. We are then forced to take special note of the fact that this reconstruction of values is something that the individual must do for himself. The reconstruction may be socially motivated to any degree, yet it remains a personal matter. Participation may easily degenerate into a form of herd action, in which the finest fruits of education are lost to sight.

At present the day may seem far distant when the school and the general public will be engaged extensively in matters of common concern. Meanwhile the school must do what it can to relate its activities to the larger concerns of the social order. The best hope for the school, in this connection, is to become more sensitive than it has been in the past to the need of reëxamining our national tradition. In stressing the interdependence of individuals in this modern world, something can be done, even in the lower grades, toward pointing out the need for widening our purposes in industrial and economic enterprises and for reconstructing our conception of the universe in which we live. With regard to this latter point, certain contrasts could be introduced to prepare for a better understanding of our tradition. Thus Franklin's proof that lightning is electricity and acts in strict conformity to natural laws gains a large measure of its significance from the fact that people previously held, and to some extent still hold, a widely different view on this subject. The same may be said regarding the evidence that diseases are "natural" phenomena. Or, again, the suggestion arising from the progressive remaking of our physical and social environment that intelligence should be entrusted with the task of recreating our standards of conduct and of values in accordance with changing conditions is a subject of violent disagreement. These illustrations serve to provide a clue to the determination of both subject-matter and method, and also to suggest how the continuity of the school with the social order, upon which our progressive schools have rightly placed so much emphasis, may be widened and directed. Eventually this growing insight should culminate in the comprehension of the basic conflicts that are to be found in every major domain of life—in religion, in economics, in government, and in the field of private and social conduct.

As was stated previously, the primary concern of a democratic educational procedure is to stimulate a reconstruction of our beliefs and habits in the light of their mutual relationships rather than to predetermine the nature of this reconstruction. The reconstruction will gravitate naturally and inevitably toward a philosophy of life or a social outlook, and it will take place with such assistance and encouragement as the schools can provide, but not according to any prescribed pattern. In a scheme of this kind we find clues for the selection of subject-matter and for methods of teaching. Can it also be claimed that such a scheme will provide a basis for social progress? It is obvious that a program of this kind, if really carried out, would not lead in every case to the same kind of social outlook. On the contrary, differences in attitude or points of view that exist among our population would tend to become more sharply accentuated and defined. But since a common program of some kind seems to be necessary, how can we hope that this kind of education would contribute to it?

The objection is plausible but has no finality. The differences in attitude or points of view to which reference was made above have always existed among our population. These differences, however, have not prevented the nation—except in the matter of economic-industrial development—from moving, on the whole, in the direction of a richer and more significant democracy. The evidence of this trend is to be found in the nature of the development exhibited by governmental functions. By and large, this development shows a growing concern for the welfare of the common man. Recognition of the rights of the common man is the basic article in our national faith, a faith that has hitherto proved more potent than our differences and disagreements. Is there any reason to suppose that this faith will be less dynamic if it becomes conscious of its larger implications and opportunities, if it gains a vision of a world in which its dream has become a reality?

It may be repeated that the kind of education which has been discussed here would doubtless carry people further apart in some respects, that it would emphasize certain differences in points of view. The point is that it would also do much toward cultivating common understandings and purposes. The time was when a liberal education meant the possession of a common body of knowledge and a common outlook on life. That time has gone by. About the only common element in present-day liberal education is that the same number of credits may be counted toward graduation. Liberal education has ceased to emphasize the possession of such a common tradition. To inherit the tradition of democracy, for example, is not like inheriting the classical tradition; it is more like inheriting a lawsuit. Yet this disturbing fact offers the opportunity of regaining, in a different form, the sense of solidarity among educated persons which is so largely lacking at the present time. All education, whether "liberal" or "technical," should help to create a sense that our traditions require reconstruction and thus provide community of understandings and interests, regardless of its content. In so doing it widens the area of common purposes by weakening the antagonisms that spring from complacent short-sightedness and from stupid loyalties to the past. Real education humanizes men. It does so, however, not by moulding them into unthinking acceptance of preëstablished patterns, but by stimulating them to a continuous reconstruction of their outlook on life.

It is in this need for reconstruction that we find the new educational frontier. At present educators are insensitive to this need, in direct proportion to their pretensions of scientific impeccability or to their sentimental absorption in the development of the individual child. A new emphasis is necessary if scientific method in education and the concept of individuality are to become meaningful. It is necessary if education is to make its proper contribution toward safeguarding the future. Without the clarity of vision that such education can bestow, there is imminent danger that class interests will brush aside the common good, or that in the storm and stress of conflict we shall lose our way and follow after strange gods. As our national faith gains a clearer understanding of itself, it will be deepened and strengthened and the genius of the American people will be set free to make its distinctive contribution to the welfare and happiness of mankind.

Chapter II

THE SOCIAL-ECONOMIC SITUATION AND EDUCATION

I

THE confusions and conflicts which have just been dealt with grow out of the very conditions of American life. They exist in educational thought because they are traits of national opinion and conduct. For the same reason, the new educational emphasis which is asked for must grow out of forces actually at work in American life. We therefore now take up the discussion of the American social situation, past and present, and of educational theory and concepts, in their relation to one another.

Up to about the turn of the century, the most generally accepted statement of the aim of education was couched in terms of the individual: the complete and harmonious development of all the powers of the individual, physical, intellectual, moral. Then there occurred a significant shift. Increased emphasis was put in theory upon social aims and upon social forces and factors as means of realizing these aims. Education was presented as a process of transmission and reconstruction of culture; the dependence of the individual upon the resources, material and spiritual, of the collective heritage was stressed. The need for enabling individuals to take part in the task of a constantly changing society was put in the foreground of educational philosophy. The idea that the school should be itself a form of community life, and that this principle should be applied in discipline, instruction, and the conduct of the recitation, gained appreciable though far from universal recognition.[1]

This change in the underlying concepts of education gave promise of a type of educational philosophy which would have closer contact with the realities of present-day life than was possessed by the older theory. It contained within itself the seed of efforts to bring about a definite integration of activities within the school with the activities going on in the larger community beyond the school walls. The promise has not been realized in any substantial degree. Translation of the theory into effective practice has been attempted in other countries on a much larger scale than in our own. Emphasis upon the creative activity of individuals as a necessary *part* of the wider office of social reconstruction has been the element in the theory which has affected practice in this country in a serious way. In this form it has entered into the continuance of individualistic concepts, which is dealt with in the next chapter. What was the cause of this check and change? Why, even when the social concepts were retained in theory, were they treated in a way which left them mainly only a nominal force, their transforming effect on practice being evaded? Why were they so often used merely to justify and to supply a terminology for traditional practices? The reason which lies on the surface is that an abstract and formal conception of society was substituted for the earlier formal concept of the individual. General ideas like transmission and critical remaking of social values, reconstruction of experience, receive acceptance in words, but are often merely plastered on to existing practices, being used to provide a new vocabulary for old practices and a new means for justifying them.

[1] Emphasis on the earlier concept of the individual, though often in an enriched and emancipated form, is characteristic of much of our prevailing philosophy of education, especially in scientific and progressive education circles, this emphasis being marked since the close of the war. This tendency is discussed and criticized in the next chapter. Accordingly this chapter is limited to consideration of the socialized strand in educational philosophy.

Any social conception remains formal and abstract which is not applied to some particular society existing at a definite time and place. Factors of time and place do not receive recognition as long as nominal social conceptions of education are not connected with the concrete facts of family, industry, business, politics, church, science, in this country. If we are not to be content with formal generalities (which are of value only as an introduction of a new point of view), they must be translated into descriptions and interpretations of the life which actually goes on in the United States to-day for the purpose of dealing with the forces which influence and shape it.

Failure to accomplish this task results in an unconscious but deplorable lack of sincerity in prevalent educational philosophies. Theory made much of the need of participation in social activities and interests through breaking down the isolation of school from life. Actually pupils have been protected from too intimate contact with the realities of the institutions of family, industry, business, as they exist to-day. Just as schools have been led by actual conditions to be non-sectarian in religion, and thus have been forced to evade important questions about the bearings of contemporary science and historical knowledge upon traditional religious beliefs, so they have tended to become colorless, because neutral, in most of the vital social issues of the day. The practical result is an indiscriminate complacency about actual conditions.

The evil goes much deeper than the production of a split between theory and practice and the creating of a corresponding unreality in theory. Our educational undertakings are left without unified direction and without the ardor and enthusiasm that are generated when educational activities are organically connected with dominant social purpose and conviction. Lacking direction by definite social ideals, these undertakings become the victim of special pressure groups, the subject of contending special interests, the sport of passing intellectual fashions, the toys of dominant personalities who impress for a time their special opinions, the passive tools of antiquated traditions. They supply students with technical instrumentalities for realizing such purposes as outside conditions breed in them. They accomplish little in forming the basic desires and purposes which determine social activities.

The deeper and more enduring education, that which shapes disposition, directs action, and conditions experience, comes not from formal educational agencies but out of the very structure and operation of institutions and social conditions. During the earlier—the pioneer—period of American life, these social forces were for the most part unified, and they operated quite directly upon individuals. The school specialized in providing what life in general failed to furnish in an adequate way: namely, the instrumentalities of learning. Schools, in spite of their seeming remoteness from life about them, actually supplemented that life in an admirable way.

The causes which brought about the confused diversification of the earlier simplified and unified office of the school also explain why the social concepts of education were relegated to a formal plane and were not applied in the special conditions of our place and time. Social life has been too confused and divided to encourage this translation. On the one side, the influential forces at work in industrial and business activities, so influential as to be dominant upon the whole, are directly antagonistic to the social ideals professed in educational philosophy. On the other side, the lag in school practice due to inertia and to maintenance of older conceptions of the cultivated gentleman prevents the adequate recognition within the school of the part played by science and technology in modifying, even revolutionizing, conduct and belief outside the school.

It is our conviction, accordingly, that (1) any educational philosophy which is to be significant for American education at the present time must be the expression of a social philosophy and that (2) the social and educational theories and conceptions must be developed with definite reference to the needs and issues which mark and divide our domestic, economic, and political life in the generation of which we are a part.

The demand upon educational theory has both a critical and a constructive side. Theory must face present realities in their discords, defects, and perversions. But it must also face them with an eye to detect the new forces which are operative, the new patterns which are forming. With respect to individuality, it will not only recognize that individuals now find their lives disintegrated because of absence of defined and unifying objects of loyalty, but it will also consider the ends now forming which may bring unity and order into belief and action. It must search out, in other words, the forces and patterns which, if they were promoted, would on the one hand remake society and on the other enable individuals to find themselves as they find a place within a society which is in process of forming.

The demand for a philosophy of education which shall grow out of intelligent acknowledgment of both the conflicts and the new-forming patterns of social life did not find its origin in the present crisis. But one aspect of it is illustrated by a breakdown so great as to compel consideration of needs and problems that were more easily covered from view in days of complacent "prosperity." An example of what is meant may be drawn from one aspect of present economic society. The crisis has affected untold numbers of teachers very directly. They face a demand to use their income for relief of relatives and friends, for general relief of the unemployed, at the very time when their salaries may be in arrears or seriously cut. These facts might be dismissed as part of a general situation which concerns teachers only as it concerns all other citizens as constituent parts of an interdependent community. But there is another phase of the matter which surely has direct educational significance.

The general burden of taxation is so directly felt that there is widespread demand for drastic curtailment of educational services. There is an actual, not merely theoretical, danger that the most significant expansions of the last forty years in school activities will be seriously impaired. In some cities they are already undermined and eliminated. Under the plea of economy, there is already going on a reversion to the curriculum of the three R's. This is a question which affects education as education and not merely the fortunes of teachers and administrators within the school system.

Here assuredly is an illustration of the way in which economic conditions have such obvious impact upon the work of education that educators as educators need to become acquainted with the workings of our industrial and financial system; to discover what is wrong and why; and to be interested from the standpoint of their own calling in methods of social action that will improve conditions. As far as the depression tends to undermine, through its effect on the experience and development of millions of future citizens, what teachers are striving to accomplish; as far as it is a symbol of conditions which are hostile to the realization of educational aims, it is a definitely educational force which teachers have both the right and the duty to face and to reckon with. There is, however, danger that the very obviousness of the illustration just used will narrow our apprehension of the point illustrated. Change the instance from the time of *depression* to times when economic forces are working inequitably even when there is no marked depression, and from conditions which present themselves in the school to conditions which affect the life of children and youth out of school, and the principle still holds.

The illustration is taken from conditions which militate against the realization of educational aims. But the extension of the social philosophy of education into the realities of contemporary life should not be restricted to negative conditions. It is a commonplace that our country has an abundance of natural riches, that it has an extraordinary equipment of machinery, of skilled engineers and trained workers. It is well known that we have both the material and the human resources to give to all that degree of security and reasonable comfort in life which afford the physical basis for cultural development. Technically speaking, the crisis which is attacking the enriched curriculum is needless. The educator, then, as educator, not merely as human being and citizen, has a direct concern with all the positive agencies by which the work of education may be protected from adverse influence and rendered constructively effective. The philosophy of education must discover and ally itself with the social forces which promote educational aims, as well as uncover and oppose the vested interests which nullify ideals and reduce them to mere flourishes or to phrases on paper.

Only by such an extension of the intellectual and moral horizon of educational theory can the demands of the social conception of education be saved from unreality. Only in this way can those who consciously take on themselves the responsibility for transmitting and remaking social values carry their work forward. Only in this way can they experience the great emotional drive which is implicit in their function but which is now dulled by convention and dissipated by inner confusion and conflict.

It is for this reason that we are impelled to begin our exposition of educational philosophy with an account of the social institutions and arrangements which condition the work of education. Since these conditions exercise the greatest and most enduring educative (including miseducative) effect on the life experience and on the culture which prevails, any serious theory of education must begin with them rather than with the school system as such. Since the field is broad and complex, we shall approach it through an historical survey of the social scene. The object will be to elicit the essential elements in our national democratic tradition; to disclose the changes in our industrial life which have worked against them and have deprived them of vitality; and to indicate the potential forces which can be employed to give our historic social heritage new meaning and force under present changed conditions. In this way we shall arrive at a conception of the intrinsic nature of a democratic society educationally considered, and of the implications of the aims and values of such a society for the profession of education and the work of the American public school.

II

Human history records no expansion like that which has occurred in the United States in the less than 150 years of its existence. From the quantitative point of view the expansion is unparalleled. We have grown from a group of colonies on the Atlantic seaboard to continental size, from a few million to almost fifty times the original number. The qualitative change in the habits, occupations, interests, and values of the people is even more significant. The growth of the nation has coincided in time with the change known as the industrial revolution. Not only have the two been contemporaneous, but the United States has contributed more to effecting the transformation than has any other people, and it has experienced the consequences more fully. It is *the* industrialized nation, *par excellence,* of the world. In the past forty years the transformation has gone on at an accelerated pace, so that from an agrarian nation we have become a manufacturing and distributing people with the center of gravity transferred from open country to the congested city.

In the early days of our existence, the remoteness of the

American continent from Great Britain contributed to a spirit of political independence which was intensified by commercial conditions and was consummated in the formation of an independent nation. Both negative and positive conditions favored the development of a philosophy of free and representative government, a conception which at that time was new in the world. By sheer force of conditions the democratic idea grew to include much more than a republican form of government. It became a social ideal, asserting the right of all individuals to equality of opportunity and to the widest possible sphere of freedom of personal action unhampered by external interference and control. The belief that social welfare and progress were best served by allowing every individual a wide area of personal choice, initiative, and action was fostered by both internal and external conditions.

A century ago the population was sparse; land, with fertile fields, with forest and minerals, was abundant and unappropriated. Enormous natural resources invited human exploitation; individual energy was stimulated even to the point of reckless waste. A continent needed conquest, and the need excited and rewarded the ambition of all but the congenitally lazy and apathetic. Nature seemed to make equal opportunity for all a reality; it was easy to suppose that, barring illness and accident, individuals won or lost in the industrial race according to their own industry and ability. Individual success and satisfaction of social need bore a close relation to each other. Because of the abundance of unused natural wealth, the economic struggle of individuals was not so much against one another as with nature itself. In fact, individual initiative and enterprise, directed toward subduing a continent, had moral significance. The men and women who did their part in clearing away the forest, making roads, building habitations, churches, and schools, cultivating the soil, were rightfully sustained by a sense of social value. Personal success was not merely private. It was also a contribution to the improvement of community life. Outwardly, early American life seemed often lost in materialistic activity, but at that time this materialism was at least the basis for a possible new civilization in which all should share the goods of life more freely and more fully than in any prior state of society.

As long as life was predominantly rural, democratic ideals were readily embodied on the political side of community life. The old town meeting, as is often pointed out, was as close an approximation to political democracy as the world has ever seen. Neighbors who knew one another, who were judges of one another's characters and achievements, met to confer about matters of common interest: their own roads, their schools, their taxes. Public interests, being so largely local, were genuinely public; they were open, not concealed nor masked; they were close by, not remote; substantial, not shadowy. Problems might be difficult, but at least they came to citizens in terms of conditions which were familiar because they touched the lives of all citizens. It was natural to think of government as a coöperative effort of individuals to preserve initiative from being interfered with and to protect the fruits of private industry and skill. The subordination of political action and ends was a natural, an inevitable, product of the situation.

External conditions operated in exactly the same direction. The citizens of a country which had just won its independence by revolt against established government were inclined to look with jealous eyes upon all political authority. It was something to be watched, as having an inherent tendency to swell and to assume despotic power. Freedom was thought to be identical with limitation of powers of government. The conceptions of rights inhering in individuals as individuals prior to any social order, rights which set fixed limits to the sphere of government and for the sake of protecting which governments were called into being, awakened a natural response. In like fashion, the doctrine of *laissez faire* in economic matters seemed to express the actual conditions of American life and to set forth the conditions under which life might continue to prosper. From every point of view, individualism was the philosophy which set forth the intrinsic conditions and aspirations of American life in its early period.

Yet the original formulation and acceptance were also affected by the temporary factors growing out of conditions which were not eternal but which belonged to American life as it was lived on the large and as yet unutilized and unappropriated soil of the United States. Reckless abuse and waste of natural resources was bred; constant change developed into love for the excitement of aimless mobility; ruthlessness was not confined to dealings with physical nature but was carried over into dealings with fellow-men; wild speculation was always likely to encroach upon slow-going and patient industry. Complacency and undue optimism were the fruits of the comparatively easy success made possible by abundant gifts of nature. We have always been prone to attribute to the excellence of our chosen institutions and our own virtues of character results which for the most part should be attributed in fact to the circumstances in which our national life went on. The constant lure of new opportunities has rendered self-criticism an unwelcome diversion and a source of irritation.

In spite of all limitations, however, the earlier conceptions contained the core of that democratic idea which forms the distinctive ethical tradition of the United States. It includes the political aspect of democracy; this was definitely limited in the first part of the history of the republic but broadened out later to include the right and duty of every mature citizen of the country to participate in the government of his locality, state, and nation, on the ground that such participation both made the individual a better citizen and helped ensure that government would serve the public good. The democratic idea included also broader moral ideas, such as the equal right of every individual for opportunity to make his own career and develop his own personal being; moral individualism, which asserted the right of all to personal freedom of development without allowing fixed classes and castes to develop; faith in the possibility of an abundant life for all, not only materially but culturally; belief that government is an affair of voluntary organization for the common good, so that the people have the right to change their institutions when they find that they are failing to meet the common need, Jefferson and Lincoln agreeing that this right extends even to revolutionary action; faith in individual inventiveness and adaptability; an attitude which welcomes change as an omen of future good rather than resists it as a sign of degeneration from a superior past.

Such beliefs as these are integral in the national democratic tradition. They are denied by some who are skeptical about the soundness of democracy as a moral ideal; by some who appeal to biology as authority for the belief that a division of classes is inherent in human nature; by some on the ground that history has demonstrated that the ideas are unworkable; by others on the ground that experience shows that such ideas can be realized only in primitive, agrarian conditions, and that when society becomes complex and large fortunes are established, there must follow either anarchy or else a strong centralized oligarchy consisting of the economically successful members of society. Still others hold that the ideals can be realized only by a complete and violent revolution which will put total power in the hands of the proletariat. We are not concerned here to defend the democratic faith against either Fascist or Bolshevist attack. Not till we have turned our backs upon what is most significant and distinctive in the tradition of American life will these ideas be abandoned by the American people. But educators must concern themselves with forces which undermine and contract the essential elements of the democratic faith, which in the end may cause them to be destroyed in fact even when retained in name.

Our dominant individualism, in both its sterling and its less desirable aspects, found expression in the development of our public school system: in administration, in subject-matter, in methods, and in ideals. Even a brief consideration must note at least such factors as the following in the educational philosophy which, even when unformulated, operated in our schools and gave their dominant tone.

In the first place, remoteness from the sources of our inherited culture, distance from Europe, produced dependence upon special agencies for maintaining culture. Old-world culture was not deeply embodied in the customary indigenous arrangements of our daily life. It did not transmit itself vitally and unconsciously as it had done in the Old World where it originated and was at home. Hence there was a great, almost a superstitious, faith in schools as the special and almost exclusive organs for keeping intact the borrowed culture. Just as our excessive dependence upon law-making is the correlative of absence of stability in our exceedingly mobile community life, so our dependence upon schools has been the reflex of the precarious state of traditional culture.

But since, nevertheless, life was still going on and actual habits were being shaped by the occupations and interests which employed the time, energy, and serious efforts of men and women, there resulted a split between life and traditional culture. The schools, devoting themselves to mastery of distinctively intellectual tools, operated through the medium of a reverence for books, while life outside shaped character. Of course, something of this work is characteristic of school education wherever it exists. But the peculiar conditions of American life rendered attachment to the bookish tradition and to the importance of mere mastery of the linguistic tools of culture both thinner and firmer than it was elsewhere. Life in the open, in the neighborhood and local community, through participation in the duties of the home and the farm, through contact with industries still carried on by hand tools in the home and neighborhood and demanding individual skill acquired in actual apprenticeship, was the force which shaped character and which counted in the development of personality and power. The school had a precious but relatively specialized office to fulfill: to teach the three R's and to equip youth with the technical intellectual arms which life, especially under the conditions of pioneer life, failed to provide. A similar division of labor, amounting to dualism, was found in method. Life outside the school stimulated individual energy and ambition, possibly to an exaggerated extent. School was a place for passive acquisition. The chief business of the school was to help pupils absorb what they did not come in effectual contact with either at home or in the local community.

In the third place, the dominant purpose of school education was to prepare individuals for successful achievement, for getting on, in the struggle of life. Preparation for success, help in the struggle to "rise," was almost inevitably the function of the school in pioneer days. Parents made great sacrifices to send their children to school and keep them there in order that their children might have a "better chance in life" than they had had. It was everywhere taught that diligence and faithfulness in learning school lessons was the surest road to success in adult life. We laugh now at the legend that schoolchildren were once taught that each one who did his work properly had a chance to become the President of the United States. But the legend is genuinely significant of two traits that once marked American life: belief in unrestricted opportunity for all and belief that the school afforded the best and surest means for converting opportunity for personal success into a fact. The counterbalancing "social" factor was the belief that the literate person made a better citizen as a matter of course, since ignorance (identified with illiteracy) was admitted to be the source of poverty, crime, and other social defects.

At the same time, belief in the right of every individual to start equal in the race of life with other individuals, unhampered by conditions of birth or the economic status of parents, was a marked force in the spread of a universal and unified system of common schools, in the constant increase upward of provision of school facilities, and in making schools free, supported by public taxes, not by payment of fees. In the Western States, which were created after the establishment of national independence, the same idea operated powerfully in the institution of the educational ladder with the tax-supported State university at its apex. The social conception that the republican form of government required universal literacy and the conception of the moral claims of individuality united to create the ardent faith which has prevailed in the United States in the possibility and the necessity of state-supported education on a wide scale. In the region of education the idea of inherent limitation of governmental functions has not been permitted to interfere with collective action.

III

In contrast with the facts and forces of our earlier agrarian culture stand the transforming forces which came in with machine industrialization. The revolution in industrial affairs developed in this country at an extraordinary rate of speed. The new agencies which it provided for mass production, for the utilization of unused natural resources, and for the quick distribution of persons, materials, and commodities over a vast territory, answered so completely to the felt and obvious needs of the time that the advance of industrialization took on all the marks of an unplanned and inevitable advance of natural forces. Certainly no one foresaw, much less planned, its ulterior social consequences. Every one was busy in turning the new forces to immediate account in fulfilment of some immediate need.

Nevertheless—more correctly, all the more on this account—the industrial and financial transformation has affected every phase of social life. It has doomed many of our earlier habits and attendant aspirations and beliefs to extinction as surely as great geological changes have extinguished so many of the earlier forms of animal life. It has nullified our original democratic ideals *in the form* in which they were originally stated and held. It has introduced and caused to prevail forces which are totally alien to the practices and the beliefs of our old agrarian culture. It has created a multitude of problems which have to be solved by new methods of thought and action if the American tradition of equal opportunity and free development of all potentialities is to be kept from becoming a mere phrase. It has tended to limit the earlier individualism to the strictly economic sphere, substituting material gain for development of personal character, conceiving initiative, energy, and independence in terms of material success only, and distorting the struggle of man with nature into a competitive struggle against other individuals in which those who lose in the race are put on the level of physical means of production and distribution.

Much recent indoctrination from highly placed sources has identified the doctrine of American individualism with strictly economic activity of a competitive kind, and has taught that success in obtaining wealth is the natural measure and criterion of moral qualities. In many respects American youth have been taught to regard the men who acquire unusual material substance and the men who contribute to the production of wealth by new inventions and the like as the characteristically American personages to be admired and emulated. All that was conceived necessary to justify such teaching was that the persons in question were born poor or handicapped, instead of with silver spoons in their mouths, and made their way or "got ahead" by their own efforts. Probably nowhere in the world at any time has there been so much teaching of an intimate relation between moral qualities and material reward as in this country.

So effectually has the idea of intrinsic moral stamina been identified with individual effort in the economic area that the more privileged elements of society have constantly resisted all efforts at social insurance of workers, prevention of child labor, old-age pensions, etc., not primarily on the obvious ground that these measures might lessen profits, nor on the legal ground that they violated freedom of contract (an idea bound up with the natural rights conception), but always principally on the moral ground that they would weaken the moral fiber of sturdiness and independence of character. Even organized labor has opposed social legislation on the ground that it is better for workers to win benefits from their employers in a direct way than to have them conferred by "paternalistic" legislation, as they have chosen to call it. Meantime, however, employers did not permit their moral ideals to interfere with securing from government favors in tariffs and franchises, etc., while even these were justified on the ground that they provided more opportunities for laborers to work and to rise in the social scale.

The development of machine industry necessarily brought about concentration. This tendency is reflected in the growth of cities, and within the cities in the congestion of population in crowded quarters, only the especially well-to-do living in habitations exclusively possessed by themselves. This concentration is further seen in the shift of production of goods from small shops, where men worked together in close companionship, to huge factories with their impersonal character and with subordination of the mass of "hands" to superintendents and bosses, and to the general adoption of a semimilitary discipline. It is exhibited in all the phenomena of standardized mass production. It has led to the concentration of wealth in corporate forms in order to secure the capital needed to carry on mass production on a large scale and to relieve individual investors of undue personal risks. There has followed in turn the concentration of great wealth in the hands of the few, with an accompanying concentration there of effective power in the direction of social affairs, the setting of standards, the moulding of public opinion.

In spite of this practical transformation of social conditions, amounting to a revolution, the theories, watchwords, and slogans of the earlier agrarian period have been maintained and cherished. The industrial and commercial class which made use of governmental power for franchises and special favors had definite reasons for gaining control of governmental agencies. Corruption followed, inevitably. The *theory* of *laissez faire* has been constantly combined with the *practice* of "porkbarrel" government. Sometimes a considerable measure of public benefit resulted, as in the Homestead Acts which followed the Civil War. A frequent outcome has been an inextricable mixture of idealistic and materialistic motives and results. Thus the unrestricted policy of immigration was supported in part by genuine belief in the country as a refuge for the oppressed of all nations, the land of opportunity for those who had not had a chance, and in part by a desire for factoryfodder, for cheap and docile labor. The instance illustrates the peculiar union of general social planlessness and definite planning and control within limited private areas which has characterized much of American life.

In multitudes of respects, of which the matters cited are

sample instances, the earlier national ideals have under the impact of the new industrialism, been maintained in verbal form and in accompanying sentiment, often intense, while departed from or distorted in fact. In consequence they tend to become mere hold-overs having a strong emotional appeal which can be aroused and manipulated for special purposes, but do not give guidance in thinking and action chosen and directed by personal insight. These ideals need now to be reinterpreted in the light of changed and changing conditions.

We need to realize, in the first place, the nature and extent of the change effected by the industrialization of the country. The change has taken place so rapidly and in many ways so unconsciously and so unintentionally as far as the mass of persons are concerned (who have passively experienced its effects rather than actively directed its course) that almost all, including educators, retain intact old convictions and watchwords as if they were still applicable. Hence we are confused in the face of any emergency which social realities present to us. In our ideas and sentiments we live in the past, while we are compelled to act in the present. There is such disparity between the two that we are necessarily torn and divided without knowing what is the source of our difficulties. The conflict is especially marked in the case of those who profess liberalism; for their hopes and aspirations, being generous, make them concerned with the development of a better and more human future. But their intellectual tools and weapons, their conceptions of liberty and equality, of democracy and individualism, are derived from past conditions which have been destroyed by the industrialization of the country. Cynics and pessimists may argue that the basic conceptions are mere illusions. Those who have faith in the national tradition of democracy will desire to slough off whatever social changes have rendered inapplicable and to reinterpret the essential ideas in terms of present life. This work cannot be done apart from educational agencies.

There are, however, various ways of accepting the social conception of education in name and denying it in fact. One way is that of the academic intellectualist. He is sufficiently impressed with the vogue of the social concept to desire to attach himself to it; but in substance he remains a traditionalist. So he calls attention to the fact—and it is a fact—that number, linguistic forms, words, history, etc., the material of the accepted curriculum, are social tools, such important social instrumentalities that social life could not be carried on without them. Every other consideration and subject is, upon this educational philosophy, an "extra"; the school may be obliged to take it up, but that is only because some other institution is failing in its duty, not because it belongs in school. In principle the school is a fenced-off sanctuary devoted exclusively to "teaching" and "learning" the great intellectual means by which civilized society is maintained. Of course society would relapse into barbarism without the transmission of the arts, skills, and understandings which make up the traditional curriculum. The essential point of a social conception of education, however, is that these subjects be taught *in* and with definite reference to their social context and use; taken out of their social bearing, they cease to have a social meaning, they become wholly technical and abstract. It is then a mere matter of accident for what ends they are used outside of the conscious educational system. There is nothing to protect them from being tools of private advantage and material success, or even being put to anti-social use. Moreover, apart from reference to their place and function in social life, the educator has no guide to help decide what parts and aspects of the great complex of intellectual subject-matter shall be selected nor any guide in choosing the methods of instruction and discipline which build up attitudes in the pupils. The inevitable effect is conformity to and duplication of the existent order with all its limitations and evils.

Another method of avoiding the practical implications of the social conception consists in failure to take account of the changes which are going on in the concrete institutions of society and of the causes of these changes. Or, putting the matter positively, those who accept the idea that education is a social operation must, if their acceptance is sincere, consider how family life, the church, the production and distribution of goods, agriculture, the means and modes of amusement and recreation, ends and means in politics, have been affected by the development of science and technology, these being the two great causal forces at work. They must ask how far the changes which are taking place are themselves the inherent product of these forces, and how far they are the effects of beliefs and attitudes which are themselves the result of prior education of human nature and which therefore are capable of modification by change in educational aims and methods. In short, they must definitely orient the work of education, both critically and constructively, to the concrete social situation in its needs, defects, conflicts, and problems as well as in its positive achievements. The first step in the accomplishment of this task, without the performance of which education in the schools will remain aimless and confused, is a better understanding by the teaching profession of social issues with intellectual courage to face them.

This is not, of course, the place to consider in detail the nature of the modifications going on in family life and sex relations, in the church, business, commerce, finance, the press, the theater, and organized sport, government and politics, because of the impact of science and technology. And yet the substantial material and effective method of teaching must be determined on this basis. Otherwise a philosophy of education employing social concepts will inevitably become formal and tend to be an affair of phraseology without specific bearing on the conduct of the educational system. Science and machinery have affected the traditional doctrines of the church; they have profoundly modified family life in all urban communities; they have made child labor in factories sufficiently remunerative to call children away from school; they have taken multitudes of women from the home; they have left millions of children no place to play except the street; they have encouraged as a by-product the organization of gangs that easily become criminal; they have through physiology and psychology modified sex and parental relations; they have, in connection with the dominant motive of private profit, introduced on a large scale alluring forms of commercialized amusement that leave children and youth passive but excited at the time when they are also deprived of normal outlets for action. Close and vital contact with the realities of nature have been eliminated for youth in the cities and much reduced for those in the country, as standardized finished products of mechanical work constantly gain in distribution. Inventiveness in technical things, tools and machines, has been stimulated to a great degree, but inventiveness in social forms and methods has been discouraged rather than promoted. A certain degree of literacy has become a necessity, and so universal and compulsory instruction has been favored. But, at the same time, a premium has been put on control of reading matter and publicity devices by those who would gain the management of public sentiment and opinion. The public which is literate in use of linguistic tools but which is not educated in social information and understanding becomes a ready victim of those who use, for their own private economic and political ends, the public press. Direct pecuniary profit at the same time causes the public to be the recipient of an incalculable amount of trash and trivialities, esthetically if not morally degrading.

IV

These are casual illustrations of the immediate effect of the forces of science and technology upon basic customs and institutions of society. We cannot extend them here nor go into any detailed analysis. But it is necessary to consider some of the outstanding *mis*educative results which have attended the diversion of the earlier agricultural individualism into the competitive economic individualism of present society. For the school system has to reckon with the consequences both negatively and positively: negatively, since its own work is conditioned by them; constructively, since without a knowledge of them it cannot see clearly its own place and function in the making of a society whose institutions will have a better effect on the experience and the attitudes of its members.

1. They—science and technology—have helped form a society in which chronic insecurity is such a factor in the lives of the majority of men and women that the insecurity and the fear it engenders have come to be counted as the chief motives which drive men to work, achievement, and thrift. Under the very conditions in which stability and security are imperative needs of the masses, there has thus developed positive antagonism even to schemes of social insurance which might mitigate insecurity.

2. They have created a popular mentality which regards acquisitive motives as the normal ones in human nature and which correspondingly depresses activity that is moved by direct interest in work itself for its own sake, productive activity as such. Appeal to pecuniary profit is so universal and seemingly so necessary in a society like ours that other potential forces of human action are slighted and shoved out. The greater number of persons taking part in productive activity engage in it under such conditions that labor in itself is regarded as an evil to be endured for the sake of ultimate exter-

nal reward. Even the laboring classes do not regard it as the purpose of their organizations to achieve control of the conditions and plans of industry but merely to get increased pecuniary reward and reduced hours of labor, and if possible to bring it about that their offspring become members of the possessing and employing class.

The counterpart of this conception of productive activity as something to be undergone for reasons outside itself is that countless thousands believe that the real satisfactions and enjoyments of life are to be found in "leisure" which is thought of as a period of amusement and idle relaxation if not dissipation. It is but a short step from this attitude to the psychology of the racketeer and gangster whose motto is "get by the shortest possible course, the one which involves the minimum work and the maximum excitement."

3. Emphasis upon acquisition has intensified the motives which oppose to the greatest extent the tenor of all deliberate religious and moral teaching and create a state of ethical confusion and conflict. It has also exaggerated the significance of business and money, materialistic in comparison with cultural aims and values. It is not too much to say that the official and the popular views of human psychology have been seriously corrupted. Habits and attitudes which in fact are the product of social conditions interacting with native tendencies have been treated as if they were innate in the human make-up and incapable of modification. It is constantly repeated, and finally generally believed, that most men would not engage in productive effort unless driven by hope of personal gain or the pressure of imminent loss and disaster. The failure of Soviet Russia was, for example, predicted on the purely *a priori* ground that any system which tries to eliminate the profit motive *must* fail.

The extension of this theory of human motives was distinctly unfavorable to higher culture. Science came to be prized mainly because of its use in money-making applications and was correspondingly disregarded in its contribution to an enrichment of experience and to the method to be adopted in all matters subject to intellectual inquiry and test. Art tends to be pushed to one side as an extraneous adornment, valuable as an evidence of polish and of ability to engage in display and "conspicuous consumption." In other cases, art is deliberately cultivated simply as a means of escape from hard realities which overwhelm sensitive spirits. It is a matter of common notice that as a nation we are laggards in interest in ideas as ideas. Such interest as does exist is likely to be specialized and thin even when intense, or else is employed as a self-conscious emblem of superiority to the common herd. Interest in seeing ideas applied is of course an added value when the application is in the humane interests of life, but usually "application" is limited to economic matters, and the entire meaning of the "practical" is degraded by the limitation.

4. Emphasis upon individualism as primarily economic in character and as having value in other respects only in dependence upon the economic has induced apathy and incapacity of thought in collective matters. In spite of talk about regimentation and suppression of ideas, there was never a time in our history when as many persons had concern for intellectual things and strove to be critical in their thinking as now. But this thinking rarely takes social effect. Indeed, many intellectuals pride themselves upon keeping their thinking "pure" by keeping it remote from social problems and needs. In consequence, there is relatively little ability to think effectively upon collective matters to a collective effect. There is a painful contrast between personal culture and culture that is socially grounded and effective. In consequence, no small part of our present crisis is due to the fact that social belief and thought are dominated by convention and outworn tradition and by notions that are deliberately put in circulation by publicity agents of

the dominant pecuniary group. Our literature is marked by the growth of a critical and discontented spirit, but one which has contributed little to the integration of a new social culture.

5. Competitive tendencies in human nature are stimulated to an excessive degree. While the individuals may find their operation in conflict with official religious teachings as to the proper attitude to be taken toward one's fellows, the official intellectual apologists for our economic order teach that the whole social welfare is best promoted when every individual looks out for himself.

6. The whole tendency of the *laissez-faire* system, as this works in our industrial and financial life, leads to distrust of the effectiveness of planned endeavor to control social conditions. Substantial and active faith in intelligence is undermined by this distrust. A defeatist psychology comes to prevail as to the possibility of securing and maintaining social values by organized collective effort, while extreme phantasies are created as to the prospects of private and material success for the individual. The same psychology of intelligence which forms inventiveness has been stimulated in physical matters by our social arrangements. In the making of tools and mechanical devices we have been prominent, but there has been comparatively little inventiveness in social affairs. Here we have been largely content to depend upon tradition and accident. Nothing like as much creativeness has gone into the formation of ends and purposes as into mechanical means for ends externally determined. Since foresight and planning of consequences are conditions of a recognition of responsibility for results, an indirect outcome of the absence of systematic social planning is absence of any conviction of personal responsibility. When things go wrong on a large scale, the blame is put on uncontrollable natural and social forces, and the same forces are depended upon to bring a turn in the wheel of fortune. Because the individual does not participate in collective projects of

social planning and control, he feels himself submerged and paralyzed by forces too large and blind, apparently, for any control. The final result is a spirit of fatalism combined with one of reckless speculation.

7. Finally, there is generated a growing pessimism about the possibility and the value of democracy not only as a form of government but as a principle of social relations and organization. When industry and finance are managed autocratically and for private pecuniary gain rather than as coöperative enterprises for mutual service, political democracy, in a society so dominated by industry and finance as is our own, is inevitably degraded to something formal, external, more or less mechanical, and hence comparatively easily manipulated by those who have material prosperity as their goal. In their relative helplessness under the conditions of power conferred by concentrated wealth and consequent control of the machinery of production and exchange, the masses "rationalize" the decay of democracy on the theory that the small number of industrial captains in control will know how to spread the blessings of prosperity to others. Political democracy thus tends to become a shell. The old ideal endures in the form of a pathetic hope that under the régime of "equal opportunity" one's children at least will become members of the economically governing class. Non-participation in the direction of the work done by men and women breeds indifferent, routine, and passive minds.

v

The picture just drawn has been intentionally sharpened to bring out the darker side. Many qualifying and offsetting conditions have been omitted. This course has been taken not only because of limited space, but because the brighter features of the situation are constantly brought to our attention and are even used to cover up the blacker traits of our social organ-

ization and life. It might have been stated, in what has just
been said about the effect of our economic system upon mental
and moral dispositions and beliefs, that the breeding of an
uncritical optimism is essential to the perpetuation of the system. Even statistically and in so-called prosperous times, the
proportion of economic failures to successes is at least ten to
one, and it requires a continual stream of propaganda of success stories to prevent the rise of widespread doubts as to the
soundness of the system. The schools have repeated and represented the existing system with faithfulness, so that the
great need in the development of a directive educational philosophy is a clearer recognition of the needs and problems which
call for educational readjustment in connection with social and
industrial reconstruction.

An honest facing of the defects, needs, and unsolved problems of the situation will not, however, breed pessimistic hope-
lessness as to the possibilities of a rebirth of our original native
ideals in a form consonant with present conditions. It will not
create despair as to the possibility of active participation of
the educational system in creating a better social order. For
it will reveal that the evils noted are not the intrinsic products
of the two great forces which are operating, namely, science
and technology, but of certain inherited customs, legalized institutions, and generally unquestioned traditions which developed before the rise of modern industrial society. The evils
center about the principle of private labor for private gain,
a principle which was natural and on the whole probably more
beneficial than harmful under the conditions of the origin, but
which has taken on a malign form when linked up with the
tremendous expansion and centralization of power effected by
technological industry.

Science in itself is method: a method of inquiry, discovery,
testing. Yet to most persons it seems something apart, isolated,
peculiar, esoteric. To very many it seems to be a combination

of the miraculous and the merely curious and strange, so that the "popular science" of the Sunday newspaper is often a mass of absurdities concocted for a supposed sensational value, and swallowed with avidity, to be displaced in a short time by other trivialities and "wonders." In its application, to be considered shortly in the discussion of technology, it has had a revolutionary effect on daily life. But in itself as a method of observation and reasoning, of investigation and verification, it remains the possession of a comparatively small number of specialists. It has not become the organ of everyday ways of thinking in formation of beliefs. It is not a part of the popular mind. The ways of thought of the latter remain much as they were before the rise of science. Some of the important conclusions of science have, of course, dispelled from popular belief many things held to be true before its rise. In some matters of religion and a few of moral belief this effect has been important enough to be disturbing and to call for a certain amount of reorientation. But conclusions of science are accepted for the most part on authority and not because of personal command of the method by which the conclusions were reached.

The cause for this enduring remoteness of science as method is a matter for most searching thought, especially since, after a long period of resistance from ultraconservatives, the teaching of various sciences has obtained a foothold in the schools. The reason which reflection directly suggests is that science has been limited to things remote from human life, so that its results touch human life only through the medium of some mechanical application rather than directly. In consequence science in itself assumes a purely technical—that is, compartmentalized—aspect. That the physical sciences should develop and should obtain prestige prior to those dealing with man and society was so much in the nature of the case as to cause no surprise. But it should be a matter of surprise that the idea of the possibility and desirability of impartial and coöperative methods of inquiry should hardly have made an impression on the public mind. It should be a matter of surprise that, while it is assumed as a matter of course that beliefs regarding physical things should be reached through a skilled technique of investigation and testing, the great mass, including even scientific men eminent in their special fields, should rest content with moral and political beliefs which express tradition, dogma, emotional appeal, and the vested interests of classes. It should be a matter of surprise that, whereas it is taken for granted in the physical field that planned invention and control of natural conditions should follow from discovery of facts and relations, the very idea of inventiveness and planned control in the social area is ignored or recognized only to be frowned upon as dangerous radicalism.

The difference of attitudes points to some deep-seated source of resistance on the social side. The dead inertia of custom and habituation counts for much. But resistance is active and often aggressive. These facts point to class interests which fear the free play of critical inquiry and constructive invention in social institutions. Otherwise a universal organ of observation and thinking would not have been changed from an instrumentality into an end in itself and given almost superstitious reverence as something apart, while it is opposed as the method to be used in the institutions and arrangements of society.

The conclusion is that education possesses in scientific method a potential agency for ridding the present situation of its confusions and conflicts and for making the transition to a society which will be emancipated from many of the undesirable traits of present life that have been indicated. To make this potential actual and operative, the method must be simplified and generalized. This will take place when *experimentalism* is realized to be the heart of science as method of discovery and test. Experimentalism is the cause of the victories won by science in the physical field, while the social field is kept as a preserve sacred from the free use of experimental procedure. The result is unbalance, distortion, and misuse of the physical fruits of science. Those who hold the remaking of institutions and traditions is as much the office of conscious education as is the transmission of values attained in the past will not see their ideal realized even in a fragmentary way until the formation of an experimental attitude of mind becomes the unified and unifying goal of education in its intellectual phase.

The vested interest which most definitely and actively blocks emancipation of method and prevents the experimental attitude from becoming universal is business as an institution carried on for profit. This welcomes "science" as long as it produces discoveries which can be utilized in ways that will show on the credit side of the financial ledger. It stimulates—and appropriates—invention within the same limits. But the publicity, the coöperativeness, the common and gratuitous sharing which are inherent in the scientific method of inquiry and verification are hostile to this end of private and competitive gain and so are resisted as subversive of law and order.

The factors which have brought society to its present pass and impasse contain forces which, when released and constructively utilized, form the positive basis of an educational philosophy and practice that will recover and will develop our original national ideals. The basic principle in that philosophy and practice is that we should use that method of experimental action called natural science to form a disposition which puts a supreme faith in the experimental use of intelligence in all situations of life.

A second basic principle is the use of technology for social ends. Modern machine industry is, of course, the product of technology, and this in turn is the result of application of the findings of scientific method. There are those who personify the machine much as our savage ancestors personified the forces of nature, and thus surrender their minds to a new form of mythological animism. In itself, the machine is of course but the effective supplementation of the energy of human muscle and nerve by the inanimate energies of heat, electricity, chemical reaction. The only basis on which the machine can be condemned logically is that of a passive and pessimistic philosophy which regards all exercise of energy as intrinsically evil. The present widespread blame of the machine for our present evils is a projection of the unwillingness of human beings to blame themselves for permitting the development and growth of legal and political institutions which make machine-industry the fountain head of widespread insecurity, poverty, fear, physical and mental crippling, with subjection of the many to the privileged power of the few.

Inherently the new technology is simply skilled control on a wide scale of the energies of nature. It contains within itself the possibility of not merely doing away with the evils which result from our present economic régime but of ushering in an order of unprecedented security and abundant comfort as the material basis for a high culture in which all and not merely the few shall share. It is as certain as any fact can be that we have within our power the means, including technical and managerial skill, by which the natural resources of the earth may be used to save all from dire want, from paralyzing insecurity, and to guarantee the essential conditions of a life devoted to higher things than the mere struggle to escape destitution for one's self and one's dependents.

It is not necessary to recite here all the evidence that the man-made legal and political system under which technological industry operates is the cause of our troubles rather than machine-industry itself. On the negative side the evidence is overwhelming that material success is not the attendant of superior character and that poverty and unemployment are not the results of inferior character. The sole alternative is that the social system is at fault. There have been times when it was utopian to indulge in a belief in a state of society in which all dire want and its attendant evils would be abolished. Our present technology brings the hope wholly within the region of possibility. The educational profession has therefore a direct concern in all that concerns the use of technological resources for the formation of a more secure and more humane order. Because of conditions which have been indicated, our professed and professional educational aims are fated to impotency with respect to both social advance and the systematic development of personal character unless the power inherent in science and technology is utilized for ends which are not controlled by economic institutions where competition for pecuniary gain is supreme.

The net conclusion of the discussion is:

An identity, an equation, exists between the urgent social need of the present and that of education. Society, in order to solve its own problems and remedy its own ills, needs to employ science and technology for social instead of merely private ends. This need for a society in which experimental inquiry and planning for social ends are organically contained is also the need for a new education. In one case as in the other, there is supplied a new dynamic in conduct and there is required the coöperative use of intelligence on a social scale in behalf of social values.

In this conception there is neither an explicit nor a lurking assumption of an opposition between individuality and social ends and values. The opposition is between the public and shared on one side and the private and isolated on the other. This opposition works to the detriment equally of individuality and society. An extension of activity on behalf of public community interests by the organization of collective social agencies is necessary under present conditions for developing and sustaining mature, intelligent, unified personalities.

We have stated that present conditions need not be a source of permanent depression and pessimism. Since science and technology have equipped us with the means of establishing a sound material basis for our civilization, our problem shifts from a material one to a moral one: the challenge is now to good-will, intelligence, and courage. Conditions present us with a magnificent opportunity: that of forming a society wherein continuous experimental planning with respect to our abundant resources and material and technical skill further a democratic faith to full life and action, while nothing else will do so. It has been pointed out, particularly by Dr. Counts, that our original democratic institutions were furthered by a happy conjunction of circumstances. The circumstances have changed. We can no longer depend upon external conditions. Our continued democracy of life will depend upon our own power of character and intelligence in using the resources at hand for a society which is not so much plann*ed* as plann*ing*—a society in which the constructive use of experimental method is completely naturalized. In such a national life, society itself would be a function of education, and the actual educative effect of all institutions would be in harmony with the professed aims of the special educational institution.

A society in which science and technology are employed under social direction for social ends will emancipate "individualism" from the alien forces which have gathered about it. It will restore its original moral significance. Individuals find, as we have said, their lives broken and confused because of the absence of clear and coherent objects of allegiance. They are torn between the ethical and religious principles which instill regard for the common and public good, and conditions of economic life which compel exclusive regard for private good. A community wherein coöperative intelligence is steadily used in behalf of promotion of a shared culture will eliminate this deep division in life. It will also render unnecessary that escape to special and isolated realms of science and art which is now the sole recourse of many who put culture above material values, since it would integrate these values with the purposes of the common life. Faith in promotion of shared values and devotion to a constantly growing and varied method of experimentation will supply the void which now exists in the life of so many individuals because of collapse of those objects of traditional loyalty which once held men together and once supplied meaning to individual life.

In opening new avenues to trained intelligence, such a community would fill the gap which now exists between theory and practice, between the intellectual and the executive type, and thereby also promote the integration of the individual. At present those concerned with social science and philosophy confine themselves to specialized fact-finding and isolated theorizing, with no responsibility for the execution or even the formulation of policies of action. On the other hand, the practical executives in business and government are largely concerned with immediate accommodations and manipulations, adherence to catchwords and worn-out traditions, unillumined by generous and informed thought. A unified individuality is hard to maintain where intelligence which is public by nature cannot operate effectually for public results, and where the ever-urgent demands of practice compel compromise, evasion, and conformity to ideals that do not command spontaneous loyalty.

If education were to awaken to a sense of its identity with the cause of a community which employs science and technology for experimental planning and action in the common interest, the effect upon it would be equally sound and integrating. Direction would be given to an aimless situation; unity would grow in a system now distracted by a multiplicity of special movements that are not held together by any single purpose; simplifying order would appear in a congested situation; definiteness and continuity would accrue to efforts that are now wavering and oft interrupted.

Harmony would be effected between actual practice and professed theory. Our present philosophy extols education through participation in community life, the winning of insight and understanding through direct taking part in the realities of life. But under existing economic conditions, it often seems the part of humanity to protect children and youth from too close contact with surrounding realities. For the defense of the young we maintain the school in isolation from life even while we proclaim that the isolation must be broken down. In a society which continuously planned its activities for the common good, educational theory would of necessity be carried into operation.

The change would affect also the subject-matter of instruction. In spite of all educational endeavors, there are many subjects in our schools which remain academic and aloof and which are pursued in a pedantic spirit, or from the traditional identification of culture with a polish belonging to the few in distinction from the mass. On the other hand, so-called practical and vocational subjects and courses are introduced which lack depth and intellectual substance. They are not used to contribute to an understanding of society or to recognition of the scientific foundation of callings that are socially important in the modern world. Instead, they are used for the superficial purpose of enabling individuals to "adjust" themselves externally to a profit-seeking civilization. In a planning society, the plans and methods of maintaining and furthering the life of the community would form the natural core of the course of study. The split between personal culture and the vocational would disappear.

These are examples of ways in which programs of social

and educational reconstruction meet and correspond. Each must develop in intellectual reference to the other and as far as possible in practical connection with the other. The first step in clarification of philosophy is to see the entire educational enterprise in the perspective of that form of social life which is needed to save us from present evils and is required by forces which already exist. Such a vision is preliminary to action which will develop the new society. The detailed development of an outlook and program of this kind demands the combined thought and effort of all educators in connection with students of social affairs. But certain conditions stand out which map the field and define the problem. Intellectual and practical reconstruction will be compelled to take account of the following factors in our society.

1. Society has become in fact corporate. Its interests and activities are so tied together that human beings have become dependent upon one another, for good or for harm, to an unprecedented degree. This is a statement of fact, whether the fact be welcomed or deplored. This interdependence is increasing, not lessening. It must be taken into account by education. We must not only educate individuals to live in a world where social conditions beyond the reach of any one individual's will affect his security, his work, his achievements, but we must (and for educational reasons) take account of the total incapacity of the doctrine of competitive individualism to work anything but harm in the state of interdependence in which we live.

2. Not merely the material welfare of the people, but the cultural and moral values, which are the express concern of the educational profession, demand a reorganization of the economic system, a reconstruction in which education has a great part to play.

3. The crucial problem is no longer one of stimulating production, but one of organization of distribution with reference

to the function of consumption and use, so as to secure a stable basis of living for all, with provision against the hazards of occupation, old age, maternity, unemployment, etc., in order that an abundant cultural development for all may be a reality.

4. Strictly speaking, the idea of *laissez faire* has not been carried out for a long time. Monopolistic ownership of land and of values socially created, privileged control of the machinery of production and of the power given by control of financial credit, has created control by a class, namely, control over production, exchange, and distribution. Hence general and public repudiation of the doctrine of *laissez faire* in behalf of the principle and practice of general social control is necessary. Education has a responsibility for training individuals to share in this social control instead of merely equipping them with ability to make their private way in isolation and competition. The ability and the desire to think collectively, to engage in social planning conceived and conducted experimentally for the good of all, is a requirement of good citizenship under existing conditions. Educators can ignore it only at the risk of evasion and futility.

5. The interdependence spoken of has developed on a world-wide scale. Isolated and excessive nationalism renders international interdependence, now existing as a fact, a source of fear, suspicion, antagonism, potential war. In order that interdependence may become a benefit instead of a dread evil and possible world-wide catastrophe, educators must revise the conception of patriotism and good citizenship so that it will accord with the imperative demands of world-wide association and interaction.

6. We are in possession of a method of controlled experimental action which waits to be extended from limited and compartmentalized fields of operation and value to the wider social field. In the use of this method there lies the assurance not only of continued planning and inventive discovery, but

also of continued reconstruction of experience and of outlook. The expanded and generalized use of this method signifies the possibility of a social order which is continuous by self-repairing, a society which does not wait for periodic breakdowns in order to amend its machinery and which therefore forestalls the breakdowns that are now as much parts of social activity as storms of nature are of the physical order.

The fact that all the changes which we have spoken of are connected with whole-hearted loyalty to the method of intelligent experimentation saves us equally from external and dogmatic inculcation and from colorless neutrality in the face of issues so crucial that the very values of civilization are at stake. Intelligent experimentation is based upon possession of working hypotheses. These hypotheses are themselves the fruit of careful study of actual conditions, a study conducted as honestly and impartially as is possible to human beings. The convictions which we set forth are arrived at in consequence of our own survey and analysis of conditions; they are offered not as dogmas which must be accepted but as hypotheses to be thought out and to be tested by their reasonableness, by their connection with actual facts and their fruits in action as far as they are adopted. The alternative to them is neither abstinence from all conviction, under the name of amiable but aimless impartiality, nor the assertion of something else as an absolute truth. Rather is the alternative a resurvey of the facts to show that these have been misinterpreted, that important considerations have been neglected, or that the conceded facts point to other working convictions than those which have been advanced. In this spirit we invite the coöperation of the profession even though the outcome of that coöperative work be a modification of the principles herein advanced.

Professor Rex Tugwell has said: "If we know as educators that society is likely to work coöperatively, that it is to create its future by a constant use of planning and shaping activities, and if it is to press continually for amelioration, we can revolutionize education—and perhaps in time society—by preparing our students for the tasks involved. We prepare them not by insisting upon conformity, but by resisting its encroachments, by free consideration of alternatives, by generalizing vocationalism, by opening their minds to the consideration of social materials. What we want is to have them learn to approach and manipulate the factors involved, how to look forward, fitting things together, how to aspire and how to reach toward their aspirations, how actually to manipulate the new mechanisms which are coming into being." [2]

If to prepare individuals to take part intelligently in the management of conditions under which they will live, to bring them to an understanding of the forces which are moving, to equip them with the intellectual and practical tools by which they can themselves enter into direction of these forces, is indoctrination, then the philosophy of education which we have in mind may be adjudged to be an instrument of indoctrination. Otherwise, not.

We too easily forget that at present there is an immense deal of actual indoctrination, partly overt and even more covert, in our schools. The outworn and irrelevant ideas of competitive private individualism, of *laissez faire,* of isolated competitive nationalism are all strenuously inculcated. We are demanding the abolition of all such indoctrination, on the ground that it is injurious equally to the health and growth of genuine individuality and to that of collective public order. We are not proposing that other doctrines should be arbitrarily imposed in their place. We are proposing that those materials and activities which enter into a philosophy of education and which find their place in the schools shall represent the realities of present, not of past, social life, and we are asking that there be freedom of intelligence in teaching and study so that the

[2] Unpublished ms.

subject-matter of study and school activity may be followed out into the conclusions toward which this material itself points. If the method we have recommended leads teachers and students to better conclusions than those which we have reached—as it surely will if widely and honestly adopted—so much the better. We have done what we can to see and note the facts and to point out whither they lead in the way of plans and directions. This fact is an invitation to others to pursue the same course further. Instead of recommending an imposed indoctrination, we are striving to challenge all the indoctrinations of conscious dogma and of the unconscious bias of tradition and vested interest which already exist.

Upon one thing we take our stand. We frankly accept the democratic tradition in its moral and human import. That is our premise and we are concerned to find out and state its implications for present life under present conditions, in order that we may know what it entails for theory and practice of public education. Events often move rapidly. The alternatives to such a philosophy as is here projected (and sketched in further detail in what follows) is likely to be a society planned and controlled on some other than the democratic basis. Russia and Italy both present us with patterns of planned societies. We believe profoundly that society requires planning; that planning is the alternative to chaos, disorder, and insecurity. But there is a difference between a society which is plann*ed* and a society which is continuously plann*ing*—namely, the difference between autocracy and democracy, between dogma and intelligence in operation, between suppression of individuality and that release and utilization of individuality which will bring it to full maturity.

Chapter III

THE NEW CONCEPTION OF THE PROFESSION OF EDUCATION

I

THE previous chapters will have made clear our belief that the educator can fulfill his function in society only in conjunction with the clarification of the cultural tradition in which presumably he helps the new generation to find itself. To-day that tradition is stunted and obscured in a welter of conflicting tendencies. Having begun as implementing the ways and means of a preindustrial life, a promising culture has been overtaken and almost overwhelmed by the imperious demands of an untamed material civilization. These two forces, a budding democratic culture and an overgrown *laissez faire* machine economy, present the incongruous scene into which we induct the young. And this means, of course, that we induct them into an intolerable confusion. Except as we first deal with this confusion, life holds in prospect but little for the young under our care.

But just in this need does education find its opportunity and task. America is engaged in growing a culture. To be satisfactory, this culture must fix its roots deep in our past, must find its ways and means realistically within the limits and the possibilities of our technological age, and must set its goals in the service of a new conception of world humanity. In this enterprise the educator has a peculiarly strategic share. He may, indeed, have to provide much of the leadership which such a movement requires. His of all professions can least carry on its work without assessing the integrity of the culture. As we shall see in later pages, the education of the child involves a peculiar responsibility for the character of the cultural context in which his personality is realized. So dependent is the work of the educator upon this enveloping matrix that his very sensitiveness to his task impels him to concern himself with the culture. And as we view current conditions, what needs to be done has chiefly to do with bringing order out of chaos, with achieving a unity and direction out of a tradition and civilization full of conflicts. This is, to be sure, the common task of both old and young—indeed, a natural common purpose of worth-while living everywhere. Nevertheless we must be impressed with the special challenge thus put to the educational profession.

During the past few years students of education have been heeding this challenge and moving toward a clearer realization of it. But a more thorough conviction and release in this direction will depend upon the remaking of our theoretical outlook so as to give full significance to the factor of a common culture. Only then can we speak with desired clearness and point regarding the strategy of the profession's advance along the new educational frontier. These three aspects of the profession's reckoning with its function will constitute the subjects of the following sections of this chapter: (1) the manner in which its students have already thought in that direction; (2) the needed clarification of view regarding the place of the common culture within the social and educational process; and (3) some indicated steps in the plans whereby the profession may move forward in realization of the corresponding larger undertaking.

II

Educators have groped toward a social-cultural view of their function from interestingly different angles of experi-

ence. There are, first, those who have felt the impossibility of
teaching the young for better things in social life so long as
that social life as represented by the mature in society not
only does not support better things, but, on the contrary, defeats them at almost every vital turn. This is just another way
of noting the confusion and conflict in our culture. The educator who has been disposed to think the situation through has
come to believe that only as this confusion is cleared up is it
possible for our people through their schools to meet squarely
the demands of youth for a life fit to live. This clearing up
becomes, in turn, the task of the whole society, mature and
immature together. Beliefs, convictions, ideals, common consents, and mutual understandings are indispensable to a wholesome society of persons. These find their crucial expression in
the intimate and basic life relationships of people, in the family, in adolescent development, in occupation and economic
function, in religion and in art, and in community approval.
It is accordingly in these areas that the unity and integrity of
our life must be worked out. But in these areas it is adults
who are responsible. It is adults through whom the reconstruction of society will have to go on. The schools of children cannot alone and in abstraction from the vital areas work out the
new unity. The schools are but a part in the whole sensitive
population working together toward such goals. The glory
of life, then, which we seek to hold out to an oncoming generation, is not the achieved unity, but it is a society of responsible persons setting a noble and inspiring example of devoted
effort in the direction of such unity; not in mere academic abstraction, but in the intimate life areas themselves, in the family, in the business world, in political life, in social life, and in
neighborhood membership. In a word, these educators are
saying, "If we would wholesomely educate our children, we
must as a condition thereto wholesomely order the civilization and culture in which they come to maturity."

A second angle from which educators have come to this conclusion is represented by those who have studied in economic and social theory and have faced the necessities of our age from that angle. These are persons not content to work merely through the logical systems of theory in their fields. They have worked toward some type of expression of beliefs that will function, of programs that may correct our ills. Not content "to do nothing about it," they find the natural route to effectiveness in the study and promotion of the educative process in society. Such zeal for action and life devotion in sensitive students of society would in former times have led them into the missionary field, at home or abroad. Now it seems to lead rather into social work and into education. And these usually bring with them a zeal for a program, a social program. They are not content to spend their energies upon the abstractions of the learning process, the measured achievement in particular subject-matters, the intelligence quotients of the young, or detailed methods in class-room management and teaching. They are persons of large purpose and ideals. They want to be going in a direction of which they are aware, and they chafe at the partial life of merely academic abstraction. These persons are finding the patterns for their zeal on the social front. The moment they ask where education is going— what it is about—their own background and the conditions of our time lead them into the social problem. Considerable inspiration and direction have been brought by these persons into the new emphasis in education.

A third route by which educators have come to see their function as concerned more directly with the culture pattern is, strangely enough, through their study of psychology itself. The evolutionary concept, coming largely through biology into the study of human psycholgy, brings with it the strong, naturalistic mode of interpreting behavior. The individual, the person, is not independent of his environment. The human personality emerges in the total situation, being part and product in and of this situation. The environment is thus integrally essential in psychological study. This has, of course, been taken into the reckoning in the stimulus-response theories. But for the past twenty-five years the strong individualism in our "intellectual atmosphere" has kept the true logic of this position from coming through to its indicated conclusions. If the environment is of such admittedly large importance in the emergence of a personality, then this civilization and culture in which we grow up is of prime consideration in education.

That so obvious a conclusion should have been so long held back from realization challenges thought to explain. There seem to be at least two conditions blocking this realization. First, the dynamic view of civilization and culture releases itself from static entanglements much less readily than does the dynamic view of the individual as abstracted from his cultural *milieu*. The culture changes only with wide common consent, and this comes slowly. Indeed, the very idea that man can do anything about the culture has been slow in coming. So the lurch ahead in the dynamic study of individual psychology has in a sense followed the course of least resistance. Today, however, this is not supported by the "atmosphere." Both the failure of the "dynamic individual" concept to *release* the individual, and rapid developments in economic, social, and political conditions have shifted the focus to these latter areas.

A second condition which has blocked the realization of the place of the culture in the psychology of the individual has been our devotion to the methods in thought which neglect the essential function of the reorganization and reconstruction of purposes. We have been so intent upon getting facts that we have failed to see that facts serve purposes. Science, accordingly, is ever prone to be socially conservative. A thoughtful study of our recent history leaves little doubt that the releases through science into new technological purpose have on the whole been in the service of social conservatism. But here, again, acute conditions are forcing a shift of focus. We are compelled to look to our social purposes. Plan economy has come to stay. The example of Russia has been a stimulus to this end, but even without Russia our own conditions would have brought it about. The bulwarks of conservatism, economic and political, are crumbling all around. New conceptions, new visions, new ideals, new world and local cultures require to be born. It is in this realm of human values and preferences that purposes are generated. We can no longer avoid attention to the methodology of human purpose, and inevitably this brings with it the problem of the reformulation of social ends and ideals. Psychology cannot much longer resist the pull of circumstance into this area of the needed understanding of the social process. Particularly is educational psychology bound to move in this direction, for its findings in individual learning are clearly but symptoms of the deeper, slowly moving process of social-culture learning. Not to neglect the individual, we trust, but, indeed, to save our understanding of his behavior, must we move in this direction.

A significant part in the development wherein the psychologist has become more socially conscious has been played by the psychoanalytic movement. Here, whatever the final route to exact explanation, there is now no serious doubt that what a personality becomes is conditioned integrally within the cultural patterns of the society in which it develops. In this case, as in the others treated above, the thought had already reached a stage where the final push of depression sufficed to carry it forward to a plateau from which we shall probably never descend. Henceforth, both from the logic of our theoretical premises and from the more relentless logic of events, must our study of human conduct proceed in terms of an advancing cultural process in which the individual must be considered as in and of the movement itself, to be studied adequately only in terms of that movement.

Similarly has the opposition to atomism and the trend toward organismic conceptions made less reasonable any highly abstracted treatment of the individual. It is the *event* in a total situation which starts, develops, and stops—which opens and closes. We may trust our human sense to continue to count this individual as a unique personality within this total process, but now with a newly conceived context: the individual personality is the whole situation taking unique form at that point. Not all organismic theorists would subscribe to such an implication. Perhaps the implication is not inevitable. But their premises make the conclusion so likely that the pull of current circumstance toward culture-considerations is apt to find thinking yield at the organismic front far more readily than in the atomistic sector. With similar caution, it seems just to venture that the *Gestalt* psychology also carries us along the road toward considering individual behavior and conduct as articulations within a larger process of culture, growth, and change.

The third angle from which educators have approached the culture-education conception was thus in the realm of psychology. A fourth approach may be found in the field of progressive method in education. In a word, the "project" and all the fine consideration of the individual which it represents has failed to grip the profound sense of the educator. Something holds us back. This is in large part due to the abstraction in this country of the project from a vital social movement. In Russia the project seems to have come into its true character, a whole society moving ahead, the spirit of the project as taken up in the schools becoming therein a true spirit of adventure with life significance. Progressive education has turned in the past two years to face this new social context of the more adequately conceived educative process.

Not less in this same direction has been the resistance of the subject-matter interests in the school program to the "project," which would tend to make them too incidental and haphazard. To the writer, who has observed this issue during the past ten years, it has this meaning: the subject-matter people are clinging to values which must be more adequately cared for in new measures before they will relinquish their hold. These values, it would seem, inhere in the sense of common tradition which the subject disciplines represent. As such they represent something of high character, a selection from hard-won experience, something more sure and reliable to pass on to the young of a new generation. To this writer, then, the reason subject-matter has lost its once complete hold on education in this country is not that it is subject-matter. It is rather that its formulations are not vital and timely, pertinent to the age and stage of culture in which we are moving ahead. The real difficulty is the absence of an adequate tradition. The "project" idea is, then, not properly a substitute for a tradition, a gripping culture, but rather is it a method by which we arrive at a new tradition. We may be said, then, to be moving in progressive education, not *away from* something to teach, but *toward* something to teach, something to believe and to pass on. By this route has progressive education been prepared for the culture emphasis in education into which we seem now unmistakably to be moving.

A fifth way by which the new understanding of the educator's function has come is the increased appreciation of the challenge of our times to man's capacity to know. The knowledge, tested and ventured knowledge, which it is important for a person to have to-day, if he is to be well adjusted in life, is almost overwhelming in body and baffling in rate of accumulation and modification. The conscious process of education, of learning, cannot be allowed any longer to stop at the ages of eighteen to twenty-two. Public education, deliberate and planned, must go on through mature years. It cannot be left to chance. It cannot be entrusted to the occasional sense of need and an impetus received in the school years. And when adults study into their problems to learn seriously in pertinence to them, they find themselves in the heart of questions about the character of our culture. The unavoidable extension of planned public education into adult years is but another way of stating the responsibility of public education for the direction and character of the culture process.

Thus from at least five different angles the educators have come to a fuller realization of the larger social function which must be theirs. In no other way can they be true to themselves or faithful to the requirements of the times in which their function is cast. So large and uncharted a task is cause for hesitation, but conditions will not permit us to stop. To the meaning of this social, cultural function we may well devote more definite attention.

III

The five approaches to the issue, as we have seen them in the section just studied, reveal upon closer study no little confusion regarding just what education on the culture frontier may mean. It was advisedly stated that they are "gropings" in a general direction, efforts far more definite about what they wish to get away from than about the goals toward which they are striving. And yet in the degree that the movement becomes positive, the need for definition of goals in terms of culture becomes imperative.

Interestingly enough, the exponents of these groping efforts have sensed something inadequate for their needs in the more progressive educational theory of the past few decades. Correct or incorrect as their interpretations may be, the fact is stubborn that to them something has been lacking from complete satisfaction. The criticisms are various. One is that the theory, by insisting against indoctrination, has failed to make way for due consideration of essential social stress in education. Another finds the theory intellectualistic, not allowing for buoyant experiences of art and appreciation. A third is distressed at the isolated individual of educational psychology, identifying this conception too often with a philosophy of education which stresses the central place of the individual personality in a desirably run society. Still others hold that the considerations of the prevailing progressive theory have avoided coming to grips with current social forces, becoming in that degree largely ineffective, if not misleading. Again, progressive educational theory has been identified with the negative vigor and the positive indefiniteness of liberalism. And finally, it has become so exclusively associated with method that these critics find it giving too little place to the stimulation and ordering of stable content. Strangely enough, practically all of these criticisms issue from essential sympathizers with the theories criticized. The philosophic outlook of all seems congenial up to a certain point. Probably this common outlook but reflects the essential restlessness of our times.

It would be too sanguine to hope that these difficulties could all be resolved by the simple expedient of remaking the prevailing liberal philosophy of education so as to make more central the factor of the common culture. But it is probable that the point in many of the criticisms would be largely met by such a remaking. Certainly the resistance to indoctrination grows out of an interest in a common tradition. It is possible that some at least of the sensed need which leads to the charge of intellectualism and the "escape" from problems into "creative" experiences of art, may inhere in the stark personal isolation attendant upon a competitive social life, individualistic to the exclusion of buoyant common cultural experiences. The Crusoe individual of psychology would be supplanted by a person who focuses in a unique way the whole cultural matrix, and we should then be unashamed to study the psychology of culture change. Again, it is probable that matters of education taken up from the point of view of their integral relations in a forward moving culture would be much less able to avoid coming to vital grips with current conditions. The chapter just preceding is testimony to our belief along this line. Moreover, the positive emphasis which would offset the negative manner of liberalism must, if it is social in purpose at all, take form in the direction of much which is characteristic of common cultural patterns. And finally, the content and social stabilization sought by those who fear too exclusive devotion to method might well, as has been indicated in previous pages, be largely supplied in stages of advance toward a more unified and commonly sensed culture.

Not only is it a social emphasis in education which is demanded, but rather a special positive concern with the building of common social outlooks, common patterns of conduct and belief, and common consents. The *social* stress in educational thought has been prominent throughout this century. In fact, it came as a reaction against a too abstract and individualistic educational outlook in the late decades of the last century. There was a growing realization that authoritarianism in religion, morals, and law was destined to lose its hold on the people. Educators accordingly conceived the need for providing a way of social control better suited to the emerging liberation of individuals from previous sanctions. The static cultural forms were breaking down, and some dynamic substitute for them was being sought. By the end of the first decade of the century, the conceptions which had come to dominate the profession's thought in this line were such as socialization of the individual, coöperation in common purposes respondent to commonly sensed needs, a sociological study of education, social and anti-social conduct, and all of these led to some corresponding efforts in school programs and school practices.

By the time of America's entrance into the World War, this social emphasis had reached its peak. Caught within the general state of high common feeling at that time there was, in our schools of education, a vigorous study of the social needs of the world and of the correlative responsibilities of education. In intensive and extensive fashion the merits of democracy were explored in contrast with that in the world which had brought on the war, and there was a crusading spirit rampant, bent with Wilson upon making the world more congenial to democracy. This crusade moved into all fields, labor and the economic problem, the church, the universities, politics, international relations, all of our social institutions, our morals and conventions.

But the first few years after the war saw much if not most of this zest for the "social" emphasis in society and education go down in reaction. Added to the more or less natural reaction was a hard realism supplanting Wilson's hopes both abroad and in this country, and then the upward trend of prosperity making for the false feeling that nothing else mattered much—security seemed to lie in the economic prosperity itself.

The result was a reëmergence of individualism in intensified form—untamed competitive enterprise in economic and other phases of life. In fact, it took the crash of 1929 and the following depression to awaken us again as a people to the fact that the socialization of conduct will not be settled once for all, that it will not take care of itself and that economic prosperity is no substitute. And more pointedly still, we now see that something is basically wrong with the inherent structure of our common beliefs and practices. There is a growing conviction that we cannot successfully socialize the outward manifestations and effects of our institutions except as we basically socialize their inherent structures. An economy, for instance, built basically upon *laissez-faire* competitive dealing is not going to give up without a struggle its very being in order to have more socialized effects. A basic substitute must be found, not just surface palliatives. Here we see the need for that which has the characteristics of a common culture, deep and powerful within the conduct of people.

But there is another approach, historically, to this same issue. The change in psychological outlook from Herbartianism to the views represented by John Dewey about the beginning of the century was conceived in the matrix of a vigorous social philosophy. Another strain in psychology, however, was getting under way among educators at about the same time. It was one in which the original nature of the individual was given large place. Its purpose was to study the individual as a biological organism responding to the stimuli of its surroundings and building up habits accordingly. The original nature traits were to be so directed that they would lend their native force to conduct which was socially desirable. Above all, this psychology was to give up the myths of previous psychologies and be first, last, and always scientific. But to adhere to the claims of scientific exactitude, studies were almost perforce limited to isolated elements, factors in behavior taken out of context. And upon this basis there was built a sanguine hope, during the first decade or so of our century, that human conduct could be studied, predicted, and controlled with a precision similar to that achieved with chemical and physical forces. Just for what, to what ends, this control was to be was a question not for the psychological scientist.

With the coming of the war, the psychologist's science was thrown into the common cause. The army intelligence tests marked an epoch in the rise of the testing movement. Psychology came to be recognized as a science which might well be of assistance in any cause having to do with persons where differences of ability were of importance. In education, ability grouping came to be instrumental in furthering the cause of efficiency in academic mass education. Advertisers have capitalized the psychologist's skills and insights into people's responsiveness to the stimuli of their various wares. And the list could be extended. Throughout, it has been a study of the individual as such, and the ends served thereby have been matters of least concern, for is not this after all the essence of exact science, that it be impartial?

The conclusion must be clear that such a psychology yields little help, is perhaps rather a hindrance, to our understanding of the purposeful behavior of people. The ends served by it are essentially static ends, for such is usually the result of "impartial" science which, refusing to criticize ends, thus accepts those of the *status quo*. And the objects of its study are thus usually those which have least to do with the way in which a people moves from one social-cultural form to another, from one end or goal of common living to another.

A clear understanding of this inadequacy of our psychology has come reluctantly and slowly. For a larger part of the past thirty years the two psychologies, one conceived within a conscious and liberal social philosophy, the other representing a static, that is, a highly individualistic *status quo* belief and outlook, have existed side by side, without until recently giving serious challenge to each other. It is regrettable that such mutual challenge has been so long delayed. An earlier show of merits might perhaps have cleared the atmosphere and relieved our educational thought of the mutually dulling effect which must result when a group tries, without knowing it, to hold at one and the same time to two mutually opposed philosophies, a dynamic philosophy with its appropriate psychology and a static philosophy implicit in the dominant psychology.

Under such circumstances the impression will not down that there must have been some lack of convincing and releasing focus in the liberal philosophy of the social individual. Why did it not earlier bring on the issue with the static competitor? Why did it not set up more resistance to the reaction against the social emphasis in thought which prevailed for the decade after the war? It would be bold and probably wrong to proclaim that this failure was due to any one influence alone, but it may be ventured with reason that a chief condition of the effects noted was the absence of defined positive programs in the views of liberalism. The liberal has assumed, and with some justification, that his method is in itself a positive program. But we refer the reader to the first pages of the preceding chapter to note our conviction there expressed that it has not been enough to conceive in the abstract of better things in society; our subject-matter must be this particular society in this particular time and place. Such being the case, a method as such and alone cannot constitute a positive program for modern educators; this program must be some position drawn up as of our own times and conditions and *for* these times and conditions. Our method must be at work here and now advancing working programs which we are eager to have carried out eventually into experimental practice.

It has taken changed conditions in America and in the world to bring out this latent possibility in the more liberal philosophy found among students of education. The work of negative criticism is, so to speak, being done for us to-day by untoward conditions themselves. Convinced thus that something is wrong, the pressing question comes to be: Which way are we going? What is the way out and forward? In response to this question, educational theory forthwith assesses the ideals of the society in which it finds its subject-matter. For it is in such patterns that it finds the orientation of any programs it may propose. In a word, we here, professed students of philosophy of education, being called upon to present a positive program, find ourselves proposing some pattern or patterns of a changed culture. In appreciable measure we shall find in this focusing of critical and constructive energies the strength and stimulation the relative absence of which in earlier years rendered us less vigorous than we might conceivably have been against the static psychology, and less resistant than we probably could have been toward the reaction to the selfish individualism after the World War.

It may well be that conditions were too strong for any theory in those years, and that the fitting thing in us would be to acknowledge the frailty of our most likely theories before the on-march of a huge civilization. But *some* effect may be had by taking thought, and whatever the final word regarding the past years, we feel the force to-day of the need to enter consciously into America's great opportunity and task, the progressive building of a positive common culture.

The distinctive character of the social emphasis needed in modern education is thus not simply or solely that education shall in general take account of the social make-up and social responsibilities of individuals, but that the common forms in the social pattern shall become matters of deliberate, positive concern and effort. To forsake a healthy regard for the individual is furthest from our intention, a point which the most cursory reading of these chapters will leave in no doubt. On the contrary, the cause of wholesome individual realization waits upon the lagging support and elixir which come only with a sense of the common, the mutual. Even the extreme of "rugged individualism" would be and must be but a myth without common consent to it as a way of social life. What we would have for the individual personality must sooner or later be supported in common belief and common expectation. Yet we know little about and attend less to the emergence of these fundamentals of a genuine culture. They are left to grow like Topsy, with the result that to-day they vary all the way from the self-centered corporate development of industry to the patterns of world brotherhood in such agencies as the International League for Peace and Freedom. Conflict and confusion are the fruits. Shall we inculcate through education the spirit of "enlightened selfishness" or the spirit of "world brotherhood"? If both, one or the other will be but a slogan, usually the latter. Is it to be some constructive mergence of two such dispositions? Then what is that form? Shall we have to wait until the mergence just grows, if the fortunes of man so dictate, or is there something which deliberation can do about it? In such fundamental issues lies the predicament of society and of education. We venture the conclusion not only that it will pay to try conscious and positive steps, but that in this direction lies the most crucially needed emphasis in the education for our times.

To release thought in the interest of common culture is as much as we dare hope to achieve in a few pages. Ways and means of action will depend upon increasing understanding of how cultures take form and how old forms are replaced by new. We can here point only to the most obvious characteristics of these common patterns of culture. First, they are commonly ingrained habits responding to common surroundings with the impulsiveness of deepest habit, as ready and common as our turning to the right on the highway. Second, they "step up" the power of the individual in that they are mutually held and mutually expected. Third, interests in life become deeply vested within them, integral parts of them; the pattern cannot be disturbed at any point without involving a resistant response from these interests, intimate almost as life itself. Fourth, the impulse within them is thus a matter of feeling, quickly converted into strong emotions upon disturbance. Fifth, they make the people of any generation far more than they are made by those people. Sixth, people stand in awe of them, cautious if not fearful of violating them; they are powerful conventions often wrought into basic institutions.

Seventh, one individual can break such patterns, but no one person can either build them or rebuild them, for this would be, in the nature of the case, a matter of common consent and common habit. Eighth, these patterns as they have grown among us are to-day in such mutual conflict, with the resulting disturbing differences, as to make a common culture either superficial or non-existent. And finally, the most tangible and accessible forms which culture patterns take are the stated ideals and commonly expressed attitudes and dispositions. It is here that we may most effectively deal with the culture; indeed, this is the only place where intelligence can get a first hold on the process. And this gives us our start as we seek now more directly to find and state the function of the educational profession on the culture frontier.

IV

What steps can we reasonably expect the educator to make in taking on heretofore unrealized responsibilities within the current cultural process? Where shall he take hold? Wherein does this function differ from present practices, and how may the profession move through these present practices into the indicated larger undertaking? These questions must, in part, remain unanswered at present. Only experience and time can fill in the meanings they seek. Some suggestions, however, may be made, and some outlines ventured of the areas and directions in which this function may take form.

At the close of the preceding section it was proposed that the effective points of attack of intelligence upon the culture process lie in the commonly expressed ideals, attitudes, and dispositions of the people. To these may be added expressed desires, motives, beliefs, and purposes, for all these are of similar character. If the expressed ideals and the actually operating patterns among members of society turn out to be in conflict, the problem comes to be one, not of avoiding expression through ideas, but of more accurate and effective expression through ideas. For how otherwise can we be intelligent about the affairs of culture?

Herein lies the route by which we believe the profession will find itself moving through its current and traditionally conceived activities out into the field of responsibility for cultural change and reconstruction. We shall start with a case which is very common and especially close to the hearts of members of the profession to-day and note how, through dealing with this, we find ourselves unavoidably at the business of remaking the common culture.

Suppose, for instance, that a child comes to school seriously undernourished. The school senses the need and takes measures to have the child properly nourished. Is the school, just as such, performing in this case an educational function? Would not this be the function properly of any conscientious citizen or part of society, and when the school so acts, is it doing anything more than fulfilling a very general civic obligation? Is the educator therein functioning as citizen or as educator?

We ask this question not to quibble over terms, but because we believe that to face the real problem involved may go far toward clarifying the meaning of education.

There is a danger that the movement of the educator into the current social situation may lure him into short-sighted action. Already, in fact, is he saying that we must stop being "professorial" and do something, the implication being clear: that the professor just thinks on and acts not at all. We must nourish the child, we must change our economic system, we must achieve security for all, etc.—there is so much of good health in this contention that one hesitates to chill it with criticism. But upon further thought, some critical appreciation may be necessary to save the proposal from the injury that lies within its own impulsiveness.

It seems clear that this disposition to *do* something usually resolves itself into just *saying* something different. Amusing as this may be, it does point to one of our difficulties. We are apt to conclude that because the traffic in ideas has come to stand in the way of effectiveness, it becomes therefore unwholesome to traffic further in ideas. No one so contending can live up to his own preachment, for it is not a question of whether we shall deal critically in ideas, but rather a question of *how* and *where* and *when*. In this latter form the problem becomes the problem of our book: When and where and how shall the educator traffic in ideas?

For note again the case of undernourishment. What does the school do when so confronted? It talks. It confers. It writes letters. It summons interested parties and seeks to find reasons and ways out. It decides, it plans *and then* acts. The play of ideas in such a case is, upon closer study, the most demanding part of the whole. The overt action is only the eventual issue and represents usually the smaller part of the effort expended. When, therefore, the school acts in the case of this child, it is perforce trafficking in ideas and it does so either well or poorly.

In a sense the particular individual in the case is the school's first concern. But this may not mean that the ideas and patterns used are conceived for this case alone and that they have served their full purpose when this case is solved. Far from it. The use of ideas has had to draw upon the ideal resources of the community and of all those concerned, that is, upon the attitudes, dispositions, sympathetic understandings, the sense of social duty and responsibility, the motives and desires. These all have their mental patterns and foci. Moreover, the particular case does more than draw upon the ideal resources; it leaves some effect upon these resources. The sympathetic understanding may be deepened, the sense of responsibility confirmed and strengthened, attitudes in such relations modified to include types of cases in some way different from those previously included. Whether we will it or not, the patterns of ideas operating in this particular case have not been for this case alone; they choose and challenge the resources out of the past, and they project their influence into the future. Within this setting they do have a uniqueness as of the particular case, but it is as a unique eddy within a wide and deep-flowing stream. It is *of* the stream, and it has some effect upon the further character and course of that stream. To do something for this undernourished child means thus inevitably to do something in and to the stream of civilization and culture. It means dealing with desires, attitudes, and dispositions, with beliefs and ideals, and with the patterns of conduct which find in these traits their mental foci and orientation.

To speak of dealing with the conditions of our day, with social and economic forces, with our industrialized and technical civilization, must always allow for the large and central place of ideas, for all of these phenomena do focus mentally and must be dealt with as of this character. In all such conduct, actions and the correlative mental foci are together integrally and inextricably involved. But the projecting front of the advancing process is a matter of ideas. It is what is going on in the mental foci of the life relationships concerned. Any one interested in doing things in society, just as in the case of the undernourished child, must deal with the advancing mental front of these things, else his dealing is stupid blundering. And in doing things on this mental front, he articulates with *some* effect in the whole stream of culture. When the educator goes about it to do things amid the affairs of society, he becomes an agent in the ideal life of the people and will act for the good or the harm of its further course. He must face this responsibility for the mental focus of life and not be deceived by the lure of immediate action into the choice of less strategic fronts.

It may be enlightening to compare the case of the under-nourished child with the case of a child in particular need of ability to read something which he has encountered, or of ability to write something. The reference here is not to a general ability to read and write, but to a particular case of need for ability to read or write a particular thing. Taken in this light, it is difficult to find much if any essential difference between the two kinds of case. In both there is (1) a particular need, unique in part for this person, but (2) a drawing upon resources within the culture, resources in ways of doing things, always with the correlative mental foci, and (3) a change wrought certainly within the individual's conduct and usually in the resources themselves. If we start with the recognition of this essentially similar nature of the cases, it is possible to point to some differences which may have large significance for our view of education—significance just because the cases are basically similar.

First, the treatment of the undernourishment case ties in with the culture process just as do the reading and writing cases, but there is a difference. The culture has not been as well developed in the former case as in the latter. Society has set itself up, organized itself, to provide for the needs of reading and writing. The ideas and the patterns of action are ready to meet the need. Not so successfully, however, has society organized itself for cases of undernourishment. Consequently a different kind of attention is required. Instead of simply pursuing the laid-out work of the school as in the reading and writing cases, there must be an agitation to get the community to the place where it will act. Here the school functions somewhat differently from the usual pursuit of its established program. It agitates for the creation of a phase of culture. The immediate case is the occasion, but the implicit function is cultural. Now the school may become clearly aware of this function and study it to achieve it well, or the school may, as all too usually is the case, leave this real responsibility buried in confusion and rest complacently with filling the stomach of the child. Something is done to the culture when the school acts in such a case. If the educator sees the act in this light, he will realize that his function extends into the culture's need for reconstruction. With this in view, he will want to agitate not only for this particular case but for a sustained provision against the recurrence of *this* case and against the occurrence of other such cases in the community. On the side of the child, he will wish to make the particular event, as far as possible, an occasion for that child's acquisition of knowledge, understanding, and attitudes which, supported by his environment, will tend to prevent the recurrence of the condition either within himself or, as far as the child's powers reach, within the community. Stating it positively, the educator will want to relate the particular case to the achievement of better understandings, attitudes, and practices in the community and in the particular individual.

This analysis has suggested meanings of education which, if followed out, may yield something toward the clearer definition of function which we seek. There is first the general point that educators find themselves impelled to participate in a medium of ideas and that their chief concern is how most effectively to do this. For, to recapitulate, we have noted that such an apparently simple case as that of the undernourished child becomes a unique focusing of the ideal culture of the people upon the treatment of the one individual. We found this to be inevitable, and that our will in the matter had to do only with the excellence or otherwise of the way it was done. Treatment of the particular case did something to the culture in its onward course and did it well or ill. Moreover, we have seen that the mental foci of the patterns of conduct involved constituted the media through which this case was connected with the past experience of the race and of the community, the media again through which one part of the culture is connected with another part and through which the whole of the past and present is woven into the future course of experience. And we saw that the end of being a successful medium required that there be sustained mental foci of experience—attitudes, desires, principles, motives, ideals, dispositions, and sustained knowledge of relations. These may differ in duration all the way from the transient purposes having to do with the resolution of the particular case of difficulty to those long enduring dispositions, beliefs, and attitudes which constitute the basis of the community's cultural life. For instance, there had to be some ideas sustained long enough to achieve the better nourishment of the child at the time, but there was necessary also a basis in more enduring ideal patterns upon which to depend and to which appeal could be made.

Herein is both a challenge and a cue for the profession. Whether we will or no, we are continually affecting the on-moving course of the culture. The responsibility is accordingly there. We could not escape it if we would. But constructive minds will make of this responsibility a releasing opportunity. In a word, if we affect the culture anyway, let us do it consciously, deliberately, with a heart and with a vision. If dealing with any particular case brings us face to face with a social-cultural need, shall we not go forward with unshackled will to act responsibly toward meeting that need? In retreat there is only ignominy and drab deterioration for the profession. Ahead there is a world to possess.

But does the whole of this task fall to the educator? Is he to have a monopoly of the opportunity which it presents? Far from it. Indeed, such a conclusion would contradict our fundamental belief that this onward movement of intelligence in the making of a culture is eventually a way of life for a whole people, old and young, for every occupation and in every condition. What then of the profession as such?

Generally speaking, the answer to this question may be in such terms as the following: Seeing that fulfilment of its *present* defined tasks would lead it into some active responsibility for the cultural life in the community, let the profession follow this lead with faith and confidence. Timidly to wait now for all particulars regarding the future of relations with all other prominent professions and occupations in the community would be little more than a rationalization of fear. The proper caution will come as we do move out into the field of endeavor. But the way is not entirely uncharted, for we have seen that it has to do at least with the process in which the sustained common patterns of the culture are remolded to give more adequate help and guidance in particular events and cases, and, indeed, with the process in which these remolded patterns are made operative in appropriate particular events. Moreover, it is indicated that the medium through which such function is achieved is ideas. When we speak of bringing the course of human experience increasingly into better mental focus and direction, it is just another way of denoting the process in which particular human events, on one hand, and the more enduring principles and more comprehensive common ideals of conduct, on the other, are kept correlative and mutually corrective. Whatever else public education and the profession may find in its task, the study and promotion of this vitally operative common ideal culture must ever remain a chief responsibility. This is peculiarly the case in current times wherein the crying need is for the emergence of a worthy common culture.

Such is the front along which the profession will inevitably come to distribute its efforts. But there is always a strategy; the problem of a more definite sense of distinctive function is always a problem in strategy for the time and place under consideration. One hundred years ago a wise strategy would have dictated a distribution of forces and efforts in education quite different from that which may be required to-day. One hundred years hence will in turn have needs and resources of its own and a correspondingly different problem. Our task now is to find the correct strategy for the time in which we live, with a clear sense that this may be different from the strategy of yesterday and that it may endure for only a generation or two or three. What does a reasoned strategy dictate to-day regarding distribution of efforts and points of attack? Our suggestions in answer to this question come in the following paragraphs.

By tradition and still with some good reason, we turn to childhood and youth as a most crucial field of endeavor. Such is the assumption of the public school system of America, and as a point of need and opportunity it requires no defense. The school is society organizing its adult function in relation to the immature. The adult-child relation will always remain a most fertile area for the furtherance of intelligent living.

But in the study of the undernourishment case some serious questionings arose. Is it possible to be a real teacher of children, even in the apparently simple events of their lives, without assuming something more than ordinary responsibility for the kind of culture which is the matrix of their personal being, without becoming involved with the course of the whole social process in the community? Literally it is impossible. This point is so crucial and its significance so little realized that we may well recall and extend the analysis of that case.

We found that there was less essential difference between the undernourishment case and the reading case than first thought would indicate. No subject, indeed, is essentially different from the undernourishment case. Reading, for instance, is a means of communication. It is a social medium. It finds its true pertinence not in general but in particular cases of communication. If taught thus intrinsically in the child's life, there is no gulf that can be defended between the need for reading ability in school and the needs in the intimate experiences of communication in the whole of the child's life. And it is obvious that there is no gulf between the kind of need for nourishment in the school and the kind of need for nourishment anywhere else in life. Moreover, we found that the service of both needs drew upon the cultural resources of the race and community. If reading seems to draw more directly upon that culture than does the nourishment case, it is only seeming, for the mental foci of the conduct patterns aroused by the latter case are just as truly cultural as is the play of symbols and meanings in reading. Indeed, the two are identical in much.

The inference from this similarity is far-reaching. Whatever the subject in school, a real intrinsic manner of conceiving and teaching it would involve responsibilities within the corresponding cultural functions in the community outside the school. If the child is undernourished, the school has, properly, to do something about it outside the school. Likewise if the conditions outside of school, in the home, in social groups, operate to impede the development of good use in language, the school's duty to the pupils requires that it give attention to those influences in the community. This becomes highly obvious when a moral trait is involved. The school can advance very little further with the child than the community too will go.

A clear recognition of this wider obligation has come with parent education as promoted by those concerned with the development of small children. And it is only because our older and traditional curricula have become so isolated from their intrinsic function and crusted over with a false inner sufficiency that we do not see them in much the same light as we now see small children's schooling and parent education. Just as we cannot do for the small child except we do also, at the same time, for the parents, so can we not do for the older children except we do also for the influences in the community under which they weave the patterns of their lives.

And again, when a child comes to school undernourished, we should be stupid if we were to say to him and to the community, "This is a state of affairs which we cannot change now, but we shall feed the child when he comes to school and when he grows up he will change things in the community so that children will not come to school undernourished." Yet this is the theory on which the schools, by and large, are proceeding in relation to all those matters of personal quality and character which are so much the product of the social *milieu*. As a plan, it simply does not work. Moreover, it is essentially immoral for adults to shift the burden of their responsibility for changing things in society over onto the backs of unrealizing children. Without doubt the psychiatrist has some word for this disposition to justify ourselves by shifting the responsibility onto those who cannot effectively complain. At least human decency has a word for it.

How inefficient! We bring up a child and youth for a better world. But claims of this world are too strong. The youth will want to be socially favored, he will want to marry, to have and to hold a position, to be recognized and responded to in his community. Basic to all this, he will want to feel secure. These are powerful desires and motives. If he has been brought up for a different order, with higher ideals, the fine point of such a character will bend and break before the force of these basic desires in a community hostile to his ideals. The exceptions to this we may admit as proof of the rule.

The case seems clear and beyond question. When the type of character desired by the school is so dependent for support upon conditions in the whole culture, and this support is not forthcoming, the educator's responsibility moves out into society to agitate and to work for that support.

Implicitly the schools have long acknowledged this obligation without rising to its challenge. For we seem never quite to have been clear as a profession about the real function that is implied in the fact that we select when we build a curriculum. The things chosen are preferred parts of the tradition and culture. Some things are rejected, else there would have been no choice. Some things are, on the other hand, accounted good and worthy to be perpetuated. Now how can we do this without doing something to our civilization and culture? Be it ever so little at any one choice, we nevertheless do always seek to project a culture into the future which we call good. Whether we are aware of it or not, we always do something to the culture when we set out to educate. But how well or ill have we served in this regard?

We have long allowed ourselves to be made insensitive to this function, for there is no royal road to dealing deliberately with the culture. People resist it. The educator shrinks. There is pressure at every turn to repel innovation. How easy then just to be quiet. The philosophy actually prevalent in modern American school systems is easy to state: Keep things quiet and running smoothly. Touch not the controversial topic. Teach the accepted, the well known. Choose for the young those beliefs and practices to which people respond with no fears, against which no interest will rise to complain. The tendency, in brief, is to make the schools deal in isolation and in innocuous ways. The result is that the schools and the profession pursue a system of intellectual abstractions which seem destined to serve nothing save their own inner consistencies, while life goes on little affected by our thought.

But the day of this easy escape seems now to be passing. The conflicts within our tradition are making it impossible for our schools to select either the *status quo* or some deviation therefrom without drawing fire from one side or the other. The conservative and the reactionary are coming to be disturbed just as are the progressives and the radicals. In a word, educators find that to be alive at all to their task of selection is to become targets for some differing or opposing interest. Complacency is becoming less and less possible. To do anything at all significant in education is to do something to a culture and a civilization which are so confused of purpose as to respond with resistance and conflict.

If we have followed where the argument inevitably leads, the school and the educator will accept fully the challenge to assess the social order in the interest of the education of the young. There will be no institution, no custom, no practice which will be outside the field of their potential subject-matter. For the particular cases of each of the thousands of pupils will call not only for their own immediate solution but for a critical appraisal of the social forces involved in the difficulty. The outcomes sought will be the removal of the particular difficulty and provision against its recurrence through the establishment of appropriate understandings, attitudes, and operative ideals. What this may mean by way of actual participation in public solutions we shall discuss later.

V

There is another familiar case which we may analyze for its bearings on the way we think of education: the case of a dentist and his patient. The patient, an adult, comes suffering, and the dentist acts to give the needed relief—extracts the tooth, administers a drug, removes a pressure, or fills a cavity. Wherein if at all is this an educational situation? At least some learning comes from the experience to the patient. He learns something about going to the dentist's, or more specifically about going to *this* dentist. But the dentist might well increase the learning on the patient's part by suggesting the idea of preventive care of the teeth, notions of better diet for healthy teeth, the relation of bad teeth to health, the care of the teeth when young, etc.

But more, the patient and the dentist must come to some agreement about remuneration for the service rendered. This may set them both to thinking, whether the fees be large or small. One may become aware of the prohibitive nature of the prices and thus set the other to thinking. In conversation they may agree that there is a great amount of needless suffering and disease in society due to the cost of medical and dental care. They accord with each other in deploring these conditions. It is even conceivable that the one or the other might then and there resolve, as the young Lincoln is said to have done at the slave auction, to use any chance he may have in the future to strike at such conditions. Suggestions of socialized medicine and health provisions would probably come up. And this would be a step toward critical estimates of the pressures at work in the economic-political affairs of the country. Can the better ends be had within a capitalistic society? What does appear to be the most promising route for this country toward changes for the better in economic relations? And then the international situation might come up. We could indeed go on almost without end citing the educational potentialities of this one dentist-patient case, and the medium of all such potentialities is ideas. The dentist may thus be able to initiate the idea of better practice in the patient and point to the conditions in the community which will encourage him to pursue it: the number of dentists, the dental clinics, etc. On the other hand, the patient may be able to start the dentist thinking on better social and economic conditions, better provision for medical care, and ways to move toward them. Moreover, the later recollection of the one might at any time come to be a stimulus to these ideas and ideals in the other. Thus might an idea be kept alive until something happened in practice to correspond to it.

All the way from the simplest learning in connection with the visit to this dentist when in tooth trouble to the formulating and in some degree providing support for the idea of some better plan for society, this dentist-patient case has potentialities for education. That is, it has elements which may be woven into patterns of intelligence to be sustained against recurrence of the difficulties and toward the achievement of a better ordered course of human social experience.

The probability that both the patient and the dentist are too preoccupied with making a living to carry through such an educational elaboration of their case tends to prove too much : that our social-economic set-up keeps us so preoccupied with ways that defeat better living as to preclude effective thought toward needed reconstruction. This is an acute problem in public education. Some of its meanings we shall take up later.

Meantime this case could be multiplied by the whole number of the people's vital contacts in modern society, and each one would reveal upon analysis just such educational potentialities as did this one. How shall society make capital of these potentialities? Here we have a problem in public education which challenges the profession from outside the schools. Can this field be included in the educator's vision of his responsibilities? What would happen to his own view of himself in such case? What would happen in the field? What if any organized effort is reasonably to be anticipated? Can we foresee that the public will ever make the capitalizing of these rich opportunities a charge on its treasury?

Compare the dentist-patient case with what goes on in the schools for the young. Properly conceived, school education for the child would consist in just such illuminating developments in and around the affairs in the child's life as took place in the case in the dentist's office. The differences between the cases which impress us upon first thought are (1) that the schools properly are making a business of such development of intelligence, whereas it is only incidental to the work of the dentist, and (2) that in the schools the initiative and responsibility cannot be left so much with the children as presumably they can with the adult in the dental case. But are these differences as marked as at first seeming?

If we were pressed by a visitor from Mars to answer just why the dentist's office should not recognize such educational procedures as a primary function, we might have some difficulty in summoning reasons that are convincing. We could protest that there must be some division of labor and thus freedom to pursue the special functions, but beyond that we should probably make some weak and vague remarks to the effect that that is just the way things are done among us and that there are no very good reasons for it. It is just the kind of a society we have; and we have to live, so we follow its dictates.

Likewise the second difference can very soon be overworked. Just how much initiative and responsibility can we expect each adult individual to take for the way things are in this society, and how far can we expect him alone to be thinking these things through and coming to more complete views, better attitudes, and more adequate ideals? Somewhat more, of course, than in the case of the small child, but the point to stress is not this difference. Rather is it the amazing degree to which adult and child are similar in helplessness before mighty forces which tend to mold them into their patterns, for ill or for good.

The conclusion is inescapable. There must be deliberate and studied attention to capitalizing society's adult potentialities for developing an intelligence suited to her imperative needs. If this requires a division of labor—and there seems to be no other way—that division of labor and the allotment of functions must be a matter of much thought and planning. What it will be, even in outline, can scarcely be anticipated. We can review and appraise some of the things now being done which give promise and suggestion [1] and perhaps be daring enough to venture the merest sketch of outline. But the clearer program can come only with a catching of the vision by one group after another and through the experimental efforts which they will then make. And it *must* come, for there is no turning back now from the realization that adult society as well as the child requires a deliberately planned attention to its relentless need for a corrected and advancing intelligence. We can no longer safely leave it to chance or to the feeble efforts of the individual who *was* educated when he was young. The problem both for the adult and for the child is a problem of an advancing civilization and culture. The task is accordingly a social one, a collective task, and to be achieved only by collective measures, old and young moving together.

We may, by way of daring, venture that every occupation should have its "education" committee, call it what we will. Perhaps it may be called a planning committee. Little by little the interests in society are moving toward this conception. Note, for instance, the following:

"Every industrial manager has two major responsibilities.
"One is the economical and effective management of his particular business.
"The other is the contribution of wise judgment and positive action in securing stabilized progress in the economic society in which he conducts his business.
"Neither responsibility is fairly met if the other is neglected; each contributes to the other. . . .
"It is for this reason that the Bulletin of the Taylor Society is concerned both with the problems of managing the individual enterprise and with the problems of collective management of all industry.
"The emphasis at any particular time is determined by the dominant problems of the time. . . ." [2]

[1] Cf. Chapter IV on "The New Adult Education."
[2] *Bulletin of the Taylor Society,* October, 1932 (Vol. XVII, No. 5).

The larger social consciousness thus required in self-defense is a hopeful sign to-day.

Private interest, however, yields so slowly to the social imperative that one is tempted to sympathize with those who preach the need of a wave of fundamental social conversion. At least we dare to dream of the day when our society shall be so arranged that there may be fewer fundamental obstructions to the play of an aggressive social intelligence. In the meantime the part of education is to stimulate, cultivate, and promote social intelligence at every opportunity and to make opportunities where they do not exist.

Social intelligence *is* human planning. If once we begin to plan for common economic advantage, it will be a beginning only, for there is a mutuality about nearly every human interest which human sensitiveness would seek eventually to provide for. It is in this wider range as well as in basic economic relations that we may well hope for some special development of the educational function. Is there any eventually sound reason why the educational (planning) agents in and of the great variety of special occupations and interests in the country should not come together for mutual help and training? A school for such agents is not foreign to possibility. And what a liberation of intelligence it would mean. Already there is an earnest of this development: people from a wide variety of occupations are seeking out advanced schools for the study of education. More often than not, of course, they are bent upon specific knowledge to be adapted to the purposes of their special groups. This is a long way from going to school to prepare for critical treatment of the more fundamental purposes of their special groups, but is it not on the way there? Barring organized radical revolution, which our keenest observers believe to be highly improbable in America, we must catch the germ of a better order which resides in these outreaching efforts of the special interests and make them the objects of nourishing attention. And we must spread such germs to one after another of these interests, develop an atmosphere conducive to their growth, organize their representatives into inspirational and supporting groups, create some clearing-house of information and guidance. Thus we may dare to dream. For is not something like this so imperative in the logic of the needs that it must inevitably become the logic of events?

Thus far we have been a bit hesitant to state the obvious conclusion, that to try to be intelligent is the main business of society. The corollary is that society's primary and foremost occupation is education. The social process is the interplay of human impulses in the quest for a satisfactory state of affairs. To become aware of the ins and outs of this interplay and to seek its ordering and guidance through the foci of intellectual formulation is the business of public intelligence as it is also the function of public education. It is therefore with no apology that we propose the putting of the public educational function not only prominently, but uppermost, in the work that belongs to every special interest in society. Something of this sense may have been implicit in the development of the universal public school in America, but it has remained implicit. An error has been made in trusting that the education of youth would provide intelligence in adult public responsibility and function. This we now know has been an unwise faith. The business of living in this age is so everlastingly novel, confusing, and complex that deliberate study and effort to understand it in its myriad relations and to control it for larger good must continue on without a break into the mature years where responsibilities are as keen and heavy as are the human consequences of our many special efforts.

Will such a place be given to education in our country? Is it conceivable that in such scope it could become a public charge? For the short view the answer is no. But the longer view is not entirely discouraging. If some one had told the fathers on the *Mayflower* that we should ever in the new country be carrying on at public charge the education of the army of youth which now considers it the thing to do to attend high school and college and university, he would have been suspected of witchcraft. If the function of the Interstate Commerce Commission had been hinted to the first Continental Congress, the hint would have fallen on deaf ears. And instances could be multiplied to show how matters of supposedly private concern are not only becoming sensitive to public interest but are being held to public interest at the public charge. How far ahead, then, shall we have to look to see society making education its chief concern?

We need not think of the educational profession, even finally, as having all this range of activities represented in its membership. The larger conception of public education as indicated above will always have many and varied phases. These will indeed have always the same common denominator: an essential concern with the integral and mutually corrective relations of particular events and the common ideals and purposes of the people. They will all be in the business of building a vital common culture. The promotion of this function is the important consideration. In some way, in all needed ways, society must "man" this function. What organizations may be required for this purpose and what the organizations may best be named must depend upon a great variety of need and of circumstance. Whether they be called "educational" and come to be represented in an "educational profession" is not of first importance. Our purpose is to make clear the point that all such efforts are to be accepted as genuine phases of a properly conceived public education and particularly that there is an essential identity and a direct continuity between the function of the educator of children and that of the "educator" in these various phases of adult concern with the common culture. And as public educators we are deeply concerned that there be an awakening of conscious, deliberate vision and effort all along this continuous front of cultural reconstruction.

We do believe it to be an indicated task of organized public education that the profession as such shall have a large share in keeping society stimulated and alive to this function. In doing this, the profession will bring intimately together a far wider variety of specific functions than it now does. It will include as one important branch those particularly charged with the education of children and youth. Other branches will appear through the various special educational professions, legal, medical, engineering, clerical, economic, social, business, and their subdivisions. Others will represent industries and labor with their increasing efforts at the education of their participants. Others may well come from schools of government and diplomacy. The germs of all these sources of representation in a profession of public education, as we have conceived it, do already exist. Each of these branches of schooling is showing promising signs of recognizing its wider public and cultural relations. In this sense each is beginning to give place to the public educational bearings and responsibilities of its particular calling. The encouragement, the organization, the mutual stimulation and support, and the growing private and public provision for this emerging interest in a genuine public education seem to us imperative needs of our times.

Such a profession would furnish a generating source of local and world cultural advance beyond anything we have yet experienced. With self-preservation pressing even grasping business interests into more common consideration of affairs, with world conditions making economic, social, and political planning the only sure route to self-defense, and with science and technology already revolutionizing our present common ways of getting on together in society, the need for coming together on positive common programs of advance calls for the highest and most effectively organized leadership. Every occupation and every distinct interest in society may well have part in this same task, but organized leadership is needed. Some considerable part of this leadership, though indeed not all, will come through an organized public educational profession. It lies inevitably within the logic of the educator's task.

The type of outlook and effort which constitutes what we believe to be the essence of public education and which the profession will organize to promote happens just now to be brilliantly illustrated in the Lytton Committee's study and report on the Manchurian issue. Lord Lytton himself has stated the crucial point:

"The issue at stake is a much larger one than whether China or Japan shall control the future destinies of Manchuria; it is whether the principles of collective responsibility and the maintenance of peace and justice between nations shall be preserved or sacrificed. The choice lies between the continued organization of peace by coöperation or a return to the anarchy of competitive force.

"The problem is obviously difficult; it is not impossible, if firmness on the essential issues is combined with patience, tact, and sympathy in adjusting the details. The success of the negotiations is profoundly important for the peoples of the world. . . ."

Here we have an agency bent upon formulating and making operative large ideal patterns of culture while dealing with an acute particular case. This, we propose, must be the pattern and the tenor of public education in any and every community where particular cases and common cultural patterns present the need for progressive mutual adjustment.

When the task and the opportunity of the profession, whether concerned with the child or with the adult, is so imperative and in outline so clear, we should not hold up action until all possible overlappings of effort and function with other occupations and professions shall have been anticipated and provided for. Such would be only a rationalization of timidity.

Overlappings there will be, and considerable conflict and confusion to be cleared up, but further caution will come most properly as we set out upon the endeavor. And early generalizations as to division of labor are apt to prove restrictive. The first consideration is to get the function attended to. Then a hundred cases of overlapping may easily result in a hundred significantly different divisions of the labor. We have seen enough of the way ahead, through grade schools, through universities and professional schools, and through organized education in other public relations, to start in the indicated direction. And this onward movement on the culture frontier we confidently propose to the educational profession.

Increase of encouragement comes with getting clear that the medium through which the profession works is primarily one of ideas. It is through ideas first, through formulation of a new mental focus, that we move forward. To do this vitally, to do it with increasing breadth and inclusiveness, and to make the doing of it actually liberate existing and potential current forces in society toward the realization of the goals and ideals thus formulated, constitute the heart of the profession's function. When the legislator and the government executive work with students of economic and social science, the latter bring to bear upon the thinking of the statesmen a perspective and an understanding of relationships exactly got by holding themselves detached from immediate decisions and the immediately "practical." The wider and long-time view is thus in a position to influence current decisions, giving them the advantage and the direction of vision.

No generalizations should be made regarding the extent to which the special student should go toward lending support to one side or the other of the issue, just as no reasonable generalization can be made concerning the amount of "detached" thinking toward perspective and vision to be done by the one who deals with men and affairs. The statesman-philosopher is

desirable as truly as the philosopher-statesman. Each partici-
pates in the experiences of the other and in so doing renders
more adequate his abilities for making his special contribution
to the common problem. The public educator in such a case is,
by our definition, the one whose *primary* service is with the
advancing front of the ideal culture.

Be it said that the profession here envisaged is not a mere
fact-gathering organization. It is rather a profession which,
individually and in groups, devotes much time and energy to
thinking through toward more adequate cultural goals, being
equipped therefore with unusual means and opportunities for
looking widely and thoroughly around, for getting facts and
for sensing conditions. This can be done in the small local
community as well as in national and international areas. Such
devotion to perspective, rooted deep in the generating forces
of modern society and overtly active where the cause will
thereby be served, comes close to being the heart-throb of the
profession as its possibilities are seen and felt.

We have reserved until now the discussion of certain of the
functions of the educator which are his regardless of his place
in school or society and which belong not to any individual
alone but are a collective task of the professional group. First
among these is the pursuit and maintenance of a critical understanding of modern society. Whether approached through
instances in the life of the child or through cases in adult
affairs, this is a relentless obligation. All social institutions,
customs and practices have deep and serious effects in human
lives. Deliberate education becomes aware of this. It chooses
from among effects and accordingly turns a critical eye upon
the conditions which produce them. This process of description
in the light of consequences must never relax.

To the reader of the early pages in our book,[3] it will be clear

[3] Pp. 68-70.

that we are describing here what we have done there. There we assessed the present social order in the light of the criteria of good which impress us as strategic for our times. No more definite illustration than this could be given for the point just made, that we feel the educator is obliged *as* an educator to appraise critically the society of his own day. And this cannot be done once and for all time nor for all persons. It is a common undertaking and must be continuously sustained, else the occasional formulation of to-day will tend to become the orthodoxy of to-morrow and the changes which surprise one who sleeps but a night will go unattended by careful thought as to their human consequences.

It should be added, however, that it is not alone this broader description that is needed. Every teacher of children will want to get an accurate understanding of the particular influences at work in his community as well as an understanding of the whole civilization and culture of which he is a part. This can mean only that he will be constantly alive to how that community's institutions—social, economic, or political, as the case may be—are functioning. He will be as much interested in the business side of the people's life as in what they read and how they play. He will assess what they believe, he will be sensitive to how they live, he will be eager for their wholesomeness and health. Their laws and their customs will become objects for his attention.

No one teacher could be expected himself to achieve such an appraisal of everything in the community and in the world. It is not necessary that he should. The function belongs to the profession. Mutual enlightenment and help would be the indicated rule. Moreover, the teacher can draw upon the observations of many outside his profession. Journals, books, lecturers, and acquaintance with persons make open highways into understanding.

The thought, too, reaches back into the education of the

educator. Many a teacher of to-day went through college with hardly a respectable course in social science. In the teacher's college or normal school he has learned only bits of a badly warped psychology and a few tricks of the trade of teaching the subjects which he was taught. He has been taught not to think, indeed the less he thinks about crucial matters the less trouble he will give his superintendent. He can be heir to all this and still be rated high. Such cannot continue to be the prevailing conception of the teacher. For we are beginning now to see what the profession, to fulfill its own integrity, is compelled to do. The group of persons who are charged with critical appraisal of the modern American community must be of the highest quality, with a most thorough and vital educational experience of their own.[4]

A cry of helplessness will go up all over the land. "What would happen," the teacher asks, "if I should start out on a critical tour through my community?" There is a frown as well as a smile for this cry. First, no fear of consequences need keep a teacher from learning critically what his community and his culture possess, and certainly no teacher would be worse off for an uplifting vision of better things. But it is true that the culture resists having anything very serious done to it, and the teacher may fall a victim of such resistance. There is, in this light, a too little realized possibility in the profession to-day. This is the effectiveness of organization for mutual support in efforts necessary to our great endeavor.

There is but one limit to the power of an organized body of educators: that is the limit inherent in its own sense that it represents the people. And this is a proper limit, but it needs discriminating study. We have here the old issue as to how far the representative shall reflect his constituency. The final answer to this question is found in the qualities of leadership in

[4] Cf. Chapter VIII on "Professional Education" from the *Social Point of View*.

the representative. This applies peculiarly to the teacher. We have already noted that the educator's selection of a curriculum involves an effect wrought thereby in the culture. In the degree that he is instrumental in this selective process he is asserting himself discriminatingly in the community. He could not possibly represent the present wishes of the whole community, and there is doubt that he could really represent a majority in most modern American communities. The consequence is that the palest, least vital elements in a community are apt to get represented in the teaching force. The alternative is wisdom and strength in leadership. Some outstanding educators in American communities have shown unmistakably that it is possible for a minority representative to lead a whole school system with its community on to new levels of vision and achievement. Such leadership cannot be expected from every teacher, but it can and must be expected from the group in the profession. In such case, the leadership of one becomes the criticized leadership of the many, and the power of any one of the many is thereby multiplied a hundredfold.

One of the most imperative needs of the educational profession is thus to organize for effectiveness. It has proceeded defensibly in its quest for salary increases, the one great organized achievement of education in America. And yet this is the merest hint of its potentialities. Can there be any final reason why the profession, in groups either large or small, should not bring its organized weight to bear on crucial issues in modern social, economic, and political life? Perhaps things may not then be so quiet or run so smoothly as now, but it is possible that things will in that day be constructively alive. The great deterrent is lack of vision. Nothing can long stop a group of wise people with an uplifting and impelling vision. We have practised "wisdom" and caution so long without vision that the prospect of the two combined is a bit terrifying. In a word, we wonder whether we can both have vision and be wise at the same time.

But the scene is changing, and, as we have tried to show throughout, the time seems at hand when not to work toward a vision of better things is unwise. Individual and profession alike will lose the right to hold up their heads if they do not rise to the challenge. The rough places along the way will but accentuate the thrill of the conquest.

For society is moving speedily into the business of building a new culture and this, as we have seen, is preëminently an educational task. The problem of being intelligent in the building of a new culture takes us back to our earlier point regarding the approach to action through ideas and especially to the conclusion there reached, that the whole culture exists for concrete cases and that the treatment of the concrete case in turn has an influence upon the culture. It was clear then that the basic elements of the culture are sustained beliefs and patterns of conduct. One characteristic of these beliefs and patterns cannot be too strongly pressed, namely, that they are held in common by great numbers of the people. It is this requisite common possession which sets the chief problem in any deliberate building of a culture.

The need for such community in belief and in conduct patterns is in reality the condition which has called forth the efforts of our committee. A tradition confused and conflicting, a society weighed down by an interdependence for which it is not prepared, a civilization outmoding even the habits and thought patterns of our own childhood, all cry for order and integration. An economic order which defeats the most elemental requirements of human consideration and a technological advancement which has habituated us against our own previous personal development and made us preoccupied to the exclusion of many values—all of these call for reconciliation and for such harmony as will release us from the strain of incessant conflict. Into such a situation society moves with the task of achieving common understandings and common consents. It is like establishing a better regulated traffic in streets not made to the proportions of motor driving.

We are ill prepared by our history as a people to work toward these common ways of thinking and doing. But with the individualistic frontier now gone, the new conquests appear to be more collective in character and the new frontier is in the advancing culture. We must achieve the knowledge and abilities which this function will require. As yet we have little by way of attitudes or tools with which to build. Tested knowledge is almost entirely lacking.

Here again only suggestions in outline are possible, for the clear task must be discovered by those who venture to experiment, urged on by a more or less definite sense of the need. One thing seems reasonably to be stressed, namely, that people seldom come together by the simple fact of thinking together. They may discuss the issues and seek to achieve common ground through words and indeed will find many places where they can verbally agree, but often there are more places where they cannot agree. Consequently it may not always be wise to seek agreement short of the time to act. It is the approaching need for action which brings out the real agreements and the real disagreements. This points two ways: first, toward the need for freeing minds for fuller intercourse without the pressure of impending action; and second, almost paradoxically, toward the need for experiencing together the approach to action—the test by fire, so to speak, of the common consents —to find wherein they are real. It is quite probable that such common ways of believing and feeling seldom come when the issue is drawn in symbols of abstraction. The real community comes as a deposit of doing many things together where common purposes are required.

There seem, then, to be these four stages in the process of

the forming of a common element in the culture: first, the liberation of thought on crucial points; second, the attempted formulation of a program of action; third, the doing of many things together, even though trivial, where purposes are formed in common; and fourth, thoughtful approach to actual experimentation along the line of the larger need. Other analyses of steps might be made, all differing among themselves. But the list as made may have fruitful suggestions.

It should be noted, for instance, that stage one is the core of the program of the liberal. He trusts intelligence liberated to bring the common consents needed. But many to-day doubt that the liberal here has completed his conception of intelligence, holding that the other stages, especially the second and the fourth, do but fulfill the complete act of thought in that in them is the program put to the test. This seems particularly to be needed in the process which develops an attitude or disposition, or makes ideals that are operative, or yields an impulse strong enough to serve as a motive.

For these traits are but mentally focused social conduct. If they persist as merely the mental foci with corresponding feeling and do not find themselves operative in vital conduct, they become annoying sources of conflict within the personality. They are opposed by the less welcome but more virile foci of conduct patterns which are necessitated in the civilization of our times. Conflict and a drifting social life are the normal and natural fruits of having mental orientation without the test of vital conduct in the conditions of the times. The ideal does serve to reach out ahead of overt conduct and to direct it, but if the ideal is not implemented sooner or later in the overt conditions themselves, it ceases to be operative where ideals are most needed, namely, on the advancing front of a changing world. These basic traits of a culture will function in their true place only when they find some encouragement and support within conditions as they are. They can operate to shape advancing conditions to their pattern only when they are operative within the potentialities of those conditions themselves. We seem, then, inevitably forced to the conclusion that the development of the common patterns of a new culture must take place through active common participation in reshaping the conduct of society's current and most signifiant affairs.

Engaging in the business of building a culture calls thus upon the highest of courage as well as for the most thorough deliberation, since a culture can be expected to change only when long cherished common beliefs and attitudes are shaken from their domain in conduct and other patterns are wrought in their stead. This is often a rugged domain within which to work, but there is no alternative for the educator except retreat. The conditions, however, which give rise to the need for a new culture make the task less difficult; conflict has already shaken confidence in some of the aspects of our most fundamental institutions and customs, and we even now as a people are groping to remold the common forms of belief which shall again free us. The educator has a peculiar interest in and responsibility for expediting this process. It is the supreme test as to whether society can summon intelligence to her most intimate needs.

In the service of public intelligence the educator has at length become clearly conscious of what had all the while been implicit in his work: first, that his rendezvous with childhood and youth is a service to the whole culture and involves both keen insight and responsibility in community relations; and second, that the crux of the whole front of social intelligence is at those points where adults are making the decisions and shaping the influences which in turn shape the lives of the oncoming generation. If the educator will once realize that when he educates he does something to the culture and then will follow on with the lively sense of responsibility into the paths and functions which that realization dictates, he will be close to the intelligent heart of society's urge toward a richer and more fitting culture. He will work at the task in the interests of childhood and youth and in the interests of the baffled and confused adults of the modern community. He will work with his profession to make our civilization give up its secrets and its leads, good and bad, and both singly and collectively with his colleagues he will use and multiply his powers for effectiveness in furthering the good and averting the bad.

And as basic to all this, the profession must sooner or later be uplifted and impelled by a realistic vision of what, in terms of our modern society, *is* better. It need not be an orthodoxy and certainly not an over-simplified radicalism, but it can have the power of a gospel and at the same time present a new frontier, a working philosophy of education and social progress. Our joint effort in this book is. to move toward this realistic vision, one which we can hold in common; and having reached it to set it forth with the faith that it inspires in us.

Chapter IV

THE NEW ADULT EDUCATION

I

A REVIEW and restatement of the new need for inclusive adult education as brought out in the preceding chapters will perhaps help us to see more clearly the function of such education.

Public and private thought and action seem in our times unsettled and confused as never before on so sweeping a scale. Education cannot remain indifferent. In the confronting situation two factors stand out as especially causing this confusion, the one more general, the other more specific.

The more general factor unsettling our times is the modern development of exact science and its application to the affairs of men, partly to break down our traditional ways of thinking, even more through manifold invention to break down our traditional ways of living. One special group of problems thus arising has had peculiarly unsettling effect. The medieval world passed on to its successor a binding legacy of authoritarian thought and outlook. Monarchy could not be questioned; the duly anointed king ruled by divine right. In secular thought Aristotle held sway. In moral and religious affairs divine revelation through book and church was the one sole and sufficient foundation. In lesser matters traditions ruled. Under it all lay philosophic authoritarianism founded on the assumption that all important matters were somehow fixed in the essential nature of things and could not be changed. Since the thirteenth century the general progress of thought has been to break down one after another of these authorities. The extraordinary industrial development coupled with the great vogue of science has, in our own times, practically completed the destruction. The last stronghold of tradition under the guise of authoritarian morals and religion was at length all but destroyed by the World War. Probably never before has so large a proportion of a people been so completely at sea as to what to think on fundamental matters.

But this is not all. Since the achieved results of scientific thinking increase, at least for the nonce, in geometric ratio with an analogous increase in invention, actual social life, especially in this country, is subject to continual change in a range and degree quite new to history, and the prospect is that this state of affairs will continue as far into the future as we can see. These ever new conditions generate ever new problems, so much so that the need for continual attention to insistent social and public problems becomes a fundamental characteristic of modern life.

As we face, then, the fundamental collapse of authoritarianism and the unending stream of ever confronting problems, the need for present adult study becomes urgent. The idea that a dozen years more or less of schooling toward the beginning of life could, in a world so at sea and still always changing, supply sufficient education to last for the rest of life has become absurd even for those who try to conceive education in this inadequate preparatory fashion. If we think of study and learning—and those of this book do so take it—as inherent in the effort to grapple intelligently with any confronting difficulty, then clearly new study and new learning must take place with each new difficulty faced. This continual process of study and learning, especially as intelligently directed to the best possible cumulative results, is what we call education. The conclusion seems then inevitable, at least for those of us who accept democracy, that for a decent civilization we must contemplate a state of affairs approaching continual all-inclusive adult study of life's problems. Education so conceived is exactly a way of life in which shared intelligence is consciously applied to the best attainable direction of life's common affairs. Universal adult education becomes, then, exactly a name for this way of living.

The more specific factor in our present confusion and unsettlement suggested above is a fundamental and irreconcilable conflict recently introduced, in degree at least, into the very heart of our economic life, and this in result unbalances all else. The nature of the conflict is clear to view. On the one hand is our modern industrial system with its new technology and the resulting extreme degree in which it binds all our fortunes together. This, our sole and supporting system of production, will not work—the depression is our proof—except as all the parts in it do in fact coöperate, fitting mutually and appropriately together. And herein lies the conflict: while coöperation in thought and act on the largest possible scale are thus inherently demanded for the success of our economic life, our still dominating outlook and our business practice alike embody and express an older and contradictory individualism. Our present system of ideas, our everyday morals, our working political ideals and party practices, our business ethic and practice—all these were built to serve, not our modern system of inclusive large-scale coöperative production, but a quite different system of unlimited competitive rivalry. In production we need an essential coöperation; in profits we have an essential warfare.

But the conflict reaches still further. When broad-thinking parents, teachers, or citizens try, as they must, to educate for the wholesome and intelligent public spirit needed to cope with this situation of conflict, they find their efforts greatly hampered if not effectually overborne by the contrary educative effects of the surrounding business system. It is not business men as such but the business system that is here under review and condemnation, for we are all involved in the system and together responsible for it. The struggle for private gain necessary under the present economic régime and the great rewards possible under it educate inherently and—in tendency at least—inevitably to selfish indifference to the public good if no worse. We literally pay people to seek private gain at the expense of the public welfare, and our pay educates them accordingly—and in effect we all do it, we are all responsible for the results.

In the face of this powerful miseducation inherent in our present business system, any effort of home and school acting alone to improve social conditions simply by the education of the young seems foredoomed to failure. We cannot hope for it. Granted sufficient coöperation elsewhere, the home and school can do much; alone, however, they are impotent. Nor is this even yet all. Besides the unconscious evil educative effects of our competitive system to thwart substantial improvement, there is often to be found the more or less active effort of selfish vested interests to prevent even a study into the system. Inertia and tradition add their weight, and the total combined opposition to improvement becomes very great. Under such discouraging conditions, cynicism is but too often the result. Human nature is declared unequal to modern demands. Politics are too dirty to touch. Democracy is counted a failure.

In the face of all this difficulty and discouragement, what if anything can the educator do? Can he stop short of the adult world?

First and clearest perhaps of all, the complex of conflicts and problems involved in this situation demands that the educator as such rethink his own position. He literally cannot know what or how to teach in the realm of social and moral affairs except as he can himself bring his own mind to some order in the face of the inherently conflicting demands. And everything else that he may do as educator becomes involved, at least in the relative emphases to be given and in the implications to be got and applied from the social situation. And here again is education led to the adult world from which these perplexing difficulties come. The various conflicts discussed in the preceding paragraphs pervade the modern world, with consequent frequent maladjustments. As already suggested, the proportion of parents in this country now unsettled in their fundamental beliefs and outlooks on life is very great, with the result that growing children often get from their elders and from life about them a most disturbing insecurity. Positive conflicts are only too frequent. A modern-type school, for example, will study some problem of social injustice, with the class discussion pointing clearly to a desired change in the social practice. Conscientious children thus stirred to a new moral sensitivity may, when discussing the matter at home in the evening, find— in consternation—that the family income is derived from the practice of this very injustice or from some other much like it. Strain is at once inevitable. The trouble, we know, is broader than the father's responsible reach, but to the child and his moral relations with the family the result may be tragic. When such things are possible and true, the school as such cannot be indifferent. In order to carry on its own work it must somehow deal with these surrounding disturbing conditions. It must somehow extend its function from the child to the adult.

Such an extension of school function need not cause surprise. New situations may be expected to demand new types of responses. New social situations will call for institutional changes. For example, in the period now ending the American school has been effecting, in theory at least, one clear-cut instance of an extension of institutional function. As has already been brought out in this book, in earlier times the school's duty as regards education was well defined as supplementary. Home and community carried the inclusive burden, the school furnished the literary addendum. But now that situation is changed. Family life in that earlier day, including as it did a much wider range of economic functions, brought parents and children together in a sharing of life activities which was educative in high degree. Only the shadow of this former education, taking the country over, now remains. To make good this loss the school has been compelled to extend its function. While the American school does not accept the whole care of the child—manifestly, it cannot—it does accept a real care for the whole child. That is to say, the American school at its best now accepts the idea that its active concern properly extends to include not only books and the other customary learning, but also the child's physical health, his moral health, his personality adjustment, his esthetic welfare, his vocational welfare, and so on. So that all aspects of reasonable well-being are now included in the aim of the best school thought and endeavor. Where such breadth of view has found supporting wealth, as is true in certain of the best schools, both public and private, school medical inspection for example takes thought for every kind of physical well-being, advising as to teeth, hearing, eyesight, organic weaknesses, contagious diseases, etc., etc., and counts all of these integral in a proper educational outlook.

And even now is there still further extension of school function in process. Not only must the school as such be sensitive to all the varied needs of the growing child, it must seek to see that the needs are met. It must consciously deal with conditions. It must enter further into the adult world. Wherever people need to learn in order to meet life, there education has a positive obligation. Some needs as already indicated are now being met in the enlarged school program, certain of these for now many years, as in the case of school music, school libraries, school playgrounds, medical inspection, dental inspection, vocational education, vocational counseling, schoolroom lunches, etc., etc. These extend the school into life. Others lying outside the school in the home are coming to be met by "visiting teachers," who go to individual homes to study and advise upon especially difficult personality cases. Still other needs will be met by more organized efforts between school and parents, meeting in study groups. Still further outside of actual school work, public educational authorities have ofen coöperated with other civic groups to work for public libraries, better park facilities, community musical programs, better conditions of child labor. All these we have become more or less accustomed to. But in it all we have seldom generalized even our own practices. If we do that, the next steps will perhaps seem but easy.

Is there a final extension to the work and function of education into the adult world? Preceding chapters tell the story. When we think closely on these things, we seem bound to conclude that the proper educational care of the child knows no excluding boundary to shut out any aspect of life which does in fact affect the child's well-being. The school need not accept care for all the aspects—it manifestly cannot and will not—but education as such will study all such aspects and be concerned that suitable measures be somehow taken to care for them. If young parents need help in the nurture of their children, the profession of education in some of its reaches will study this problem and help those parents in their study. If child labor is anywhere a problem, the profession of education—more consciously and insistently than hitherto—must accept a leading responsibility to arouse and direct public opinion. And this widening process leads on by inevitable steps from this regard for the whole child considered in himself to a new and active regard for the social and economic conditions that affect child welfare, and this perforce includes regard for the welfare of the child's parents. For family conditions certainly affect child welfare.

But we must go even further. The whole surrounding and enveloping social life and culture educate the growing child. We saw this above in the miseducative effects of competitive business and more generally in the discussions of Chapter III. If culture is thus powerful for education, and words can hardly exaggerate the fact, then the educator must be profoundly and fundamentally concerned that the culture be the kind which shall best educate both young and old. But this culture is primarily in adult hands. It thus appears that wherever and however the educator may start his thinking, he is led inevitably on the one hand to the determining conditions of social life and on the other to the adult population and its improvement. The crux of all social improvement lies in the interaction of these two. If intelligence is to serve, adult education, it would seem, is the master key. The profession of education must take up new work.

At this point, however, a new difficulty arises. We may seem about to put the entire burden of directing civilization upon the educator. A sense of humor if nothing else must somehow rescue us. Where shall we draw the line? The educator's proper function seems to radiate from two foci: one is the child and whatever concerns him, the other is the educative process and how it can best be directed to help civilization. These two foci give the initial definition of the work of the educator, but as we have seen wide extensions are inherent. The demarcation seems as follows: As in the one case the educator will not assume the whole active care of the child but only a responsible concern to foster that care as may be residually needed, so with the other the profession of education as such will not carry the whole burden of civilization, nor even of education within civilization, but will assume an active responsible regard that education, wherever it works, shall serve our civilization as best it can. And this too will be interpreted residually and in proportion to strategic need. Any conditions whatever affecting life may become the concern of educators as such if it appears important enough and the active effort of the profession of education seems needed in connection. The criticism and promotion of our social ideals is one area in which we shall always feel the deepest concern.

One further distinction of function remains. We saw in the opening pages of this chapter how a proper democracy working amid the breakdown of outworn ideas in our changing times will wish the whole population to pursue the educative way of life. And this is of course but another way of calling for an inclusive program of democratic planning, the shared effort of all to apply common study and learning to the direction of our common concerns. A question arises in connection: How do we distinguish adult education as the whole people studying their inherent problems from adult education as one of the professional concerns of educators? The answer seems clear. Education wherever found is best conceived as a self-active process. If we accept democracy, we shall wish as widespread and effectual study of common problems among the whole people as can be got. This is both the democratic and the educative way of life. But the art of studying together is a matter which can itself be studied. Research in such will be needed, materials to help group study must be prepared, leaders and organizers will require professional preparation —in short, at least for the coming decades if not forever, we shall need professional workers to foster and guide at least some of the processes of the wider adult study. Both these aspects will be considered in the coming pages, with emphasis on the professional as befits the purposes of this book. But in it all education as a function of society finds its *raison d'être* and its guidance in the more inclusive principle of Chapter II that society is to be conceived as a function of education.

Thus under the changing conditions of the modern world continual social study becomes the inevitable consequence of continually arising social problems. Education whether public or private can no longer be conceived as stopping when adulthood is reached. Universal adult study of life's problems having become necessary, the profession of education must accept the enlarged responsibility. Adult education, of a new kind and degree, enters as a necessary constituent of any inclusive social and educational outlook. The task next at hand is thus to explore the needs and possibilities of this new adult education.

II

The term *adult education* as usually understood may to some prove a stumbling-block to thought in this discussion. If some quite new term could be found which carries no implication of early lack of opportunity, thought and effort might both be helped; but so far no adequate alternative has appeared The present effort, then, is to take the existing term and try to widen and deepen the ordinary conception back of it.

The general conception herein presented is that the whole population need to become students of life and civilization in a new sense and degree and that the profession of education must so enlarge its hitherto customary thinking as to accept responsibility for helping as best it can in this new adult field of study. Practically all aspects of life must be studied, but at the present our social-economic situation seems to furnish the most pressing problem, on the one hand to get possession of our own soul—to effect an integrated social outlook and find satisfactory objects of allegiance—and on the other, to find how our society may by continual planning better and better harness our ever growing technology to the best interests of society. Our inclusive aim may perhaps then be expressed as the effort to help our people—all of us working together, no imposition from above—by study of the situation to change the character and outlook of our citizenship as did our Revolutionary fathers in their day. The demands on us and the attendant difficulties are even greater than they knew; the possible outcome—if we can but achieve it—may likewise be greater.

Already a great amount of adult education is now going on among us, much of it too familiar to attract attention. Possibly more account of this would customarily be taken if the inherent place of education and the educative process in life were more adequately conceived. Our first step will be to take stock of the varied forms of this existent adult education, see its possibilities for the purposes we have in mind, note its deficiencies, and get from it any suggestions we can for the better pursuit of our aims in this connection. It may help to group some of the more typical instances under a succession of heads beginning with those least conscious of themselves as education and going by stages to the more and more conscious efforts.

First in this list comes the education inherent in ordinary life itself. This is so remote from the text-book conception of learning that we shall probably do well to examine it at some length, partly to see more surely how it is true education, but even more to see in it its wider possibilities. The discussion in the preceding chapter [1] will help at this point.

Suppose a newly married couple are beginning housekeeping. That they have literally innumerable things to learn all older hands at the business know only too well. The verb *to learn* as here used points to the educative effect, and properly so. Each new experience: with real estate agent, with gas man, with furniture store, with stove, with ice-box, with marketing—each such brings its demand to see and understand things in new light. Each instance reaches for its management back into the learner's past experience and outward into what the group culture has to offer. From suggestions thus got,

[1] See pp. 102 ff.

selected and adapted in the light of the situation at hand, the learner contrives what is for him, or her, a new response—however old it may seem in the race experience—and so builds himself or herself into a somewhat different person with new and wider social connections and responsibilities. It is but a commonplace to say that life thus takes on new meanings.

Now the education so demanded is as wide and inclusive as there are varied and significant new experiences presenting themselves to be met and managed. The actual educative result and its quality will depend on how well the many situations are met, that is, on the quality of life lived in meeting the situations and in the promise thus given for meeting other situations well. This point can hardly be overemphasized. Education has two sides, corresponding to two aspects of life. First is the on-moving, the advance being made, the gain in quality of life being effected. Second is the registering of this advance in the very being of the person himself. We now understand that in each significant response the whole organism, in some true sense, coöperates to make the response a success. Learning then goes as far as does this inclusive responding, and each such instance in its own measure remakes the learner's whole being, each remade part being also newly connected with each other remade part throughout. Thereafter the learner by so much sees differently according to the new insight gained from the learning experience, feels differently, decides differently, acts differently. The test of the advance lies in the way in which succeeding situations of life are consequently met. Each such advance made—be it much or little, good or ill, rich or meager—is registered for the future. Self and life are always in process. This is what we mean by the fact of education.

How adult education as a conscious affair can help people lies in the process just described. The danger is that our newly-weds will either ignore their new possibilities or will meet their situations simply by following tradition, or just as bad by hiring others to think for them. If we can help these beginners to study better their successive experiences, they will in general meet them better and the gain will be capitalized for the future. If we can help them to find and study the best that others have done in similar situations, thinking will be further stimulated and fertilized. If we can so help them and all others of their kind that wider interests and better habits of study shall become general among our people, our whole civilization may change. This constitutes in general the aim and process which the profession has before itself in the matter of adult education.

As to actual learning, by all the principles of psychology we learn best when the situation at hand in fact stirs us. For these newly-weds there should be definite but very friendly opportunities to study the various aspects of home-making, each carried as far as an aroused interest would care to go. House planning, house decorating, gardening, cooking, serving, with preparations later on for the baby, and then the care and nurture of the baby—these are obvious possibilities, each to be taken at its time. But we are perhaps even more concerned that these first needs shall be so managed as to lead on to further and deeper study, on the one hand, of all that makes life good and fine in the living; and, on the other, of the social, economic, and political conditions that keep actual life from being what it might otherwise be. An intelligent program of adult education will study life and its possibilities and seek to present such a program of lectures and study, on the one hand, and of observation and discussion and practice, on the other, as will in fact help people to take hold of life consciously to make it better.

An actual community situation may indicate how under good guidance a wider study of affairs might arise than now ordinarily obtains. A small community found that it was about to be left off the route of a projected state highway, unjustly as it appeared to the villagers. Study immediately arose of the highway routing and how it was determined. It soon appeared that geographical and economical considerations were not the only factors at work in the case. Interactions between highway location and construction on the one hand and political influence on the other seemed clear. The actual working of state and local politics came forward for consideration. Indignation at injustice and possible corruption was aroused. The name of a particular official came henceforth to be taboo to certain of the citizens. Votes were shifted in the next election. In the actual instance, the matter stopped there, at least for the most part, except that there was probably some increase in the feeling of cynical helplessness common to such situations. But under suitable study and leadership such a case might easily lead through a real study of actual politics back to underlying problems of the economic background. And such study should lead to concerted action. If this local group could know that it was part and parcel of a wide group studying seriously the actual social situation, if regional conferences could occasionally be held, if nationally known thinkers were seriously discussing such problems, if publications of assured standing were helping in the mobilization of thought along such lines—if all these things could be, there need be little doubt that far-reaching effects would be possible. This way of study and action, many, many times repeated throughout the country, furnishes the democratic hope for remaking our economic system and otherwise rebuilding our social life. In the degree that citizens can so unite for study and action, in like degree can best expert thinking be better spread on its merits and defensible action taken. In the same degree can each participating citizen find for himself a cause worthy of thought and effort. So, further, can each one thinking through his own problems to satisfactory action in pursuit of a worthy cause come to terms of internal integration with himself. Finally, it is in fostering such a way of life among the people in general that adult education in the narrower professional sense finds its guiding motive and justifying cause.

One phase of the education of ordinary life demands special attention, and that is the possibilities inherent in vocation and its many connectednesses. As matters now stand, we ordinarily expect that a man will, if necessary, study his work sufficiently to make a reasonable success of it: most probably meet this expectation, while many go on to steep themselves thoroughly in business. But study to secure private gain, if that be all, is likely to lead to the narrowing rather than the broadening of the range of meanings seen. What we here wish is something quite different. We wish as far as possible that men engaged in any one line of work, or even better in complementary aspects of work along any one line, shall study the many varied social bearings of that work. A chief condemnation of the existing business scheme is that in fact and by accepted implication it releases men engaged in it from considering morally all the consequences that legitimately flow from their acts. It may be a matter of wage scale for employees, it may be an affair of winning over a rival in a deal. "I am sorry, but business is business and I cannot do otherwise," is a sentiment often heard in excuse for what on other grounds seems blameworthy. As long as the profit motive rules, we shall not be able to get any full or free consideration of all consequences; it is simply impossible. But something can even now be done, especially perhaps when the varied opposed interests meet together in honest thought about their common concerns. If only it can be made to succeed, possibly no study will do more to broaden views than such a shared search by employers and employees into the actual effects of the existing economic régime. And there are many other possibilities.

What is possible even now from such wider studies may

be seen from an actual case. A certain group interested in finding better ways of life got together certain of its members, men in business, to study the social bearings of their business practices. The more they studied the apparent results, the more they felt the need of more exact knowledge and more adequate interpretation. Being thus stirred, they engaged an expert student in the social field to come and trace out for them the further-reaching effects of their own scale of wages and conditions of work on the lives of their employees and their employees' families. Various results of the study carried over into their business. For example, the architects in the group began to study housing conditions and their effect on human happiness. This led to a further study of city planning and eventually in fact to such concrete results as the model villages of Sunnyside and Radburn near New York City. And even yet there is more in sight.

It needs no further words to argue the possibilities here. Vocation and all that it potentially means forms one of the strong natural centers for study and personal integration of life. Each profession, both as a whole and in each locality, has thus its possible public service. The same is true for each line of economic service, with the special advantage that mutually interacting agents can talk over their contact points hitherto so often provocative of conflict. The wider adult education will see here unlimited possibilities for the future, as our social life is put progressively on a planning basis. The specific profession of education can meanwhile do all in its power to foster the development.

In the matter of conscious intent to influence action the commercial efforts to sell come perhaps next in our survey. Advertising and face-to-face salesmanship constitute the principal instance. From the point of view of education it is the limitations that here most impress us. Appeals are often of a low type, and only too often positively misleading. One who is interested in improving the economic system would see here a wonderful opportunity to study public waste. A conscious adult education might well study this question of waste and go on easily thence to study of suggested plans for reconstructing our economic system so as to utilize technology and abolish waste. In the degree that the people generally become intelligent in the matter, the course of appropriate action would, we believe, be furthered. The extraordinary possibilities now seen in commercial advertising suggest too the possibilities in it that an intelligent society might find for itself if it but mobilized the press, moving pictures, radio, all in one consistent program of social enlightenment. When we think of how universal attention could be directed to a worthy cause, how directly reliable information could be spread— when we think of these things, we almost shudder at the possibilities going to waste. Possibly in time a better social order will learn how to use these agencies for the common good.

We are thus led to consider these last-named agencies as they now work. Even as matters stand they are extraordinarily influential. Probably of all agencies educating in non-face-to-face affairs it is this commercially motivated group, the press, moving pictures, radio, theater, etc., that wields the greatest influence. A veritable army is here at work alluring people powerfully into experiences which do in their way educate. But what shall we say of the education they give? For our purposes the following facts—speaking generally—stand out regarding these agencies. They are commercial efforts at pecuniary gain. In order to get this gain they must sell themselves, and the wider the sale the greater the gain. They sell by pleasing. That the social effects will be bad as well as good hardly needs argument. On the bad side will be the temptation to appeal to the lower ideals and taste of the majority rather than pursue the highest attainable ideals. Our present work conditions aggravate the difficulty. The widespread boredom from uninteresting work, with its insistent demand for compensating excitement, furnishes an easy mark for such exploitation. So these agencies in order to sell themselves tend too much to seek the striking, the startling, the scandalous. Even the best newspapers, for example, cannot disregard this aspect of news, and the cinema and (in this country) the radio suffer analogously.

But there is a good side. Information is through these agencies certainly made fluid as never before. What printing has done in 400 years to raise the lot of the lowly is a story often told. Possibly the like influences may now be extended to other lines. Actual information is certainly a large ingredient in intelligence. Nor is this all. It appears more than possible that readers of the low-type newspaper come on the whole gradually to demand something better. Some newspapermen confidently so claim. And nearly all people who read higher-type literature think they improve in the process. If this is general, the process of improvement is inherent. But be that as it may, this much is true: the higher the demands among the people themselves, the higher will be the character of response in newspapers, cinema, plays, or radio offered. This fact affords a positive opportunity. Anything that consciously directed adult education can do to raise the popular demand made upon newspapers, for example, will surely result in better newspapers. And these in their turn will bring better educative results to the people. The process of advance can thus be mutual. If professional adult education can then succeed in getting more and more people to studying life earnestly, all these agencies here under consideration will be favorably affected and become in their turn better educative agencies. These considerations point to a very hopeful means for improving our social-economic situation. If we can get the people to study the economic problem, the newspapers, etc., will find it out in the new interests and demands thus created, and they in their turn will seek to meet these demands. In this way as elsewhere can professional adult education effectually help the cause of wider citizenship education.

The radio seems to demand a special word, since its public status in this country is still in the making. Unrestrained competition in broadcasting is of course impossible. Public control is essential. The question not yet settled with us is whether this control shall subordinate public service as now to the private gain of advertising or whether the radio shall be run for public service. In the opinion of many, including these authors, the waste in our present régime of broadcasting, based as it is on advertising, is nothing less than a tragic disgrace. We can have vastly better service if only we will become alert to the possibilities. Possibly we should adopt the British scheme of public tax support and management. Possibly a better plan can be devised. Our present arrangements are meanwhile unspeakably bad.

It will not be necessary to give detailed discussion to the various remaining groups, important as they may be. Next come the avowedly propaganda bodies such as political parties, peace societies, the Anti-Saloon League, organizations to fight the 18th Amendment, etc., etc. While these do in a measure educate, the danger is that they will present one-sided facts and arguments and so mislead and confuse. The worse of these belong, perhaps, about in the class of the worse newspaper, and analogously perhaps with the higher. The effort of conscious adult education to raise the standards of these propaganda bodies may not be highly effective, but at any rate their campaigns will furnish good subject-matter of study for adult education groups. Our fathers thought that even the wiles of the devil could be made the means of grace. So here probably if we do but try.

Closely related with the foregoing are various bodies doing propaganda work on the side—the churches, chambers of commerce, parent-teacher organizations, the American Legion, the D. A. R., Rotary and Kiwanis Clubs, etc. That the range here is very great is notorious. At the highest these may approximate the best study groups later to be discussed. At the worst, they seem more despicable than the worst among those avowedly organized for propaganda. Conscious adult education can again study the programs and claims of these various bodies as was suggested for the group preceding. But more can be done. At least some of these bodies are anxious to study in order to be sure of the social programs they would advocate. Possibly adult education authorities would be welcomed in helping these to map out such study programs, in supplying speakers, etc. Where there is a will, there is usually a way.

Correspondence schools deserve perhaps a special word. Here again is the range great, from the most honest and careful down to what seem at a distance something like conscious frauds. The amount of money paid out by the American people is said by some students of the subject to amount to $25,000,000. Possibly the best thing here would be for organized adult education itself to enter this field under the highest possible auspices so as to ensure—until general public support can be got—that no exploitation is involved. At the present time some of our higher universities engage in correspondence work in order, so it would seem, to make money for use elsewhere in the university. Even at the best such a shift of money seems a doubtful policy. At the worst it is indefensible.

In pleasing contrast with much of the work already studied stands the next group of organizations, those committed in advance to study in order to find out what their members are to believe. Among such we find the League of Woman Voters, the Foreign Policy Association, the American Association of University Women, parent-education groups, public forums, and the like. There are, of course, many varying degrees of seriousness of study even within otherwise admirable organizations. The general conception, however, stands clear. These organizations hold that ordinary, well-educated heads of families should consciously study the various problems that life presents. This is of course exactly the key element in the conception of the wider adult education herein advocated. The organizations now under review may be said to represent in voluntary and spontaneous fashion exactly what the adult education movement in a more organized way will seek to foster. Study groups, discussion groups, lecture associations, discussion forums—these will remain probably through all time as among the best conscious efforts to raise the standard of popular intelligence.

Higher in the scale of careful study stand the various learned bodies or associations, the American Economic Association, American Philosophical Association, American Political Science Association, American Historical Association, etc., etc. These for the most part are clearing-houses as it were for the university study of these various fields. In this sense they represent the country's intelligence at its best, the most careful and exact study possible to be made of the problems of human interest. Adult education can go no higher. This is a clear illustration of a field of adult study where the adult education movement as professionally directed will not give but receive. What it receives from these experts it will use as it tries to help others to study. In fact it will seek in every known way to bring the popular thinking preparatory to action as near as it may be in quality and content to such thinking as characterizes this learned group at its best.

Much closer within the typical conception of adult education as professionally conducted stands "university extension." By this we mean the effort of the colleges and universities to offer their advantages of study as widely as feasible outside the group of full-time college and university students: afternoon and evening and Saturday courses offered both on the campus and off with a minimum of excluding regulations. This provides one of the key instances of the professional adult education practice as herein conceived. The State of Massachusetts has been a leader here in offering such under the auspices of its State Department of Education apart from any college or university, and the plan seems worthy of high commendation. Delaware too is doing much. Of course elsewhere, in Wisconsin for example, much the same widespread study has been got under state university or other university auspices. Possibly the time will later come—we hope so—when any reasonably sized group can study under state auspices, free of tuition charges, within their own home town anything whatever of significant worth.

Child-study groups constitute a further already flourishing line of adult education, and the promise here is very great. Nursery schools have recently come into being and they will render real service, but possibly their greatest service will lie, hand in hand with other schools, in helping parents to study the better care of children in the home. It is of course true that much remains to be done both in securing more knowledge of child care and in the techniques of helping parents. But recent progress is distinctly gratifying. Already much reliable knowledge is available and the movement of study is under way. The school of to-morrow will more and more accept responsibility for work along this line, and the gains seem great. Parents and teachers need to educate each other to a fuller understanding both of particular children and of education in general. The more we accept a responsible regard for the whole child, the more each child as such will be studied. The more we try to join the school with life, the more will school and community need to work in coöperation. The more parents and teachers study life together, the more will the school be permitted to undertake with children. At present, American prejudice against new thinking is very great. The school is now kept so neutral as to be dull and even forbidding to youthful interest. Adult prejudice is a bar to social progress. We must broaden the range for both child and parent. Eventually the whole life of the child must somehow be unified as to intended educative effect. Eventually the whole adult must similarly get consideration. The parent study group is a definite start to bring both results. Once the coördinated task of child education can be accepted, progress in the education of both child and parent will come much faster. And the mutual interactive educative effects on parent, teacher, and child can and will be highly significant. History and civilization and economic life if studied openly, really studied that is, should hasten the day when conscious planning of life and its affairs shall become the rule. Many difficulties attend, but the possibilities are great.

Finally in our list we reach the movements now consciously calling themselves adult education. So far, as intimated at the outset, these have naturally enough hitherto thought rather in terms of the under-privileged. From this point of view they have done excellent pioneer work. The time seems now ripe to go forward to a broader conception that will at least potentially include the whole adult population. From the point of concern of this book, the chief interest of adult education will, then, lie henceforward not so much in the under-privileged as in the people generally. The under-privileged will of course not be slighted—rather the contrary—and "reëducation" along new trade lines will also always be a feature, but the main interest at any one time will lie wherever the main social problem lies. At the present time this seems to center in the reconstruction of our economic system. At a later time the emphasis may be in "the good life," that we may learn better how to live. Our ever oncoming social problems will give us a steady stream of demand for study. The chief thesis here maintained is that our population generally must learn *to* study and *how* to study as an ever continuing part of ordinary life. It is exactly to foster such study among our people as a whole that the profession of education takes on the new work of adult education. But the educator here, as elsewhere, does his best work as he makes himself progressively unnecessary. The profession of education as it works in this new field will try to make ever more people independent of it in their wish to study and act and in their skill in so doing.

III

At this point in the discussion, certain skeptics and critics will rise to question one or more features of our position. Some for instance will affect to see in the whole presentation simply a revival or continuance of the "liberalism" once flourishing among our intellectuals, but now everywhere in decay. These will ask, perhaps with a condescending "Oh, yeah?" if we have not heard about "tired liberals" and of the general bankruptcy of that position. To these cynics our reply will be that, while we share some things in common with those liberals, we still differ radically on our one fundamental point. They recognized certain evils and sought through reform measures of honesty in politics, the fair deal, industrial democracy, and the like to remedy these evils. We recognize the same evils, but we believe them deeper rooted than these liberals saw, namely in the very structure of our *laissez-faire* profits system economy. We count too that technology now offers greater opportunities than could then be seen. Under these circumstances we propose to attack these root conditions which not only cause these long recognized evils but now stand in the way of great advances. And also we too believe in democracy and the fair deal, but we propose to apply these to the underlying system itself and not merely to its surface outcroppings. We count therefore that some form of economic planning run ultimately by all for the good of all offers a real basis for getting rid of dishonesty and poverty and insecurity, all at the same time. We aim to call such attention to these underlying conditions and to the possibilities of planning as will allow others to see what we see, check and if need be improve our thinking in connection, and then, we hope, permit all to go forward together in appropriate action. We have not, like some ex-liberals, accepted defeat and turned cynic. We still believe in reform and in democracy, but our reform and our democracy must face actual conditions and cut to the root of the difficulty at hand.

Still another group of critics will accuse us of proposing to use educational agencies for partisan propaganda. True education, these say, will engage in study and research to find the truth, not in propagandist efforts to spread in partisan fashion prior chosen doctrines. There is so much warranted in just fears along this line that we cannot fail to be sympathetic, but we believe that confusion of thought pervades the charges as made.

The common thought about propaganda and indoctrination has come down to us from the past when men thought in terms of orthodoxies as fixed-in-advance and clear-cut rivals. Acceptance or rejection was an out-and-out either-or affair. Propaganda thus came to be thought of as the effort to win grown-ups from heterodoxy to orthodoxy, while indoctrination was the method of fixing orthodoxy once for all in the minds and hearts of the young. It was in this period of our thinking that the state adopted neutrality as between rival church orthodoxies, and the public school became so "neutral" that it refused to consider live issues, even though this refusal meant continued indoctrination of now out-of-date positions. But a change in thinking has come about. History has convinced the modern-minded that doctrines themselves have their life histories of birth, acceptance, and decay. With this conception of continued change and becoming, propaganda and indoctrination do not fit. Instead the public school must accept responsibility for the building of intelligence in and for the wise choice between growing and decaying doctrines and programs. Neutrality, in the sense of avoidance of this responsibility, becomes thus, as we see it, a cowardly refusal to face inherent duty. It is amid this shift of thinking that many are now confused.

As conscious education, whether of young or old, faces then such a situation as our hang-over economic system, it cannot be neutral. To do nothing is in so far to perpetuate outworn and now hurtful doctrines. And probably most American schools do in effect thus join hands with reactionary influences to maintain the *status quo*. As in such a situation we seek a defensible positive program two things must characterize our educational endeavors. On the one hand, we must distinguish a proper education from anything that is in effect prejudice building or mere training; we cannot in general rest content with the unthinking acceptance of what is learned. On the other hand, we must help any we touch, whether old or young, to study the rival claims of contending new ideas that progress in thought and action may more surely take the defensibly best road, while the individual himself shall in the process thereby best learn to help forward such progress.

The first of these two considerations lies at the heart of respect for personality: we must help each one to the best of his ability to be an intelligent judge in his decisions and policies. Anything less is but to degrade the citizen to the status formerly accorded to serfs and slaves. And this ethical consideration is backed by another, it may be said, more practical in nature. One who has thus thought all round a question before reaching a decision will on the one hand choose his positions more wisely and on the other will know better the limitations of his choice. It is a commonplace how unintelligently the unthinking will apply principles which if discriminatingly used would prove most efficient. The situation as regards children would call for further consideration, but we are here concerned with adults who can think before they decide.

The second consideration reaches the heart of our present problem. The world of affairs always presents us with a great variety of ideas in all stages of their life career. Some we may say are dead and ought to be buried. Others are now decaying but still have some good in them which should be saved for use elsewhere. Others further are in the full flower of acceptance; these we should use for all they are worth. Finally, still others are struggling for recognition and acceptance. Surely no educational program worthy the name could omit the positive duty of helping its members, whether old or young, each according to his own stage of development, to criticize these confronting ideas so as to learn better what to do about them. Here it is the ideas struggling to gain initial acceptance that most concerns us. The claim that educational endeavor must wait and do nothing until the rest of the world shall somehow have chosen is to ignore the fact that in our kind of world ideas are all the time being born. Certainly, if education has any valid meaning for life, it must help both young and old to deal with the origin of ideas and with choices among rival ideas, whether these be old and possibly outworn or young and possibly very hurtful or possibly very significant. There can be no escape. Education must accept its duty.

The principle is, of course, to be applied according to the conditions. If, for example, the educator finds himself in a backward community, he will deal with his people as there they are, trying as best he can to help them choose, as befits freemen, as intelligently as possible what to reject from their hitherto accepted ideas as well as what to accept from the new ideas that demand consideration. Since the learner must choose and so must learn to choose, the educator will help him as best he can both to choose reliably in the case at hand and to learn in the effort how to choose better next time. That the educator is himself further along in his own thinking is simply an asset. The learner must still think, and the educator must still help him to think. To call such a process propaganda or indoctrination is to call in question the quality of the teaching help that the educator gives. At the worst this might be the worst kind of propaganda or indoctrination, at the best it will be neither. That the educator knows in advance where he believes the learner should come out should be a warning to him to watch his steps, that his teaching be true teaching, but this is no reason why he should ignore what he thinks. Otherwise we throw out the baby with the bath: in order to avoid the possibility of partisanship we should be forced to prefer instructors who are either ignorant or unable to reach conclusions, exactly those from whom we pray to be delivered.

Or suppose again a group of adults who in their thinking have already reached the general conclusion that a planning society is a social necessity. Shall they stop study? Or shall they go on to the next step and ask what specific measures for planning, among the many proposed, can best meet the situation? And if yes to this, might they call in to help them in their thinking some one who has studied plans and believes that he has found a specific program better than any other yet proposed? And if they do so ask this man to help them study, does he by accepting thereby become a propagandist for his plan? Does not the answer here as before depend on how he leads the study? He may be a propagandist, or he may help them really to study and weigh. And suppose the next step, that this group from their study of plans shall themselves adopt one which they wish put into effect, are they then to be estopped from further study? Should they not rather begin on a study of practical political or other social means for actually putting their program into operation? And if yes again, might they not call on adult education headquarters for a man versed in such matters to help at this stage?

That difficulties and problems will arise in connection with any widespread program of adult education is but true, especially if so controversial a question as changing the economic order is widely studied and stressed. Attempts will be made to suppress open study and discussion. Political and financial pressure will be exerted. In short, the struggle for academic freedom, hardly as yet won for all our colleges and universities, will be begun all over again in the realm of adult education. But this is itself only another instance of the growth of an idea in a new setting. The profession of education will have to organize in this new field to gain acceptance here for the right of untrammeled study based on fairness for all. This is but life: struggle, growth, counter struggle, forever. Our aim and effort is to introduce effectual intelligence into the process.

Is not then the conclusion clear that in a changing world, where ideas grow and flourish and decay, education can and should help people to deal intelligently with any idea or program at whatever stage of acceptance it may then have reached? And does not the charge of propaganda or indoctrination at any stage turn exactly on how the educator manages his teaching and not on whether he thinks he knows where intelligent study will lead the learners? We of this book would answer both of these questions in the affirmative and define propaganda or indoctrination in connection as any effort to secure acceptance of any idea in such fashion as does not thereby help, as best possible, to make the learner an independent judge of such matters. With this understanding we deny emphatically that the educational program we herein propose is properly to be called one of partisan propaganda.

There are still other questions that critics will raise as we propose a program of widespread adult education. Some will ask, belatedly now to be sure, whether we really expect minds long out of school to study and learn; and references to James will be brought forward with his intimation that already at twenty-five we begin to be old fogies. Fortunately the studies of Thorndike and others enable us to assert that we have no need to fear nature on this point. So far as this goes, the parent of forty will learn as well as the child of fifteen and probably better. The main thing with the old—as well as the young—is that they be interested to try. We can confidently believe that the more they study with success, the more they will wish so to study; and the more the results of such study accumulate, the more successful will further study be. Here as elsewhere is it true that to him that hath shall be given.

But the question of ability to learn takes another and more serious turn. Some among us assert that, irrespective of age, most people by nature cannot think reliably, and they further add that the trend of affairs is to leave all important matters more and more to the determination of experts. These objectors therefore call on us to renounce democracy in all its forms as now outmoded. The issue is too important to be ignored. The position taken by this book is in conscious and intentional antagonism to that of these critics. It is herein held that nearly all people do think—and fairly reliably—about such of their own affairs as lie within the range of ordinary experience; that effectual intelligence, of the more gifted as truly as of the less gifted, is largely a social product built into the individual as a result of his personal experience of sharing with others in common concerns; that accordingly each person, less gifted and more gifted alike, can and does successfully judge and use ideas and other tools which others have devised. We do not deny but affirm that expert knowledge has properly a very large and growing place in modern life, but we do deny that either the psychology of thinking or the distribution of native intelligence or the history of social and political institutions warrants the conclusion that the many should live in unthinking subservience to any group of experts however selected. We believe that the most realistic position to take, certainly in this country, is that the people generally will at least have to accept any new policy that is to be put into operation. We have no proletariat in the European sense, so we cannot have a dictatorship of the proletariat. Nor is it easy to take Fascism as a serious proposal. No Mussolini could maintain dictatorial power in this country. It is not our way. But let us consider the problem further.

That the present working of democratic political institutions is bad we may readily admit, but so also—as at the moment everybody knows—are the workings of our economic system. Indeed, it is open to doubt whether business is not now in worse bankruptcy than government. As for causes, it seems quite probable that the failures in both cases have a common root and source, namely in our hang-over business system of unlimited competition for gain. This, as we have already seen, sets people to working against each other and educates them accordingly. So that abiding disposition, as truly as the lure of immediate advantage, leads the common run of our citizens, whether in business as such or through politics (which increasingly becomes applied business) always to seek each his own gain. And often they unite in predatory groups to get this gain at the expense of the rest of us, as witness the Congressional log-rolling for "pork barrel" and tariff, not to mention the cruder forms of selling protection and exacting graft. Under such circumstances really common interests fall before the more obvious and immediate private gains. It is this corruption of politics by predatory business that probably most accounts for the present failure of our governmental machinery. It is accordingly more than a problem of political government that confronts us. Rather are we once more led to the question of remaking our fundamental underlying economic system.

As fast as this conception of our trouble can be accepted and people can see what has come to be the strategic fact of our times, namely, that our fortunes are tied together and not, as now we are taught, opposed to each other—when these things can be effectually grasped, a different situation confronts us. Even our political situation enters a new phase. It remains of course true that full incorporation of the new conception can only come as actual change is effected in the working economic system, with its correlative new educative effect. But a new conception can be sufficiently well grasped to mean a new program with a new orientation of thought and feeling. With so large a proportion of our people even in boom times—one-half of all families in 1927 we are told —living below recognized standards of comfort, with the present widespread distress, with the recognition that insecurity under existing arrangements confronts practically all—with all these things true, it ought not to be difficult for an intelligent study, on the one hand, of our existing evil conditions, and, on the other, of the possibilities inherent in our technology to bring such a change of conception and attitude in the majority among us as shall demand effective change of system.

The position herein taken, then, is that our people do have sufficient native intelligence to see both the evil condition with its potent injustices and the possibilities of new and better things, and that once they see these clearly they will demand unified action to give up the old and move on to the new, and that once the demand be clearly voiced there will be no lack of leaders to execute the will of the people so expressed. Is there then no difficulty or danger? Both are possible: if the people do not understand the matter, unwise steps may be taken; if action be unduly delayed, anger and resentment may lead to hasty and even violent measures. It is then a situation and not a theory that confronts us. Technology has changed the world in which we live. An outworn business system retains the technology for the advantage of the few, when this should, both morally and efficiently, be used for all. We confront thus two alternatives: keeping the people in ignorance and thus either maintaining the existing system with its injustices and periodic breakdowns or "slipping over" some dictatorship; or we may try the other alternative of helping the people as far as possible to understand the situation that changes may be made both knowingly and intelligently. With all the means of publicity at hand, with ever larger numbers going to high school and college, the idea of keeping the people generally in ignorance is fantastic. The invention of printing 400 years ago made that thenceforth forever impossible, not to mention more modern means of spreading ideas. The only reasonable thing is to accept the American people for what they are, with their belief in democracy and their determination to rule themselves, but equally with their broader democratic notion of justice and fair play for all; and then proceed to use whatever endeavor we can muster to foster an intelligent study of our condition and of the means for improving it.

If history teaches anything, it is that wisdom is a collective affair and that leadership is varied, each kind mutually calling forth the others in ever greater degree as accumulating approval calls out ever greater efforts and accumulating results allow ever better criticism. There is thus one leadership of interested concern, which when it becomes sufficiently strong will call out the leadership of study with resulting proposed programs. And these programs in the degree that they seem feasible will evoke still stronger interest. Thus do the two leaderships of interest and expert thought mutually bring each other into fuller being and degree. And both will provoke—probably simultaneously—the third leadership of statesmanship which puts programs into action. Here then are at least three leaderships and they may act—nay, do act—at any level of intelligent knowledge.

The important thing, then, for us is that all these leaderships shall act at as high a level of effectual intelligence as possible. And it is exactly to meet this situation that we are here most concerned to foster adult education. It becomes, then, the business of all pertinent experts to put the funds of their knowledge at the disposal of the people as the situation is being studied and the new policies are being determined. This general position of interactive study and leadership with consequent appropriate group action we call by the name of democracy, without thereby committing ourselves in advance either to our present governmental arrangements or to any other specific set of devices in preference to another whereby the processes of shared decisions or their execution may best go on. In this sense of democracy we believe that a fair study of history will uphold it as better for us than any alternative yet tried or proposed for the management of social affairs.

And it is exactly in keeping with the foregoing position on democracy that this whole discussion on Adult Education has proceeded. As we look forward to certain necessary changes in our institutional forms, it is of course possible that some violent revolution may be the actual means by which such changes are effected. If the beneficiaries of entrenched injustice are so misguided as to force it, they may bring on such a violent revolution. But we of this book are working on a different theory. We wish to get as large a proportion of our people thinking as intelligently as possible about our social and economic problems in the belief that our safest hope for wise and effectual policies is the public intelligence that follows public study. In such study there will be amplest room for the highest expert knowledge to function. We wish all we can get. Once widespread study has sufficiently aroused and built widespread intelligence, effectual steps can be begun to change our system as intelligence may at that time indicate. Meanwhile any who would help to guide such study among the people must use the utmost intelligence they can muster for pointing out what seem to be promising lines of study. The most promising hypotheses must be examined in all their pertinent bearings. We shall thus use our present best thinking not as propaganda or indoctrination but as the best available means for fostering the best possible study to secure the best possible action.

IV

A few words as to possible steps in organization may conclude the chapter. The work herein contemplated comes properly within the enlarged conception of the profession of education as discussed in the preceding chapter. That it does so belong properly to the profession would seem to need no further word of argument. This means, then, at once that the institutions for the higher professional study of education should take this up as a proper object of study in the search for aims and methods as well as for the preparation of suitable personnel. Beginnings here have already been made. The American Association of Adult Education has already been studying more or less consciously along this line. If it should take a more definite stand in the matter, progress could probably be accelerated. Most of the agencies already at work in the field need hardly more than lift up their eyes to see that they have latterly been working more and more toward the general lines of operation herein contemplated, except as regards the particular social-economic emphasis of this book. That, however, is easily the next step. Some, of course, as for instance the labor colleges and most other labor efforts in education, have already been working consciously at this problem. As regards actual workers already in the field, it is not easy to say which best represent the line of future growth. Most probably there will be many lines of development. The Smith-Lever workers are coming increasingly to see that the whole life of the people is their concern rather than any mere increasing of the yield of wheat or improving the canning of fruit. The government will always be very sensitive to what opponents will call social-political propaganda, but actual study will spread itself in spite of stand-pat fears. Probably the Smith-Lever people need to become more conscious of their own trends and of possible next steps. Municipal colleges offer a great opportunity, and the work is growing much more rapidly than most know about. State extension, whether under university or state department auspices, is assuredly a proper line of future development. Present economy measures will postpone the advance, but not for long; the need is too great. The State work in Delaware is significant in this connection. It is reported that in one rural county as many as one-eighth of the white adult population was last year enrolled in positive work in adult education and that for the state as a whole a majority of the legislature took part in this study. This last fact had one interesting result. When the economy program proposed to cut from the budget the appropriation supporting adult education, this majority rallied to its support and defeated the proposal. There is reason also for believing that otherwise and in general these particular legislators showed a larger social vision than did most of their fellow-members. Possibly these things are a foretaste of the results that may be expected when study and planning are permanently married.

However, for a good while to come all governmental agencies in this country will probably lack somewhat the necessary freedom of study that the situation especially calls for. In keeping with the genius of American institutions, voluntary effort probably must lead the way, at least in many localities. Some church efforts here hold excellent promise. Past efforts have built in large numbers a strong urge to render service to their fellows. The old lines of such service increasingly fail to satisfy. Many pastors and rabbis will welcome the idea of organizing within their congregations discussion groups to study social problems. Already some interesting experiments along this line are in process, and the further possibilities seem great. Parent-teacher groups, as has already been suggested, offer another rich field. Schools can hardly go forward as they wish unless the parents go with them. Groups can start with the study of children and go on to a study of the times and what they demand. Intelligent teachers, if they will, can help here in practically every school community in the country. Very probably city school systems will soon have an expert in charge of all such efforts. Here organized school effort can help adult study in general.

The public library is so powerful an ally in all study movements that especial mention should be made of it. Already it is doing yeoman work in reading lists, general advice, special book services, and the like. Somewhere, whether in library associations or in universities or in state or federal departments or in the A. A. A. E., special study must be made of the best reading helps that can be devised in connection with study groups. The schools of education certainly must study the whole problem of organization, of helps, of study manuals, of bibliographies, and the like. This will, of course, be a never ending occupation.

To encourage the idea and foster steps some active central committee must be at work. Just at this juncture it probably would be impossible to find a more useful course for a foundation to back. The profession must, of course, study its own processes and direct its own efforts, but a central committee reasonably supplied with funds could help with the study and encourage needed experiments. If democracy is to continue and succeed amid the new conditions, a higher standard and more diffused social intelligence will certainly be necessary. An intelligently directed adult education movement seems a certain necessity.

Civilization by all signs faces a new era. Our economic system can by proper planning yield hitherto undreamed-of wealth. Until the present hour the majority of men have been tied to superstition and other hindering authoritarianisms, on the basis of which real study has been counted either futile or wrong. Now we begin to be free. In the past the majority have been condemned to grinding labor, now plenty is possible for all. Life beckons as never before. At the moment we stand helpless before new problems. Possibly most among us still mistrust study and thought. But study to see the new possibilities and to realize them intelligently in action is the one great thing we need, and it must somehow be the study of all for all. In this study to help all and the intelligent steps consequent upon it a distraught civilization can find a unifying cause worthy of its supreme effort. The new professional work of adult education finds its precise reason for being in the effort to foster this wider study and action of all in the interest of all.

Chapter V

THE SCHOOL: ITS TASK AND ITS
ADMINISTRATION—I

THE school to-day faces a new task.. It must find its place in the scheme for social reconstruction which is needed to lift society from its present chaotic state. New conditions set the task with great definiteness. The social-economic situation has taken a form which the school can ignore only if it is ready to recognize that as it fails to contribute to the regeneration of society so does it become ineffective itself.[1] To this sorry end the school is not likely to go. It must be quite clear, however, that unless reality is faced such an end will result. And reality in the present social-economic situation makes sharp demands. The individual citizen must be brought to a realizing sense of the values that are implicit in the struggle for security by the common man in a society where corporate action has now become a basic characteristic. He must likewise be sensitized to the fact of international interdependence in the world situation. He must achieve an abiding concern for the educative effect of all social institutions as men plan together to establish a social order in which life for all may flow from a stable source. Furthermore, he must rise to a method of action which naturally brings old values up for reconstruction as changing conditions necessitate new attitudes.

The school, to be sure, is not to be asked to accept sole responsibility for the remaking of society. It has too long been

[1] A summary statement of factors that the school must now take into account is to be found in Chapter II, pp. 68-70.

our habit to "pass the buck," as we say, to the school on crucial social issues, and we have come now to realize that at its best the school is but one educative influence in the life of the students whom it touches. Unfortunately, as it is now organized the school is so out of relationship with society that more often than not it is the least effective of all the forces that play upon the student as he achieves the attitudes and dispositions which give character to the social process. This fact, however, need not lead us to disregard the school as a positive instrument for bringing the desired educative influences. What it really does is to compel the educator to turn to his own ground to seek out the nature of the contribution that the school may make to social reconstruction. The educator must be sensitive to the conditions that have precipitated our present social confusion and difficulty. He needs to recognize that the school is not the all-important agency it has too long been assumed to be. He needs to realize that as a member of the social order he has an obligation to bring about its steady reconstruction. Finally, he needs particularly to recognize that within the school situation he may move positively to accomplish tangible results in the direction of bringing to the social process individuals who are not only increasingly more capable of dealing with it intelligently but who are increasingly disposed so to act. This represents a distinct contribution, one that gives to the school a significant and directing program, and to the educator an impelling purpose.

It is to this task that the school must give its attention. In so doing it will discover that at certain strategic points a new emphasis is demanded. So insistent is this fact that a reconstruction of the school activity becomes at once a necessity. This we cannot fail to recognize; a statement less emphatic would but ignore the reality of those new conditions that bring our educative processes up for scrutiny. But we must likewise recognize that the school cannot ignore the reality of attitudes bred by a social order in which the individual pursuit of profits has been a dominant motive in action. It is thus entirely clear that the school is not free to change its character overnight. It is equally clear, however, that the educator faces the moral necessity of determining the direction in which the school is to move. This is inevitable. We of this book, therefore, faced with entrenched attitudes that are insensitive to a social-economic situation which compels the adoption of new values, have elected to throw our emphasis upon the attainment of a way of life which progressively reshapes the social forces to bring security to all and thus make possible the development of a culture in which all may educatively share. It is in these terms that we have set the task for the school, and we need now to ask what we may reasonably expect of the school as it seeks to develop individuals who will participate in the progressive reconstruction of the social order for the purpose of bringing a larger measure of satisfying life to all.

As earlier stated, the reorganization of the school processes is demanded by this point of view. This brings definitely to the fore a sense of direction for the total school activity. But it does more. It indicates specific reorganization at particular points, in each instance providing a way of turning the total process to the task in hand. We must expect the school to rise to a realization of its responsibility for contributing to the remaking of the social order. We may then reasonably expect of it emphasis on such a reorganization of its own activities as will bring the student to a consciousness of the character of his present world, with an allegiance to a mode of action which attacks the reconstruction of social values in an intelligent and sincere manner. Specifically, then, the school must launch a positive program for dealing with the present confusion both within and without the school by pointing up its reorganization at least in the following ways:

1. It is reasonable to expect the school progressively to orient the student in the life of which he is a part.
2. It is reasonable to expect the school to provide situations for the purpose of leading the student progressively to direct his action by an integrated and unified attitude to which he increasingly gives his allegiance.
3. It is reasonable to expect the school to encourage the development of independent interests, intellectual, esthetic, or practical, on the part of its students.
4. It is reasonable to expect the school to set up an environment in which all of its members, through active participation in its organization and control, may move progressively to a more complete appreciation of the deeper significance of the democratic way of life.
5. It is reasonable, finally, to expect the school to face frankly the fact that it will not contribute significantly to the reconstruction of the social process until it launches a positive program of experimentation directed toward the reconstruction of its own procedures.

Each of these obligations is applicable to the total educative situation, and though each needs to be amplified and illustrated before its full import may be apparent, it can be dogmatically stated at the outset that each is concerned with the central interest of the school. They thus place in the hands of both teacher and administrator the means for moving positively toward the formulation of a school program that will contribute immediately and significantly to the progressive reconstruction of the social order.

It is reasonable to expect the school to orient the student in the life of which he is a part.

It is a commonplace that the individual, meeting life as he emerges from the infant stage, is able to grow, to participate in the life that surrounds him, only as he finds out what the objects and activities of his environment mean to those with whom he associates. The parent uses the babbling sounds of the infant as an entering wedge in the development of the language which is to lead increasingly to participation in a more inclusive world. Later, he works to increase the area of understanding by bringing about an appreciation of toys that are safe, household articles that are harmful, yard boundaries that are reasonable, sleeping hours that are restful, distasteful foods that are healthful, and the like. Commonplace as this is, however, the purpose of the parent, the orientation of the growing individual in a bewildering world, is one that has never properly permeated the activities of the school. As a result, the school, concerned primarily with subject-matter, suddenly finds itself "shadow-boxing" with life.

In fact, the character of the present social situation has made orientation a central concern of the school. The individual formerly got his bearings in his world merely by taking active part in the relatively simple activities of the family and the community. Life in the home, however hard, was simple enough to permit ready and educative participation. So, too, in the community. The variations in the social pattern were few, and home and community worked together to help the individual appreciate the significance of the activities and attitudes of the group. The school had little to do with this, except as the limited knowledge with which it was concerned gave support to the social pattern. This has all changed in the present. The social pattern has lost its simplicity. The development of new instrumentalities has changed the character both of the home and of the community. The extension of knowledge has cut under the old authorities that gave currency to the values men cherished. And as men live together under these changed conditions new ends emerge and demand attention. The resulting conflict in attitudes and dispositions has repeatedly been pointed to in this discussion. It is significant here because it throws into relief the reason for insisting that orientation must now become a central concern of the school. The complexity of life on the material level, together with the competing values that stir to action in the realm of attitudes, have made necessary the operation of a definite agency to bring about that orientation which is essential to a progressive understanding of the world in which one lives.

The school has not completely failed to recognize the nature of the task which it now faces, as we see in the fact that its program has here and there been "loosened up." Contacts with the life that surrounds it have been more and more established, and those who work in the educative process may find themselves, and not without reason, resenting the charge that they have constructed an artificial environment for the student. In elementary education in particular there has been a disposition to move in the direction of establishing continuity between the school and the world outside. The fact remains, however, that at those points where life takes on chiefest zest, namely, where enthusiasms are engendered, the school has been careful to remain in "safe" territory, quite removed from dangerous controversy. This means, of course, that however much the individual may become familiar with the activities that go on in the social order, he is not helped to get his bearings amid the conflicting mass of attitudes and dispositions that struggle to give character to the social process. The failure here is a serious one, in spite of the fact that the school, in thus heading itself in the direction of bringing the individual to understand the activities of his world, has made an educational gain which must be preserved.

What is now needed is that the school build on the foundation so laid and seek an orientation of the individual which cuts deeper than the surface of life. Perhaps the most effective approach to this problem is, in this instance, the most obvious one. The immediate point of departure for the school is that host of activities which bring to the family, and thus to the individual, food, shelter, clothing, recreational opportunities, and the like.

The pupil coming to the school from the average home knows next to nothing of the underlying ways in which the family secures what it accepts as the necessaries of life. Indeed, meeting as he does individuals who come from families representing all variations of standards of living, the pupil may feel confused when his thought turns to "necessaries." This same confusion may be seen, incidentally, wherever standards appear. The variation from home to home, or from school to home, for instance, in standards of conduct forces the school to anticipate an orientation that leads the individual to stable action. So, too, does the recognition of the inevitable insecurity in our social order of the individual who is ignorant of the nature of the activities that bring the family its economic status suggest that the school use these activities as centers of serious study.

Oddly enough, higher education has recently been engaged in an orientation activity that is suggestive. Colleges and universities awoke to a realization a few years back that hordes of students, possessing varied interests, varied training, and varied attitudes toward the purposes of the institutions, were upon them. The older routines established for dealing with freshmen bore no relationship to this new army of students, and the institutions had to develop more effective procedures for enabling the individual to get his bearings as he entered upon his new life. What is here important is that the purpose of this activity has been to orient the student in his new educational world in order to save the wreckage that was fast accumulating as students failed to discover the purposes of the institutions they were attending. The concern, in short, has been to help the student adjust to new purposes, to traditions that may be understood only in particular settings, to a new physical environment, to new ways of living together, to new programs of physical well-being, to new and bewildering lines of subject-matter interests, and the like. Furthermore, and this fact is of particular significance for the public schools, each institution has thus had to direct its program of orientation toward the activities and attitudes current in its own community.

Each community—perhaps better, each school—has its own characteristic environment, and the school program as it is organized to place the necessary emphasis upon orientation will begin in large measure with the social setting that surrounds it. In Florida in those sections where orange groves abound life is essentially different from what it is in those districts where only the attraction of the climate for the northerner provides a center for economic activity. And in Pennsylvania another story is to be told as mining districts, agricultural areas, industrial centers, and hustling cities appear. So, too, with every state. Indeed, each community as it takes on size shows within itself characteristics with which differently located schools must reckon. And it is within this local situation that each school will find its centers of organization as it begins upon the problem of orienting the student in his environment in order that he may take part in the life there with an understanding that breeds security and stability.

Since it is inevitable that each school write its program in its own terms, no covering scheme can be set up for all to follow. What is essential to each, however, is the sense of direction which the orientation provides as curricula are built, and teaching methods are developed, *on the job*. Airports may be visited, ice-cream plants studied, factories surveyed, municipal officers interviewed, printing plants looked over, and other similar community-discovering activities carried on. The purpose of this activity, of course, will be more than to establish a passive acquaintanceship with the economic, social, and political endeavors of the community. It should bring the individual to an ever widening view of the ways in which the members of his community go about the business of making available those necessaries which keep the individual and the family together as a participating unit in the larger life of the group. But the school has a more important concern here. Such study is to go forward in ways that show wherein technological processes together with a corporate society have transformed the character of men's work. And, in so doing, it must reveal those factors that breed actual insecurity in the present as man struggles in the grasp of individualistic concepts to gain security under material and social conditions which compel the reconstruction of social-economic attitudes. No mere orientation that leads the student solely to a view of the world as it has been thought about will suffice. Orientation has the function to-day of bringing the individual to face the conditions of the world that must now be thought about if man is to attain security.

Each undertaking in orientation will provide a center from which all manner of educative activities may flow. The writing of individual and group reports, on whatever level of accomplishment, may be counted reasonable; the representation through differing art media of things seen, or suggested; the computation of company, or of individual, earnings and what these may mean; the study of the history of differing local economic activities; the creation of plans to further recreational activities in parts of the community where these are lacking; the dramatization of any of the activities studied in order that other members of the school community, or the larger community, may appreciate their significance; the study of the relationship of the working adults to the activity under consideration; the search for information that is needed in the solution of questions raised by individuals, or by the group; an evaluation of the importance of the activity in the life of the community; the planning together of further voyages in orientation; all of these activities, and innumerable others, may move out from each effort to help the individual get his bearings in the particular world in which his school is placed.

It is doubtless clear that in activities of this character there is a vitality for the individual not duplicated when orientation *in life* is entrusted to the guidance provided by limiting textbooks. The superior quality of an educative activity which removes verbal chains from the individual intelligence need not be the subject of debate. This superiority is none the less likely to be misleading. It has too often caused the school to stop short of the central purpose in orientation. A group of students, for instance, may develop an interest in the trucking facilities of a given community and, in its pursuit, engage in a series of vital experiences that leave them with knowledge not solely of trucking but of the more general problem of transportation, perhaps even of natural resources and of local industrial activities. Their knowledge and enthusiasm here will no doubt surpass that possessed by those whose sole source of understanding has been the printed page, but even so it may readily be that they fail to see much beyond the activity itself. But the school interested in orientation will not accept this limitation. It will deliberately reach out to take the student beyond a study of the basic physical features of the local trucking industry. Problems in transportation that have arisen as a result of the relatively free movement of the truck over the public highway provide an opportunity to have the student sense, on his particular level of comprehension, the nature of the difficulties involved in staging an individualistic economic war under conditions that definitely call for intelligent planning and social control. Toward these the school will turn the individual. In this instance, as in all orientation, the particular problem under consideration will serve not only as a center for organizing much of what we now think of as "school material," but it will quite as significantly function as a means for putting the individual more and more in educative contact with those forces in the social process with which he must reckon as he is oriented in his world.

This emphasis upon orientation does not mean that students will *read* less, nor *write* less, nor *figure* less. It does not mean, in short, that what the school now recognizes as subject-matter will be lost or even minimized. It does mean, however, that subject-matter will find its justification for being on those occasions when it becomes a necessary instrument for the individual if he is to carry forward his understanding. What actually is intended, and is properly to be anticipated, is that the individual will learn more subject-matter than he now does. That this is no idle dream those schools which have turned away from the formal routines are beginning to demonstrate; and, if this were not true, the fact remains that the elementary school in particular has before it the inescapable necessity of making orientation a major purpose in the creation of its program. There will be schools here and there that are able to make a clean sweep of traditional boards and start anew. That most schools may not do this is obvious, but no school so lives within an encompassing shell that it may not reach out, perhaps only shyly at first, and bring the life of the student into significant relationship with his surrounding student life. It is reasonable to expect the school to move in this direction; and as it does this it ought to be free to write its own program.

Now while it is true that each school, facing conditions that are peculiarly its own, must organize its program with reference to its characteristic circumstances, the conditions of the present social-economic situation nevertheless compel a course of study that uses as centers of orientation those aspects of the social life, home, vocations, and the like in which the student must inevitably participate. That is to say, the school must arrange its activities in order to provide successive experiences that lead to a progressive understanding of life in the present.

It is clear, for instance, that the individual will one day face the problems that center about the organization of home life. The school may properly plan, therefore, through successive curriculum materials, to bring the student to a study of the relations of members in the home one to another under differing social-economic conditions. In this instance, successive units of work, by grade or class, pointed toward a growing understanding of home relations, may be developed around differing periods of civilization or around differing periods of our national life. Quite as appropriately, the study of differing periods of civilization may form the center of orientation for successive grades, with understanding at each stage developed about aspects of the present social-economic situation with which individuals are later to be confronted and in which they are more immediately interested. The particular turn the course of study may take will of course depend upon local conditions and upon the interests and abilities of both teachers and students, but in each instance, as orientation of the individual in his world goes forward, the course of study will get its direction from the conditions in the present social-economic situation which make it now necessary that the school focus upon orientation as a major interest.

The shift which this emphasis upon orientation suggests is, to be sure, a radical one. Textbooks have been constructed in mere informational terms; teaching activities have been formulated with the express purpose of drilling these terms into the students; administrative functions have been developed that place a premium upon teaching which successfully fixes the terms; and our scientific development in the field of the measurement of results has glorified both the administrator and the teacher whose activities bring large masses of students quickly up to the informational levels which the tester, assuming that informational accumulations set the ends of education, has established. All of this may be splendid for the

administrators and thrilling for the testers; but we are beginning to realize what we should always have known, that it is
deadening and fruitless for both the student and the teacher.
It will be no simple matter, therefore, to break through the
lines that have been struck as scientist and administrator have
thus labored together to fix permanently the traditional processes of the school. None the less, the start must be made. And
the first step in this direction is to reconstruct the school program for the specific purpose of steadily fostering the orientation of the individual in his real world of to-day.

*It is reasonable to expect the school to provide situations for
the purpose of leading the student progressively to direct his
action by an integrated and unified attitude to which he increasingly gives his allegiance.*

It ought to be fairly clear from preceding discussions that
the present social situation is in no small measure directly
attributable to the fact that we have achieved neither as individuals nor as groups that clarity and unity of thought and
action which is necessary to an ordered and consistent life. It
is not at this time necessary to review the nature of the confusion that exists in our social thought. What is here important is the fact of the confusion. Facing it as we must in its
stark reality, it is but to be expected that the school will turn
to the development of individuals who can rise above the
messiness characteristic of the present. They will need to
understand the conditions which call for a reconstruction of
our social processes, and they will need to be sincere in the
thought which they bring to this reorganization. This interest, therefore, is not to be counted as merely intellectualistic
in character. The chief concern is the development of individuals who are sensitized to the conflicts in the dispositions

and attitudes which they acquire in the social situation and who are disposed to reëxamine and reconstruct these values in the light of a scheme of social action which with defensible understanding they are learning to cherish.

In truth, the emphasis upon orientation in the school program makes necessary the further emphasis upon integration. The suggested study of the ways in which members of the community obtain those things which give life whatever security it may possess will lead out naturally to other and more significant problems. Almost at the outset of the orientation program the teacher may direct the study in ways that force the individual to the discovery that there is no unanimity of opinion in the community about what is a right and proper activity for the man who strives for security. Indeed, if the activity is to be properly educative, the teacher must so direct the study. A class, for instance, may turn its attention upon the ways in which families are housed. Contrasting situations, often marked, will be discovered in any community. These are features of the community life with which the properly oriented individual should be familiar. But as the teacher directs this orientation, he will see to it that certain basic factors intrude. Individuals living in the better residential sections may be maintaining their status there through the ownership of houses in slum districts. Furthermore, these owners may take advantage of their control of these houses and refuse to provide minimum opportunities for decent living. They may even have political and business alignments which make possible the ignoring of those regulations that have been developed to maintain sanitary living conditions as city life has grown more complex. Any proper consideration of the housing facilities in a given community will bring into the open such evidences of a bad-working profit-motivated economy as exist there; as, indeed, it will bring to light evidence of existing agencies that work to provide more adequate housing. The teacher, in short, in a study of this character will urge upon the student the competing views with their attendant consequences in actual housing in order that he may increasingly formulate an intelligent attitude toward the problem. In some instances the teacher may fully anticipate that, as this attitude takes form, the student will want to reach out into the social situation and work there with the resources that are available to improve the conditions discovered.

The same theme, incidentally, will be seen to run throughout other efforts to orient the student in his world. A proper study of the dairy facilities of a community should bring to light the causes of milk-price wars. It should discover the effects of this competition upon both the home to which the milk goes and the farm from which it comes. And in this picture, the racketeer may be expected to show his head. These factors the teacher will bring before the student in order that he may fairly view the nature of the competition which occurs in our economic life and recognize the evil results of this competition as the community struggles to keep itself right side up.

The whole point, of course, is that a program of orientation for the student in his world will bring him up against the competing attitudes and dispositions which exist there and so make necessary a further program to bring about the integration of the individual's thought. The school, then, as it sets out to help the individual get his bearings in society, will select materials that force the discovery that there is more to understanding than mere acquaintanceship with the activities to which he is introduced. Under these conditions, this introduction may reasonably lead the individual to a realization that, as men now go about the business of establishing security for themselves, they compete with other men in ways that necessitate community—that is, social—regulation. It is here that the individual will find the distress that is caused by competing points of view, and it is from this morass that the

individual will have to work his way to attitudes and dispositions which he can defensibly hold as he progressively takes
a more and more responsible part in the life of the community.
Naturally a program of this character necessitates that the
teacher be sensitive to the factors which the school must take
into account as it reconstructs itself to meet the need for reconstruction in the social-economic situation. Mere contact
with the social order will not of itself lead to the disposition to
integrate one's thought in that situation, a fact to which our
present confusion in thought bears glorious, if mute, testimony. Orientation is not concerned with the mere assimilation
of this material as final knowledge. It should provide material for further critical thinking. When it does this, then the
need for integration is at once apparent and the intimate relationship between orientation and integration stands forth.

The point will perhaps be more obvious if we remember
that it is the failure to take this step which has too often
left progressive education without a sense of direction for
the enriched program that it has developed. In progressive
schools much has been done to bring the individual to a larger
view of his community life; many activities, even some that
duplicate those of the community, have been introduced. But
unfortunately the educative results seldom reach out consistently beyond the activities into the more significant aspects
of the community life. Many excellent school newspapers are
produced the country over, and by students who have learned
to spot news, to formulate leads for their stories that conform
to metropolitan standards, to write informing headlines, and
the like. Where facilities make it possible they have learned
much about type, about linotype machines; they may even
have mastered the mechanics of "putting the paper to bed."
Similarly, they have learned to run stores, to conduct political
campaigns, to operate postoffices, etc. What the school has
failed to treat educatively is the contrasting character of the

out-of-school newspaper, for instance, which builds its policies in terms of a profit motive; how news gets colored; how editorials ignore facts; how work is done in line with pressures from above, or from without; how positions are lost when the ethics of the profession are adhered to too closely; and how all of this occurs as the mechanics of the profession, mastered in school, are carried out.

This is, to be sure, an old story; but it is one which the school needs to read again. From it is to be got that sense of direction which will provide the school a basic ground on which to build its program. This, in brief, is the production of an individual who is increasingly better able to direct his behavior by an integrated point of view toward social values. It is then reasonable to expect the school to develop individuals who progressively learn to direct their action by an integrated and unified attitude to which they more and more give their allegiance. It is likewise necessary to point out that this interest will receive greater emphasis as the individual moves upward through the educative process. Just as *orientation* will be the term most used in the elementary years, so a wider *integration* will be the point of emphasis in the more advanced years. This is not to say that either will be an exclusive function in one sector of the school. The need for orientation is present as long as the world offers to the individual things not understood; the demand for integration accompanies each new advance into sensitive awareness of situation and problem. The relatively simple integration which takes place as the elementary program undertakes to orient the individual in his world must in the upper school years take on an ever wider range so as to become a matter of major concern in constructing the program for the upper school.

The program, on this basis, will take on form as problems of integration occur for the individual and for groups. This suggests, of course, that the program cannot be laid down in advance. Indeed, it must inevitably grow experimentally. But this growth may be directed. This is the function of the emphasis upon integration. Suggesting as it does the progressive development of the intelligence of the individual,[2] it likewise suggests at once ways in which the school program may be slanted in the pursuit of this end. Whatever the final outcome may be as a school program so developed emerges, it seems fairly clear that *the play of intelligence in the world* will have large influence both upon the materials that are included in it and the methods that are followed in its attainment. As intelligence has been more and more used by man in directing his affairs, new attitudes and dispositions have been developed. All the while, of course, old values have been at work to keep intelligence at arm's length from many aspects of life; and, unfortunately, the individual has a way of smuggling both old and new values into his life by failing to examine the genesis of his dispositions. Such an examination the school should encourage, and it may at least start in this direction by bringing the individual to a realizing sense of the part that intelligence has played in giving new character to the world and by leading the individual to an awareness of those aspects of life wherein intelligence now fails to operate. Both interests are of sufficient import to warrant their further consideration.

[2] There are those in education who will be disposed to suggest here that it is futile to expect a major portion of our population to act intelligently. This attitude is a familiar one. Its merits need not be debated here; but the point ought to be made that we have as yet no evidence warranting it, nor shall we have until such time as the school and life seriously attempt to promote intelligence in social action. No one could in all seriousness argue to-day that either has, up to this time, been whole-heartedly endeavoring to achieve this purpose.

We may fairly expect that the school will acquaint the student with the part intelligence has played in making over the world.

Indeed, we have probably thought that we were meeting this demand right along. What we have done, however, is to deal with the fruits of intelligence, failing to recognize that this fruit has its least educative value after it has been placed permanently in cold storage. The concern of the school has been too much with completed knowledge and too little with the nature of the struggle that takes place as knowledge is in the making. As the individual is moving to an appreciation of his world he ought to have that appreciation deepened by recognizing the part that number, for instance, has played in making possible the industrial processes that color his life. Indeed, pitched upon the level of the student at the moment, this appreciation can begin as soon as the individual finds use for the "knowledge" achievements of the race as tools in furthering his understanding of, and his participation in, his world.

In the earlier school years such an emphasis may do no more than bring to the fore those obvious physical differences that characterize the shift from the past to the present. Such changes, of course, abound in the present. So prevalent are they, indeed, that the growing child has no real occasion to consider the conditions of life before the advent of the radio, the telephone, the electric light, the automobile and its attendant highways, the newer developments in refrigeration, the machine era in industry, the printing-press, and the like. These are things which the individual should grasp as evidences of the play of intelligence bringing to man ever increasing possibilities for a richer life. But if he sees them only in the gross, as is the usual case to-day, he is left again to deal with the results of intelligence and is not brought up to a consideration of the ways in which these resulting instruments have changed the basic attitudes of the men who use them. As the individual moves upward through the educative process, therefore, he should be taken "back stage" more and more in order that he may appreciate the struggles that take place prior to the presentation of the finished product. Even the lowly lightning rod had to fight its way against the attitudes of those who did not think that man should try to control what properly belonged in the hands of a higher power! And there are those to-day who fight vaccination for the same reason.

Each teacher, whether he deals with the activities of individuals which the newer approach to education suggests or with the subjects which the traditional ways of education insist upon, may bring this illumination to the student whom he instructs. Indeed, on each level of the student's development, this interest should be a chief one in the organization of the curriculum. Through it the student ought steadily to grow in a faith in intelligence. In innumerable ways, both within and without the school, the student will become conscious of the confusion that exists in the social situation. This result is desirable. None the less, if this fact be not anticipated by the school as it organizes its materials and activities, the result may easily be damaging to individual lives. Anticipating an individual consciousness of social confusion, the school may deliberately provide a sustaining force by bringing the student to an understanding of the ways in which man has steadily made possible through the use of intelligence a satisfying life for more and more people. Out of the effort of the school to orient the individual in his world and to foster the development of an integrated program of living should come, then, a realizing sense that, in a world which seems highly disturbed, intelligence has increasingly played an important part. Thus, when the individual later, or at the moment, runs into instances which show that man does not always make use of intelligence, he will meet this fact with the confidence born of a growing faith that he has the means available to direct his action in ever more desirable ways.

This central interest should pervade all of the work of the school. Orientation is then given a sense of direction which leads on from mere acquaintanceship with the world to an integrated outlook that springs from a deepened appreciation of the part that man has played and may play in the building up of a way of life. What we have called "subject-matter," if seen in its relation to the social situation in which the student must get his bearings, has its most significant educative opportunity as it shows intelligence at work in the remaking of the world. Thus, science on all levels is obviously replete with illustrations of the play of intelligence in bringing man new instrumentalities and new means of control. Similarly is it pregnant with the new attitudes toward life that arose as man began to use instrumentalities to control his own destiny. The so-called fundamentals, reading, writing, and number, show man progressing from a crude life in which illiteracy was the normal expectation to one in which education is directed toward the release from ignorance of all men. And thus our history carries abundant evidence of intelligence at work as a wilderness has been changed to an inhabited land. Geography, also, is no less significant on this score. So with all subject-matter, in fact. Therefore, as the school program is shaped to place the proper emphasis upon integration, each teacher will find a significant lead by searching out the changes in both instrumentalities and resulting social attitudes which intelligence, as it may be observed in his area of instruction, has brought to the world.

We may also fairly expect that the school will acquaint the individual with those aspects of life where man has failed to make use of intelligence.

This, indeed, is necessary if the individual is to get, by contrast, an appreciation of what man may accomplish through the application of responsible intelligence to life. Here, perhaps more than at any other point, the individual may sense the basic conflict in attitudes that snarls up our social order. Refrigeration, shipping facilities, display cases, legal regulations, all make possible to-day the display and sale of food under sanitary conditions; yet within the limited physical circle of almost every school may be found enterprises that violate the conditions which intelligence dictates in the distribution of food. Furthermore, over it all may be cast the sinister shadow of graft and corruption as public officials connive with individuals who would live their economic lives outside the pale of social control. The story of the development of such national law as we possess that bears upon the regulation of conditions under which food is produced and distributed shows clearly the struggle that intelligence has had with economic and political interests as these latter push aside the social use of intelligence in order that profit-seeking individualism may run its rampant course. The educative effects of such a study may easily be far-reaching. That is to say, when a group discovers that man has remained callous in the face of available means to promote a more adequate protection of the health of each individual, it may be anticipated that the group will desire to develop a positive program for giving intelligence work to do in relationship to the sale of foods. And this should be encouraged. Thus, the school cafeteria might easily, under the leadership of the given class, become a center for developing throughout the school itself a sensitiveness toward the healthful display and distribution of foods. This discussion would naturally reach back into the homes, and out into the community. Under administrative leadership that recognizes the proper place of the school in the social order [3] such discussion would be deliberately organized, with the distributor as well as the buyer par-

[3] The implications of this point of view for administration are discussed on pp. 243 ff.

ticipating, to make the problem an object of study for the entire community. It may then be expected that the proprietors participating will see beyond the profit motive that has been their sole source of orientation and recognize the possible and desired educative effects of their activity. So, too, with the parent who has been apathetic as a buyer.

In ways such as this the school must come to grips with callous spots in our social life, else it will continue to deal idly with changes that occur in the physical and material realm as new instrumentalities arise and will ignore the basic fact that such changes necessitate the continuous application of responsible intelligence to our social values. In science it is not enough to know that the radio and the automobile are outstanding achievements of man's ingenuity; that in warfare man now has the means of killing man mightily in the mass; that medical advances give life a quality of surety not previously possible; that processes and instruments are available to produce such necessaries as all men need. In history it is not enough to know that in specific years particular wars were fought; that in other years the cotton-gin, the railroad, the steamboat, the telephone, the airplane, appeared; that certain individuals passed in succession through public office; that the number of states increased in particular years as the frontier disappeared. In geography it is not enough to know that certain rivers move through particular areas; that the soils of differing states present marked contrasts; that specific natural resources are available at particular points; that geographic conditions are related to the areas within which population may increase.

What is important in all of these is that the individual rise to a realization of the fact that man has time and again refused to be intelligent at points where decent social life has been at stake. Human life has been thrown away in wars that have back of them nothing more significant than the economic interests of particular classes; natural resources have been dissipated to add additional increment of profits to over-greedy individuals; machines have been developed at the expense of individual happiness and security as much as in support of these values; social institutions have been used by their leaders to support social policy that ignores the common man; history has been misrepresented in order to intensify narrowing nationalistic concepts. Throughout the whole gamut of life man has permitted the brilliant achievements of intelligence to obscure large areas of life where intelligent action is carefully avoided. These areas the school must illumine, an end it may accomplish by having each school activity bring to the fore the contrasting failures of intelligence as the achievements are recorded and by encouraging the active and educative participation of the school and the community in behavior directed toward the amelioration of conditions that retard the spread of social sensitiveness.

The individual is actually a member of a world in which intelligence is both relied upon and ignored. In this world his values are formed, and he therefore comes to the school as a veritable educational laboratory in which conflicting attitudes are discoverable. It is in this light that the school should view the student and his world; and, dealing with him on his level at each stage in the educative process, it should bring these conflicts to his consciousness in ways that encourage him to achieve allegiance to a unified and integrated program of life. Note the conflicts as they arise: he will believe in democracy and yet find that he has definite racial antipathies; he will believe in honesty but will be learning about the essential dishonesties common in business and politics; he will respond to civic obligations, but he will learn that vested interests control civic activities; he will believe in fair play, yet with his fellows he will subscribe to the doctrine of establishing right by "getting by." He will, in brief, be the kind of citizen who now inhabits his world, one sadly in need of clarity of outlook. This clarity we ought reasonably to expect the school to provide, and it may do so by selecting its materials and ordering its processes to bring into the open the conflicts in attitudes and dispositions that arise, both individually and socially, as intelligence and prejudice run counter to each other.

Going forward on this basis, the school will make definite contributions to the immediate reconstruction of the social situation. Teachers and students under administrative leadership will think with the community at strategic points to effect changes in the organization of activities in ways that give available intelligence work to do. That is to say, the emphasis here placed upon an integrated attitude that leads directly to sincerity in action indicates at once an organization of work in the school. Whether the starting point be subjects as we now know them or the use of subject materials to further the understanding on the part of individuals of the particular problems with which they are dealing, this reorganization of work should bring into the open both the values in the present situation that have been achieved as man's intelligence has been released and the values that have been carefully fenced off from the free play of intelligence. The immediate result of this emphasis will be a clearer view of present conflicts in standards, and if the social situation is not to offset the study started in school, the school will move with the student to bring to this situation standards more in harmony with the facts and needs of society. One further result, and a significant one, is that the school, even if forced to start with subject-matter, will find that its point of interest is increasingly an intelligently formulated scheme of social action and decreasingly an orderly parade of compartmentalized knowledge. To such a conclusion does a study of present social conditions compel, as the school places its emphasis upon individuals whose behavior is directed by an integrated attitude sincerely held.

It is reasonable to expect the school to encourage the development of independent interests, intellectual, esthetic, or practical, on the part of the students.

Thus far we have called upon the school, as it reconstructs its procedures, to place a major emphasis upon the orientation of the individual in his world and upon the integration of his thought in order that he may act more and more intelligently in the social situation. These emphases throw into relief the fact that education must move forward from the interests of the individual. There can be no argument about the soundness of this approach to the educative process. Interest is central. The point that is here important, and especially when there is an active movement away from subjects as the educational hub, is that this admission of the force of interest in initiating and carrying forward educative activity need not place the school in the position of catering to sudden fancy and shallow whim. Orientation and integration, both leading to increased social insight, provide a sense of direction which ensures that the consideration of interest will not lead to the glorification of mere caprice.

The purpose involved in the educative process as thus described, the development of individuals loyal to a scheme of action that puts intelligence to work in social affairs, suggests that provision be made for carrying forward the emerging interests of the students to the point where genuinely independent interests have been established. As such interests develop and the individual gets knowledge put together in those relationships that provide control and make possible the further extension of knowledge, a deepened social insight is made increasingly possible. It has hitherto been our educational habit to start the individual out with knowledge organized by the specialist, and as knowledge has been increased, it has been our further habit to let him work with ever smaller segments of it. Always, however, the specialist's organization has been the point of introduction for the student. The impoverished and inept educational product of such an approach is all too familiar, and it is little wonder that a violent reaction occurred leading to the exaltation of interest. What is now needed, and is here suggested, is that as individual interests are encouraged they should lead on to the point where the student finds in organized knowledge those materials that make it increasingly possible for him to move about independently.

In the earlier school years the cultivation of independent interests will be in some respects limited. But this only means that in these years the product will not be comparable to that of the later years. It need not be; the important point is that the school place an emphasis that leads the individual progressively in the direction of active independent interests. The start may be early made. All that is needed is the provision of facilities that make possible the pursuit of interests as these arise. As individuals are oriented in their world, each may be expected to be captured by aspects of it that lie close to budding interests. Each, therefore, will start with his own center of orientation. The result is a familiar one in schools that have already escaped the tentacles of subjects. Modelling in clay, work in woods and metals, the use of water-colors or oils, the making of linoleum blocks, studied care of all manner of small animals, reading, writing in both verse and prose, the comparison of soils, the collection of information bearing on the control of health, the study of type, dramatization, and perhaps the combination of all these interests and more into a group interest that is concerned with bringing an informed intelligence to bear upon problems of community living—these are activities that open up when the educational emphasis shifts to the progressive growth of individuals in an understanding of their world. Thus, there have been outstanding instances when the school with a particular group as an agent has made significant contributions to a community appreciation of problems of health through posters, models of sanitary devices, dramatizations of medical advancement, conferences with adults, collections of pertinent pamphlets, articles in school and local papers, and other similar activities.

The start thus made must be vigorously followed up if the school is to rise to its full educative possibilities. The mere fact that such activities occur need not in itself be a matter of importance. What is of value is the extension of social insight through the steady pursuit of a leading interest. Activity of this sort naturally leads to the intellectual and emotional participation of the individual in the life of the community. It suggests also that the school ought properly to make actual participation in community life a vital part of the school program. Practical interests, for instance, tie in definitely with the vocational activities of the social group. Thus a student with an interest in type might be permitted to participate in a useful way in the work of a printing establishment. But this does not imply that the school can be satisfied if the sole result of such activity by the student is an innocuous dabbling in the affairs of the plant. Participation that leads to nothing more significant than this has already been too much on the educational horizon. The school, therefore, will need to exercise care in order that the activity may be educative. The type interest for the student must be but a starting point. From it may emerge continuing interests: the history of printing, present processes in lithographing or block printing, the illumination of pages, binding, machine processes, even a study of the language itself. And as each interest is followed, man will be seen not only gaining control over his forms of communication, but also contributing to a changed society in which old economic and social attitudes, like old printing processes, are inapplicable. This is only part of the desired educative effect in this instance, however. The rest concerns the printing establishment. As it organizes itself educatively, it will have to study the effects of its present form, seeing wherein intelligence may be applied to men as well as to type. As independent interests are encouraged, particularly the practical interests that play upon present vocational activities, we may, then, expect the school to arrange the contacts between students and the vocational situations in ways that carry these interests forward educatively and that reconstruct the vocational activity progressively in the direction of educative relationships to the social order.

It is important to emphasize this final point, since we may anticipate that the practical interests of students will provide many of the most immediate and fruitful opportunities for participation in the work of the community. Unfortunately, as matters now stand, the dominance of the profit motive in our economic life makes unlikely a high educative return to the individual student who takes part in it. Actual participation, therefore, as interests are developed to the desired state of independence, can be encouraged by the school only at those points where local conditions make it possible for "school and shop" to coöperate in arranging educative work for the student. This point is so clear as to suggest that vocational education as the school has too often conceived it, the mere training-up of individuals for specific participation in the present industrial scheme, has no legitimate place in an educational program that anticipates the intelligent participation of the individual in the reconstruction of the social order. Training of this character, in so far as it affects the student, reduces the practical interest to routine procedures that enable easy adjustment in a scheme devised to bring maximum profits to the industrial leader. It therefore has all of the miseducative effects of our present social-economic situation. To turn the practical interests of the student into specific vocational channels, as these now exist, is to place both the individual and the school at the mercy of an industrial order not interested in education, and it is to leave the social order in its present unsatisfactory state.

These limitations make the active and educative participation in social processes no less desirable, however, and the school should not only encourage it wherever conditions permit but should also do what it can, as suggested earlier, to make more complete participation increasingly possible. Were it now feasible, however, to arrange participation in all manner of social undertakings, the major point of emphasis for the school would be the deposit made in the intellectual and emotional life of the individual and in the agencies touched by the activity. This must not become obscured by an interest in the work itself. Educationally, the latter is but incidental. That is to say, students might properly at times of local and national elections participate in the operation and control of voting booths and in this activity get a realizing sense of the evils involved in the political situation. The significant result should be the realization that man is faced with conditions that need to be improved—and which he may improve—not merely the ability to count and tabulate votes nor the ability to check the voter as he presents himself against the registration facts of a district.

It is at this point that the cultivation of independent interests is suggestive. Out of an orientation activity that is thus directed toward an understanding of the election machinery of a community, for instance, a student might discover an interest in "democracy." This would lead him to history, and this interest, intellectual in character, should then be cultivated by the school to bring about an appreciation of the conditions under which man has developed this particular social ideal.

This might easily lead to the understanding of its progressive reconstruction as conditions have changed, and to a realizing sense of the necessity of further reconstructing it if we are to realize the American Dream in the life of the common man as he lives amid new industrial and economic conditions. The point is that the pursuit of an intellectual interest of this character, arising out of the individual's concern over one aspect of the social process, may bring to the student the necessity for an integrated outlook, an end toward which the study of history, in this instance, would be directed.

Under these prior conditions subjects would be studied properly, namely, in a way to bring the individual, already deeply interested in the field, to make such an organization of knowledge therein as would lead him to live ever more intelligently. This seems the sole excuse that the school has for the presentation of subjects; and in terms of this purpose the school may, as it is thus found appropriate, continue to present knowledge organized into subject-matter divisions. That is to say, subjects should be available as instruments for which particular students have use as they follow interests whose warmth urges them to such action. Subjects should not be required as vehicles in which all must ride regardless of where they desire to go. The school has discovered that it is futile to present the same organization of knowledge to all students, even within limited divisions of that knowledge; it needs now to permit the student to discover the exhilaration that follows upon the realization that one is building up an organization of knowledge which widens understanding and makes increasingly possible the intelligent control of social forces. Indeed, if some are so disposed, the school ought to encourage them to seek the joys that may be theirs as they organize knowledge for the fun of organizing it.

The development of independent interests, therefore, is one practicable way in which the school may bring its program in line with the growing interests of the students and still accomplish what it likes to consider genuine educative results. Indeed, it is not clear that there is any other way to achieve these results. An interest in chemistry may spring from a study of the local water supply, the medicinal content of patent medicines, or the diet followed in raising white mice. An interest in literature may develop as the student studies the feature stories of a local paper or coöperates in preparing a dramatization of the community interest in relief campaigns. An interest in printing may appear as a result of participating in the group selection of a cover for a class report. An interest in physics may be the result of a study of the local transportation system or of a survey of the differing methods of refrigeration used in the community. An interest in writing may find its genesis in the publication of a school newspaper; an interest in radio construction may follow an effort to locate interference that disturbs the school receiving set; and an interest in language may be the direct result of a survey to determine the differing national groups residing in a particular community.

Each interest thus aroused should be used as a way of leading the individual on to greater social effectiveness. This may be done by progressively moving the individual over to that control of knowledge which arises when facts get significance because of the place they occupy in a total scheme. The direction thus provided for the educative process, incidentally, removes the fear that the lead of interest will result in a smattering of knowledge. Actually, it introduces the possibility of bringing about the desired genuine educative effort that results in significantly organized and usable knowledge. The opportunity of the school at this point is a rich one, and though a radical change in subject offerings is indicated, we may nevertheless reasonably expect it at this time to encourage the development of independent interests, intellectual, esthetic or practical, as these appear.

A large part of the task of the school at present consists in the development of individuals who will meet life with a new sense of responsibility and with an informed intelligence. In recognition of this fact we have herein set certain basic emphases to guide the reconstruction of our educative processes. Orientation, integration, development of independent interests —these, obviously, focus upon the need for bringing to the social situation individuals ever more capable of dealing adequately with the conditions that face them there. But this is only part of the educational task. Quite as important is the reconstruction of the total life of the school. The orientation of the individual in his world, for instance, cannot take place in a school that stands aloof from the society of which it is a part. Nor can an integrated program of action be developed by the individual in a school that treats subject-matter as if it were complete for all time and so remains impervious to the social issues that arise as knowledge steadily increases. Neither can independent interests be fostered by a school that presents subject-matter on the assumption that all will be equally interested in it. All of this, to be sure, has been in evidence as we have tried to see what manner of reconstruction these new emphases suggest for the school. And throughout it has become increasingly clear that, as each expectation herein emphasized is realized, the total life of the school will undergo basic change. The character of this change we must now consider.

Chapter VI

THE SCHOOL: ITS TASK AND ITS
ADMINISTRATION—II

OF major importance to-day is the development of a
way of life within the school that works positively
to foster attitudes and dispositions which will offset
the disintegrating conditions now discoverable in both home
and community. It is imperative, as we have seen, that the
pupil progressively achieve an understanding of the world in
which he lives as he acquires knowledge and instruments of
expression and appreciation through the active study of those
aspects of his world that impinge upon his experience at successive stages of the educative process. This, however, is not
enough. He must likewise have the vital experience of living
with others in ways that develop a loyalty to social relationships which springs from a lively concern to coöperate intelligently in the building of a better group life. It is in these
terms that the next school task is stated.

*It is reasonable to expect the school to set up an environment
in which all of its members, through active participation in
its organization and control, may move progressively to a
more complete appreciation of the deeper significance of the
democratic way of life.*

The fact is, of course, that the school has changed its character at many points as a direct result of an effort to introduce
procedures in keeping with the democratic spirit. The socialized recitation is a case in point. So, too, are the developments

in student government, and in civic courses and undertakings. The emphasis upon a curriculum that reaches out beyond the center of college preparation to include offerings more vocational in character grows specifically out of our concern that the public school serve the needs of more than a limited group. Recently, as investigations have brought us to a greater appreciation of differing abilities and capacities, the demands for differentiated curricula have been given new support. And here the development of science in education has seemed to play into the hands of those who would organize the school to promote the democratic ideal. Other instances might be cited; these are sufficient, however, to show that the school has taken seriously its profession of faith in democracy.

It may then seem a bit odd, in the face of the obvious interest that the school has had in taking its clues from the democratic ideal, to ask here that it reorganize itself to do the very thing that it has already been professing. The necessity for this demand, none the less, is readily shown. The school has never managed to make this ideal work throughout the total educative situation. It has not, therefore, basically reconstructed its program so much as it has added new lines of activity to those traditionally accepted. As a result, the school program itself, like the world about it, is in a state of some confusion. And more recently the turn toward efficiency which has naturally enough been taken as administrators have had to deal with a rapidly mounting school population has threatened the school with a set of inflexible procedures that offset its efforts to shape a way of life for the student in which the mutual and sympathetic sharing of interests is the dominant characteristic. At this point the development of science in education, through advances in the field of measurement, has played into the hands of the administrator whose chief interest is in "results." Under such conditions the democratic ideal has had little chance to serve as a consistent guide.

All of this is serious enough. There is, however, a more basic difficulty. The school has not been sensitive to the changes taking place in the social-economic situation. This fact is of paramount importance. It has been suggested repeatedly throughout this book that the social situation to-day sets specific conditions which must be recognized as social and educational reconstruction take place.[1] The school can no longer, therefore, remain aloof from conditions that produce in the social situation definitely miseducative effects. The fact of interdependence in present-day living, for instance, suggests the need to-day of a high degree of social imagination and a sensitiveness to the implications of our conduct in the lives of others. But when we scan the social situation we discover many forces that dull the social quality of the individual's conduct. It is to factors of this sort that the school must to-day be sensitive. It will, then, not only analyze society for the purpose of discovering the educational needs of the individual, but also arrange a program that anticipates the problems the individual will face as his contact with the social order becomes more intimate.

A simple illustration will make this clear. Neighborliness, an ancient ideal, suggests that we share what we have with those in distress. In the simple life of not many years back this ideal was easily carried over into action. When illness visited the family next door, we took turns sitting up at night with the invalid, and the neighbors shared the responsibilities of preparing meals and helping to keep the household functioning. Also, we fed and clothed the destitute stranger who knocked at the door as a matter of simple Christianity. To-day the situation is quite different. The conditions of urban life and the influence of urbanization that have spread into rural districts complicate, if they do not make impossible, such direct

[1] In Chapter II, pp. 68-70, the reader will find a summary statement of the factors that we believe to be of special significance.

measures of relief. Begging and the asking of alms have become commercialized, and we never quite know whether we are contributing directly to actual and visible distress or are perpetuating a "racket" when we permit the unidentified individual to move us to sympathetic action. We have also realized that under present conditions a program of constructive relief calls for more comprehensive and corporate action than personal giving and personal service can accomplish. The fact, therefore, that the individual may deny alms to the beggar at the door of his home, refuse assistance to the blind man or the cripple on the street, or decide not to contribute to the relief drives of special groups that operate outside of the pale of corporate action need not mean that neighborliness is a forgotten ideal. It may only mean that we have adapted our actions to present conditions in order in fact to realize the ideal. These are, however, acts that have an educative effect upon the child who sees an adult apparently remain insensitive to the pleas of his fellows for aid and assistance. His impulses to share are seriously checked. The adult, to be sure, may explain that he is contributing to a charitable organization which goes about the work of relief in the community scientifically, but the child, by the time that he is old enough to discriminate, may have become desensitized at precisely those points of social contact where the adult is most concerned he should respond.

This but suggests that the school, in order to prevent an unwitting development of callous spots in individual lives, must emphasize what under earlier conditions it could properly ignore. This situation may be met by providing opportunities, appropriate to varying age levels, for students to practise service to others as a part of their normal school activity. Occasions for this are so plentiful in the school situation that they will occur to all who admit the need for taking advantage of them. And occasions may be created where they do not now exist to establish meaningful lines of communication and inter-relationship involving service for others with people and conditions outside the school. It is important to remember, however, that the school should deal with these service opportunities, both within and without the school, in an educative way. That is to say, in a community where direct relief through the contribution by school-children of clothing, food, toys, and the like is an immediate necessity, the school should not consider its task completed when baskets of food have been delivered to the homes of the needy, when local fire-houses are loaded with toys for distribution, or when welfare head-quarters are plentifully supplied with usable clothing. The students should recognize that these results are desirable in the community at the moment. But the school should go definitely further and encourage, for example, the study of differing types of relief work as the students deal with the emergency situation.

In the class-room, therefore, a critical study may be made of the relative merits of various relief forms. As a point of orientation, this opens the way for more significant study. There can next be investigated the social conditions that permit suffering and hardship to appear in the community life. And, at levels of understanding that permit this, the issues—social, religious, political, economic—imbedded within these situations may well be brought up for scrutiny. Relief, for instance, may be demanded in a local situation in which a sudden spread of disease compels concerted community action. The members of the school group should participate in the social action here of the larger community unit. This being done, the out-reachings of the activity are in order, and should form a basis for class study and discussion. What local conditions might be changed to make a recurrence of this condition impossible? What information should the average home have not alone concerning the avoidance of this disease but also in relation to the larger problem of protecting health in the social situation? What information along this line does the average home in this community have? How may adequate information be distributed? Is local, state, and national legislation appropriate? Do local groups exert pressures that interfere at particular points with the enforcement of existing health measures? Do these pressure groups stand in the way of the further proper development of these measures? How may the community keep abreast of advances in medical knowledge? What are the responsibilities of the individual as a member of the social situation, not alone with reference to health but also in relation to other values in community living? These are but indications of the educative opportunities that arise in such situations. At appropriate places they should be provided in order that the need for avoiding desensitizing effects may be met by the school as it reconstructs its curriculum and methods to foster an intelligent and sensitive responsiveness to the needs of others.

All of this suggests that the profession must carry forward a continuing analysis of the social order for the purpose of discovering the educational needs which it sets. We face to-day a new social-economic situation, one calling for a type of education that meets the forces of the present as these play upon character and conduct. This is a far cry from the school that could meet the needs of a simpler social order by presenting certain basic essentials of knowledge, such as the three R's. But the conditions of a complex society compel the shift in emphasis. Children face to-day, for instance, a major difficulty as they discover that standards of conduct compete with one another. In a very real sense this difficulty is characteristic of the present. The rural community and the country village were once composed of families that constituted a relatively homogeneous group. The life of this group was organized in terms of codes and ideals of behavior that were commonly accepted. Hardly more than a generation ago, indeed, cities to a considerable extent were but aggregates of communities in which individuals were known as personalities and community standards of behavior actually played upon the inhabitants. But the unity and consistency of village life, as well as the distinctiveness that once characterized neighborhoods within large cities, have been largely destroyed by the development of easy communication and rapid transit.

Children thus confront at the very beginning of their companionship with playmates outside the family circle conflicting standards of conduct. And the conscientious parent discovers to his regret, and perhaps with a shock, that he can exercise but a minimum of control over the environment which influences so vitally the attitudes and points of view of his children. This is obvious, to be sure, in tenement house districts, even in apartment house districts, where children are forced on the street for their play and recreation. It is none the less equally true of the suburban child who associates with the children on his block, or of the well-to-do city child who passes through the successive hands of transient nurse-maids and recreation group leaders. Nor is it a passing phenomenon witnessed solely in the lives of young children. The social situation in no way works to resolve these conflicts with advancing age; rather, it but glorifies the method of establishing standards through the pressure of the groups that are dominant in the life of the individual, a procedure that relegates intelligence in social action to the background.

These circumstances set an obligation for the school. It should assume responsibility for assisting students, at all age levels, to work out through their relations with their fellows self-directive, inner standards of conduct and behavior. In the preceding section we have seen wherein the school may proceed in definite ways to achieve this end. But it can do more. It can specifically arrange the life of the school to permit students to work together in the formulation of standards of conduct. That is to say, as conflicts and issues appear within school groups, and they inevitably will in both class and play activity, teachers should see that these are resolved in ways that lead to a progressively developed appreciation of the values and advantages in an overarching purpose that brings to pass an intelligent compromise of conflicting desires and unites in a common cause two or more antagonistic forces. Out of the regular procedure, therefore, of having groups think through common problems not only should there evolve ideals and standards of conduct that carry over into life outside the school and transform it; the student should also rise to the conscious adoption of methods of resolving conflicts in the light of a fair hearing to all interests involved. This is the essence of the democratic way of life, and the school should launch a program at once that provides ways of living deliberately intended to help the individual devise the appropriate instruments for guiding his conduct in a world of uncertain and confused standards.

The nature of the opportunity which is before the school in this connection may be more fully realized if we turn to one further illustration. The profession must recognize to-day that the spirit of competition exists in the social-economic situation in exaggerated form. This sets a new problem. The pioneer school emerged under social conditions in which competitive and acquisitive motives were given full play. The ready availability of land and raw resources encouraged men to vie one with another for the best of nature's bounty. The same conditions made it possible for competitive activity to contribute to a richer life for the group. Under such circumstances, the school, reflecting adult conceptions, went no further as a social institution than to represent a community effort to help the individual prepare himself to play effectively a lone hand when he entered the normal world of competitive activity. The means employed in the acquisition of education and culture were in keeping with the adult understanding of successful living. The competitive motive, therefore, operated in the school as normally as it did in the social situation. What the profession needs further to recognize to-day is that this motive is still dominant in our educational procedures. Marks, grades, scholarship contests, honor-rolls, and the like are to-day reputable incentives as we undertake to stimulate intellectual endeavor. Even preparation for citizenship is frequently identified with an imitation of political methods used by self-seeking politicians; and, in the realm of sport and recreation, the attitude of playing to win seems the compelling motive.

Now the school can ill afford to perpetuate the dominating motives of an older social order. It may well be argued that competitive and acquisitive motives were entirely desirable under frontier conditions. An industrial civilization, that has arisen as the conditions of the once-powerful physical frontier in American life have been pushed aside by human ingenuity, requires, however, an emphasis upon other springs of conduct. New incentives are required for at least two reasons. In the first place, the results of unrestrained competition are disastrous to-day in a way they were not in a social situation where new opportunities existed as a constant element. And in the second place, men can no longer live unto themselves alone. Interdependence is one of the conditions of life in the present that is inescapable. Our actions are inevitably bound up in the lives of others. These facts compel the school to recognize that the potential values of a corporate society are only to be realized when people learn to think and to live with reference to the conditions of coöperative endeavor.

The essential point in all of these instances is that the analysis of the social situation throws into relief particular educational needs of the individual with which the school must deal directly. Take this problem of competition. Class-room method should foster coöperative activity; curriculum materials should further the critical study of social attitudes, focusing, at successive educational levels, upon the reconstruction of the American tradition; school projects should encourage a sharing of interests; recreation activities should develop coöperatively. What is desired, in short, is that a new social atmosphere permeate the relations of students in work and play. Actually, many progressive schools have found it possible to subordinate the competitive element to other values, thus showing that external incentives for entering into intellectual and esthetic concerns are not a necessary part of the educative process. In situations of this character, culture is on the way toward being conceived as the cultivation of genuine interests and not merely an external acquisition. Also, in the fields of physical education and athletic contests an unfortunate preoccupation with playing to win is in many places receding before a healthy interest in the game for its own sake. That winning may be conceived in healthy terms is no doubt true; none the less, when a group of junior high school pupils in a certain school rushed up to their instructor at the close of an exciting game period to exclaim, "Why, Mr. ——, we forgot to keep score," one teacher could feel that an attitude appropriate to the present social situation was giving direction to the members of his class.

In a school situation known to the writers a definite move to offset the competitive influences that play upon the individual has been made by the establishment of a coöperative store in connection with a preprofessional course in business. This is in essence a laboratory in which the study of the conduct of business may be pursued. The actual operation of a business is made possible. More important, however, is the fact that the examination in class of the similarities and the differences between a store of this character and a regular business is normally achieved. Actual observation by the student of business firms quite naturally follows; as do, too, classroom discussion and study with reference to the typical forms of business organizations. But the store does not lead alone to intellectual considerations; it is itself a socially motivated project, providing an opportunity for the sharing of interests in a business situation. The profits from the store are used for social service purposes. A year ago the store sold articles which would be of use to the student body and the distribution of which would help certain organizations engaged in educational and philanthropic work. World Peace Posters and products of the Shut-In Society and the Grenfell Mission were distributed through the book-store. Incidentally, in relation to the store there grew up an employment exchange for students who needed money and had skills to sell, such as ability in relation to photography (developing, printing and enlarging photographs) or in relation to woodworking and the printing of stationery.

It is of particular interest to note that a study of consumer welfare by these business students had definite results. A number of the students joined the Consumers' Research and took an interest in the White List of the Consumers' League. This year the manager, in purchasing fountain-pens for the students of the school, used the Consumers' Research with the idea of serving the student body with the best quality at the best price. A project of this particular nature in the public school situation might easily run afoul of vested interests in the business of the community, a fact which would make possible, were it wisely pursued, the education not only of the students but likewise of the community itself. The point that is important, however, is that this undertaking definitely shows a school at work to offset the miseducative effects of competitive activities in a social situation that calls for coöperative thought and action.

This all points in the direction of the reconstruction of our school procedures. The conditions call for this. We need frankly to recognize that the school as hitherto run is not developing individuals who are equipped to participate intelligently in a social order that must undergo reconstruction in the interests of a larger life for all of its members. We may then marshal the forces and intelligence of the school and approach vigorously the reconstruction of its procedures. Ways of living that lead to the experience of sharing interests and coöperatively carrying forward community undertakings must be provided. Moreover, this emphasis must permeate the curriculum as study materials are selected. It must also find its way into the class-room as methods of study are developed. The school, in short, must come up to its problems with a realizing sense that our civilization is a moving thing. It will, then, through both its materials and its methods, be at pains to show wherein the past persists in the present and to develop individuals sensitive to the need for reconstructing our tradition as new conditions arise.

In this connection our customary curriculum and our methods are both inadequate. On the one hand, the curriculum deals with compartmentalized knowledge that has no necessary social significance; and, on the other hand, our methods have been developed with reference to the acquisition of specific sequences of that knowledge. Neither is concerned with the major problem of the school to-day. Fortunately, reorganization that is suggestive has gone forward in both areas. Subject-matter lines have been giving way as we have come to recognize the educative value of "units of work." And in the same way, the project method has refreshingly turned from stultifying procedures to the moving interests of students. These shifts in emphasis provide a valuable stock-in-trade as we move ahead experimentally to a more significant reconstruction. What we now need to do is to give to both a sense of direction which has often been lacking in their development thus far, using the interests of the individual to lead to a study of materials that play directly upon the more and more adequate participation of the individual in a world of competing values and conflicting attitudes.

Our earlier emphasis upon orientation and integration as points of attack in the reorganization of the work of the school has indicated that the curriculum must inevitably take form as the interests and problems of the students are pursued. Nevertheless, centers of orientation for the curriculum may properly be anticipated. Thus, in the earlier years "the home" might serve as such a center. This might be followed by a study of "other social institutions," or of particular institutions considered separately. Another sequence of units might be arranged so that in successive years, at the appropriate age levels, different periods of civilization would be studied. On the other hand, the curriculum might provide a series of centers that would lead to an intensive study of differing movements in American life. The particular centers are not here of prime importance. Each school will properly organize its work in terms of the characteristics of the situation it faces. What is of importance is that the curriculum at all of its stages be consciously arranged to anticipate the educative needs of an individual who faces the necessity of clarifying the American tradition in terms of the compelling conditions found in the present social-economic situation.

Under these circumstances the work of the class may be expected to take on rather definite characteristics. A group, for instance, studying the home in relationship to the present may swing out to a larger interest quite naturally by asking what conditions made it possible for man to build "a home" in this country. This is obviously not the problem of a particular subject, nor of a particular teacher. It is, however, a unit of activity that may have significant educative results for the student.[2] The resources of the school should therefore be brought to bear upon it. Facts that relate to the problem— educational opportunities, native intelligence, mountains, rivers, coal, forests, soil, lakes, harbors, winds, valleys, canals, irrigation, transportation, navigation, communication, foods, power plants, reforestation, hygienic conditions of cities and streams, reservoirs, the construction of dams to protect life in the immediate vicinity and to guarantee life in distant places, the social aspects of water as revealed in the fight between Chicago and the Great Lakes ports—all may be made available. The point of importance is, of course, that these be related to the situation educatively as specialists coöperate in an effort to bring the students progressively to more effective levels of intelligent action.

Also, the whole Colonial period would be available for exploration. The conditions of the wilderness, the influence of education, coöperative protective undertakings, agricultural methods, freedom of worship (or restriction of worship), old-world customs and ideas, the extension of the frontier, the making of clothing, navigation, freedom from compelling traditions—all of this information, and more, would serve not as mere information but as the means of illuminating the conditions in which the American Dream set its roots. Furthermore, the study would lead normally over into the arts. In fact, at points such as these the arts have the opportunity to contribute to class undertakings as integral factors in the total educative situation. The construction of a Colonial home, the weaving of cloth after primitive methods, the sketching of frontier scenes, the creation of models of early tools, and other similar activities in these and other media will contribute both to understanding and to appreciation as this study of the con-

2 The following chapter (pp. 233 ff.) presents, in a discussion of the administrative problems of a school program that builds on "units of work," definite suggestions for the coöperation of subject-matter teachers in carrying forward an activity of this character.

ditions that made possible the building of a home in this country is carried forward. It may be said, incidentally, that the arts, as means of active expression, provide ways in which the individual may identify himself with the activities of others: in this instance, leading to a knowledge of early conditions of the country that is deeper than a mere "knowledge about." A more adequate appreciation of the social attitudes of others may be furthered, particularly in the elementary grades where conceptual facility is limited, by having the art activities of the student play into the understanding of problems with which he works. Furthermore, a base may thus be set for the later development of independent esthetic interests.

A problem of this character will inevitably lead on to others equally educative. For instance, the attention of the group may be turned specifically to a study of the ways in which man has learned to safeguard his health. Here, again, information will become important as it bears upon the problem. Sanitary measures in the home, social controls in the distribution of food, the growing attention to diet, methods of vaccination, regulations bearing upon the disposition of refuse, and similar bits of knowledge will be seen in relation to a matter of major concern for the student. The play of intelligence, and the rôle of superstition, will both be illuminated as the problem is pressed; and the individual, with the school actively concerned about this end, will be forced to clarify his thought as he is made conscious of the conflicting attitudes that he himself has used in relation to his own health.

The method of a class that proceeds in this manner has been suggested as we have discussed the flexible character of the curriculum. Its chief characteristics may be stated, however, more specifically. In the first place, large opportunities must be provided for the pursuit of problems that arise from individual interests and undertakings. But this activity should be directed. The pursuit of interests should lead to problems educatively significant to the individual, and they should go forward in social terms. That is to say, the individual is to be educated in relationship to the group in whose affairs he is an active, and sympathetic, participant, a procedure that puts the individual and social aspects of the educative process into one educational frame. This particular emphasis has already been placed in much of the activity that may be discovered in the changing elementary school. It is a characteristic, moreover, that ought to color the educative process all along the line. Second, under these circumstances, the teacher will face the necessity of arousing a group awareness of a problem. It is this awareness that sets the occasion for study. We have too long tried to "motivate" students in the study of materials which neither they nor the teacher can envisage as contributing to more than an orderly passage through textbooks. We have, in short, attempted a procedure as we pursued knowledge which answered all questions so completely that none could be raised. When we turn away from the textbook and final knowledge, however, and swing toward life and a growing individual, the school situation is markedly different.

Now problems are seldom simple, and individuals are never identical, and we may therefore expect that the study will be carried on by individuals whose interests differ, whose backgrounds are diversified, and whose capacities vary. This means that students will do individual study, not in order, however, to exceed other individuals in the same activity, but for the purpose of coöperating in the solution of the problem faced. Indeed, by the time the problem is recognized and formulated by the group, the teacher will have noted that some students have had abiding interests stirred, others will be but lukewarm, some will be fertile in suggesting approaches to its study, some will already possess essential information, and the like. These are differences that should be noted early in order that they may bear upon the character of the individual study planned by student and teacher. A fourth characteristic of the work of the class will be a return to the group problem as the center of interest after the individual activity has been completed. This problem will then be faced by individuals who have important information that they may pool in working out a tenable solution. Finally, the individual ought to be given an opportunity to fit together the thought which the group brings to the problem and that which is his as a result of his special study. This last integrating activity is by no means intended to be a mastery examination in designated information. It is, rather, a definite concern that the class activity foster growth in the ability of the individual to integrate his knowledge. Indeed, the concern of the procedure at all points is to develop the student progressively to a level where he is both able and disposed to act intelligently.

Throughout this entire section the reconstruction of school procedures has been repeatedly indicated. Furthermore, specific instances have suggested the direction this reconstruction should take. It is not, then, now necessary to do more than state that experimentation with school procedures is in order. This is obvious enough. It may, however, be important to point out that the experimentation demanded in this instance is rather different from that which the experimental interest in education has thus far achieved. And the difference is just at the point of centering our experimental activity upon the development of an educational program that is guided by an underlying social philosophy. In differing ways the nature of this program has been indicated. The character of the social situation to-day sets the direction with great definiteness. It is therefore possible to note certain present interests of the school which will have to be revised.

Administrative concerns, for instance, that submerge both student and teacher, and elevate the goal of "efficiency," will not be tolerated. Similarly, a curriculum that divides the knowledge of the race into ever smaller and smaller discrete units of completed knowledge will undergo reconstruction. Textbooks that serve as convenient vehicles to bring to the student the limited, and limiting, loads of information that have passed the tests of the expert's finishing room will be removed from the tyrannical position they have too long occupied. Class activities that encourage the teacher to be the sole source of questions and that make the student the uncertain source of particular answers will be recognized to have little educative value. Educational tests that set informational limits within which teachers must move (if they are to be judged successful by administrators who believe that the use of such tests is full evidence of the scientific spirit) will be reduced to their proper subordinate position in the teaching process. All activities, in brief, will be judged in the light of their adequacy in fostering the way of life we have herein emphasized.

By way of conclusion we may state explicitly one further point of emphasis that has been implied, at least, in all of the discussion of this book.

It is reasonable to expect the school to face frankly the fact that it will not contribute to the reconstruction of the social process until it seriously experiments with the reconstruction of its own procedures.

This is clearly necessary, and in our consideration of the school task we have set the direction for this experimentation most definitely. We have charged the school with the responsibility of developing individuals who are equipped to deal with a world that is in the making, in ways that bring about the reconstruction of experience in the light of a clarified American tradition. Toward this end the school must now move. Fortunately, as we have indicated, it may move positively and directly. It may orient the student in his world. It may develop individuals who progressively achieve ways of conduct that are guided by adequately integrated attitudes. It may further the development of independent interests that lead the student to serious work in intellectual, practical, and esthetic realms. It may provide a way of living in the school that considers duly the miseducative effects of the social-economic order and consciously encourages in all of the life of the school conduct that is sensitive to the interests of others and intelligently disposed toward the needs of the group. It may move deliberately to the reconstruction of its own procedures in order that it may contribute maximally to social reconstruction. It may, in a word, provide an educative situation that develops a method of fairly considering all interests and fosters an active allegiance to that method.

Reconstruction of the life of the school in these terms will dictate activities that foster the development of attitudes and dispositions appropriate to deal with the present social-economic conditions. And it is important to point out that it will do this without resorting to indoctrination. We well recognize that we cannot avoid determining the character and the quality of many of the influences that play upon the educative experience of the student. This much is inescapable. And we may go further. A study of the environment of the school reveals individual life needs which the school program must anticipate and with which our educational philosophy must reckon. None the less, we propose to avoid indoctrination by the one means available: reliance upon intelligence. The conditions of the social-economic situation are given. Our concern is that the life of the school be so arranged that students may react intelligently in original and unique ways to these conditions. This is in direct contrast to the method of indoctrination. We want no values so fenced off that they are not proper objects of scrutiny. We are concerned, rather, that the process of education from beginning to end operate so that students think their own thoughts and live their own lives, but with an ever growing appreciation of the significance of their conduct as bearing upon the lives of others. Our view starts with a respect for the integrity of the individual, and it ends by placing upon the next generation the responsibility and the opportunity for arriving at more adequate solutions of life's problems than now we see. To the extent that the school is successful in bringing about a reorganization of its life in this direction it will contribute directly toward a more tolerant and humane social order, toward a way of life that approaches the democratic ideal.

Chapter VII

THE SCHOOL: ITS TASK AND ITS
ADMINISTRATION—III

I

SHORTLY after assuming the position of superintendent of schools in Chicago, William McAndrew announced that a school system "directly touching a total of 545,929 pupils and paid members must work clumsily on the old village conception of a one-man affair. It must adopt the motto of other big business: 'organize, deputize, supervise.' " [1]

Superintendent McAndrew was objecting at the time to the practice of individuals approaching the superintendent directly with suggestions, questions, or matters of detail that subordinates could deal with effectively. Within a short time, however, he took a further step and abolished the teachers' councils which had been established in Mrs. Young's administration for the express purpose of ensuring, as stated by a resolution of the Board of Education at the time of their inauguration, "that advisory authority and responsibility on educational subjects and the relation of the teaching body to the school system, should be vested in the teaching body." [2] In contrast with the view that teachers as a professional group should participate in the formulation of general educational policies, Mr. McAndrew put forth the following statement:

"It is scarcely to be expected that the second largest school system in America could radically depart from accepted principles

[1] Counts, George S., *School and Society in Chicago*, p. 76. New York: Harcourt, Brace and Company, 1928.
[2] *Ibid.*, p. 133.

of organization unless it should substitute for them some other plan, the success of which had been demonstrated beyond the possibility of doubt. All standard works on school management . . . repeat the obvious fact that the fixing of responsibility, groups of workers responsible to the designated heads, an orderly graduation of duties and appropriate powers, must be maintained, or chaos, confusion, and waste ensue. These books chart the school system to show the regular delegation of authority.

People
|
Board of Education
|
Superintendent
|
Assistant Superintendents
|
District Superintendents
|
Principals
|
Teachers

If Chicago has permitted to grow up a distortion of this scheme so that teachers, organized as councils, short-circuited up to a superintendent of schools, cutting out the principals and other supervisory officers, unless there can be shown benefits in the teaching unattainable through the regular organization, a return to the generally approved system is desirable." [3]

There is no question that the tenor of recommendations evolving out of the surveys of public school systems and the consensus of opinion on the part of authorities on school administration sustains Superintendent McAndrew's position. Contemporary theories on the organization and administration of education favor the centralization of responsibility and a clean-cut division of labor within school systems.

According to these views, the board of education is primarily a legislative and not an administrative body. Whether elected or appointed from the community at large, its members are expected to represent the people as a whole. Ideally it is

[3] Quoted, *ibid.*, pp. 77-78.

non-partisan and non-sectarian in character. Representing no special interest, it guards jealously the schools from interference on the part of individuals or groups who wish to promote their own selfish concerns.

To assure expert and professional administration of the school system the board of education selects a superintendent of schools, who acts as its chief executive and administrative official. To this officer, the board delegates authority for the conduct of both the business and educational affairs of the schools,[4] and from him it expects to receive recommendations regarding established policies and the formulation of new proposals. As Cubberley states,

"The board's work, as the representative of the people, is to sit in judgment on proposals and to determine the general policy of the school system."[5]

In both theory and practice the trend is away from a board so large that it requires standing committees in order to function. It is rather in the direction of the small board which can deal with all details as a unit.[6]

As stated above, the details of administration and the execution of policies the board delegates to the superintendent, who nominates in turn, for the approval of the board, the heads of all major subordinate divisions. In theory, and increasingly in practice, the superintendent of schools is considered the chief executive officer of the board. In the educational discussions of the last quarter of the nineteenth century there was a dis-

[4] For the purpose of simplicity we confine our discussion largely to a city school system. The principles involved, however, apply, with modifications resulting from size or purpose, to a single school, elementary or secondary, and to colleges and universities. While college and university faculties usually exercise more authority in practice and participate more directly in the administration of the institution than do faculties in school systems, there is little difference in the legal status of the two. Usually the faculty's action is always subject to the direct and explicit approval of the board of trustees.

[5] *Public School Administration*, p. 120. Boston: Houghton Mifflin Company, 1916.

[6] Engelhardt, Fred, *Public School Organization and Administration*, pp. 78-80. Boston: Ginn and Company, 1931.

position to favor dividing authority between a business and an educational executive. This probably reflected the desire of superintendents to emancipate themselves from business details and to center upon genuinely educational problems. Since the opening of the century there has come about virtually a unanimous opinion in favor of a unified control, with final authority resting in the hands of a trained educator.[7]

Cubberley, in *Public School Administration*, describes as follows the functions of the superintendent:

"He is the organizer and director of the work of the schools in all their different phases, and the representative of the schools and all for which the schools stand before the people of the community. He is the executive officer of the school board, and also its eyes, and ears, and brains. He is the supervisor of the instruction in the schools, and also the leader, adviser, inspirer, and friend of the teachers and between them and the board of education he must, at times, interpose as an arbiter. Amid all his various duties, however, the interests of the children in the schools must be his chief care, and the larger educational interests of the community as a whole he must constantly keep in mind."[8]

Cubberley recommends that boards of education be prohibited by legislation from interfering with the superintendent in the performance of his professional functions, such as, for example, the selection of textbooks, the organization and construction of courses of study, and the control of instruction. In many states legislation of this character exists, and there is reason to believe that with the continued expansion of school

[7] Thus in the Report of the Survey of the Schools of Chicago, Professor George D. Strayer remarks: "The Board of Education of the city of Chicago, pursuant to the provisions of the law, elects three executives—a superintendent of schools, a business manager, and an attorney. In addition to these, a secretary without administrative responsibility is chosen by the Board. Each of the three executives mentioned above is responsible directly to the Board of Education.

"The form of administration thus provided is, in the judgment of the survey staff, apt to lead to inefficiency. If responsibility is to be fixed and acknowledged, the Board should have one chief executive officer and all other executives should work under his direction and should report, through his office, to the Board." (Vol. I, pp. 9-10.)

[8] *Op. cit.*, p. 132.

systems and the increasing expansion of educational activities, professional administration will receive further safeguards.

On the whole, writers on educational administration turn to business and industry for models of efficiency in whose images they would mold school systems. Thus Dutton and Snedden remark:

"The science of administration, whether of business affairs or of government, has advanced rapidly of late, and the human element in executive control is at a high valuation. In the midst of vast aggregations of machinery and complicated devices for the speedy and skilful accomplishment of labor, the trained directive intelligence stands forth as, after all, the most impressive product of modern times. However stupendous the undertaking, one mind is supreme. In the bank, the factory, the railroad, and the industrial corporation, one head, who by natural ability and superior training is competent, directs the entire enterprise. In him is concentrated all needed authority and responsibility. To his lieutenants, chosen with equal care, is delegated a certain set of duties. They become so many additional hands and feet of their chief, and thus extend the scope of his power and effectiveness. It is fortunate that the centralization of executive power, so necessary to honesty and efficient management, should have been widely demonstrated in the business world before states, cities, or school systems had anything like the volume of business which they are called upon to perform today." [9]

[9] *Administration of Public Education in the United States*, p. 18. New York: The Macmillan Company, 1915. And Frank P. Graves, in *The Administration of American Education* (The Macmillan Company, New York, 1932), writes: "While the question is not yet as fully settled as it should be, the approved procedure, as already indicated, is to have the board of education select the best qualified superintendent it can secure, concentrate all authority and responsibility for educational results in him and require him to initiate and carry into execution all appointments and policies for the system. It is the function of the board to approve or reject his nominations for appointment and discuss and pass upon the policies proposed by him in the light of such objective evidence as he can present. His duties will thus be initiatory and executive; the board's, advisory and legislative. He should develop an educational program for its consideration and it should furnish the necessary legislation and authority for him to carry it out effectively. Sound administration springs from professional leadership and lay control. For such a general principle boards of education can find a precedent in the administrative procedure of successful commercial and industrial organizations, which, in order to survive at all, have been forced to discover the most efficient form of management possible." (P. 443.)
(These excerpts are quoted by permission of the publishers.)

Similarly Theisen [10] examined thoroughly administrative organizations in business and the city-manager form of commission government with a view to the discovery of principles that might serve as guides for city school systems. He found, as he states, three fundamental principles of administration which encourage expert executive leadership. These are:

(1) wide authority on the part of the chief executive in controlling other executives and directing their duties, and

(2) responsibility for results centered in the chief executive. "The board of control retires from active administration but retains ultimate control through the budget and through reports that must be made showing the achievements, and business or financial status of the system."

(3) The board of control demands that the chief executive and his assistants assume the initiative in matters of policy.

Theisen concludes with the moral,

"We are taught then that the form of administration which makes for efficiency in these fields is one that is centralized or coördinated. It is one in which professional leadership is recognized and in which executive functions are assigned to experts. It is one in which the board of control demands results and in which it assumes that its own function is to provide the legislation necessary to permit the achievement of those possibilities which are indicated by its leaders." [11]

The place of the professional staff, other than executives, in school systems receives little if any discussion in texts on administration. Teacher participation, for example, receives virtually no attention in the literature. It is true that when Cubberley writes of the superintendent,

"Out of his clear vision as to purposes, his more mature judgment as to ways and means and his enthusiasm as to what it is possible to do, he should give a definite trend to the thinking of

[10] Theisen, William W., *The City Superintendent and the Board of Education.* Teachers College, Columbia University, *Contributions to Education,* No. 84, Chapter II.
[11] *Op. cit.,* p. 100.

everyone, from assistant superintendent to grade teacher, who has to do with the instruction of children in the schools," [12]

his conception of the relation between the superintendent and his staff is easily inferred. Engelhardt is one of the few authors to mention teachers' unions and the problem of teacher representation upon boards of education. The latter he considers "contrary to the fundamental purpose for which the school board exists." [13] The generally accepted principle that teachers are represented by the superintendent and that all communications and all contacts with the board of education should proceed through one's superior officer would seem to define the relation of the rank and file of the professional staff in the school organization. Representation of teachers, in other words, runs counter to the "orderly gradation of duties and appropriate powers" so clearly charted in McAndrew's statement quoted above. Since, on this view, the superintendent is commanding officer, it is believed that to admit teachers to representation on the governing body would merely create embarrassing relations between superior and inferiors. It would place the hands and feet where they would of certainty impede the free operations of the mind.

The business theory of school administration involves, as we stated earlier, centralized authority with successive divi-

[12] *Op. cit.*, p. 179.

[13] *Op. cit.*, p. 66. He adds, "The purpose of the board of education is to represent the people of the district, and it appoints a trained professional staff to manage the schools. The teachers and other employees are represented at board meetings by the superintendent of schools.

"The function of a school board is to pass on the recommendations made by their appointed officials. As lay citizens they express their judgment as to the work and recommendations of their appointed professional staff after considering the effectiveness of the work done, and as to whether policies proposed, even though professionally sound and desirable, are to the best interests of the teachers and the schools of the district they represent. The board of education deliberates and determines the plan for the organization and administration of the local schools. Policies that treat of the relationship between teachers and the administration are thus considered and are formulated in the light of the best interests of the schools and of those associated in carrying on the work."

sions of labor. Authority is delegated along lines that radiate from the chief executive's office. Specialized performance thus coincides with centralized control. The flow of power, as the current of ideas, is from the center outward. The superintendent is first of all a leader, and within the sphere of their own appropriate activities and in harmony with the policies projected by the supreme command, this conception of leadership applies all along the line until it reaches the individual child in his relations with his teacher.

II

Thus our machinery of administration runs counter to the professed purposes of public education. If we ask for the motive lying back of the prevailing conception, the answer is simple: business efficiency, effectiveness. On the other hand, the dominating aim of public education is to prepare boys and girls, young men and women, adults, for intelligent participation in democratic living. How shall we explain the divergence? What in the history of public education has fostered a progressive insulation of the school from forces without the school? A board of education that reflects no popular interests? An administrative organization rigidly set off in its activities from a board of education? An organization of the staff modeled in many respects along military lines?

In the first place it represents a reaction against the disastrous consequences of lay administration. Indeed, the history of school administration is little more than a description of successive attempts to emancipate schools from lay control.

Originally the people in town meetings administered education for themselves. Here they voted to establish a school, selected their teacher, and provided the essentials for maintaining the school. Before long it became both necessary and convenient for them to delegate duties to an individual or a committee, with power to act for the town when the town meeting was not in session. In time this became a standing school committee charged with responsibility for all of the details of carrying on the school.

It was not long, however, before school committees found it difficult to handle properly all of the tasks involved in running a good school. Consequently, the school superintendency began to evolve. Thus in Connecticut, according to Graves,[14] the "school visitors" or the "school committee" as a whole were at first responsible for duties such as preparing courses of study, approving methods of teaching, enforcing discipline, and the like. In time the committees adopted the plan of assigning these tasks to small subcommittees and these still later delegated their functions to one member who served as an "acting school visitor" or "acting manager." The inferior service rendered by these representatives of the school committees resulted eventually in the selection of a trained educator with the title of superintendent. This official performed the clerical duties of the school committees as well as the administrative functions originally assigned to the subcommittees, receiving for his services a small stipend.

The school committee set the pattern for the organization of city boards of education. Since cities are commonly amalgamations of what were once independent communities, as well as new developments, the school system of the city grew by similar accretions. In some instances boards of education reflected in their make-up these accumulations of district committees, the central boards being composed of semi-independent subcommittees, and each subcommittee tending to put first the interests of its own district. In other cases a central board of education assumed from the start control over the city school system as a whole. In either event general practice perpetuated district or ward representation, and in time city boards of

14 *Op. cit.,* pp. 407-408.

education became unmanageably large. For example, as late as 1902 the Philadelphia board of education contained some 500 members.

Large boards with party representation and political log-rolling could result only in the demoralization of the schools, and in the first two decades of the twentieth century determined efforts were made to free the schools from the contaminating influences of politics.

One method adopted was to professionalize the work of the superintendent of schools. Between 1835 and 1880 this officer functioned chiefly as the business agent of the board, but from about 1880 on, with the phenomenal growth of cities, superintendents here and there endeavored to emancipate themselves from business details and to center rather exclusively upon educational administration.

They soon found themselves handicapped in two respects. In the first place they discovered, as we have already indicated, that they could not maintain a separation between business and financial management and educational administration. It became evident that he who controls the purse strings and the expenditure of funds exercises final authority on matters of policy. Second, the practice of lay administration through the medium of standing committees embarrassed and often paralyzed their efforts. In the city of Rochester, for example, the lay members of the board at one time served on the following committees: finance, qualification and employment of teachers, organization of schools and grievances, textbooks, library and apparatus, repairs, buildings, supplies, fuel and fire fixtures, printing, free academy salaries, janitors, law apportionment.[15]

This situation involved more than merely a waste of time on the part of the superintendent, who was thus forced to consult committees on details which they frequently could not under-

[15] Dutton and Snedden, *op. cit.*, p. 141.

stand. Very often it meant as well that he had to combat the selfish interests of groups and individuals who utilized committee representation for their own ends.

Consequently municipal reformers in the period of "the shame of the cities" endeavored to free the schools from lay control and to center the direction of both business and educational administration in the hands of professionally trained school executives.

It is not strange that they turned to business organization for suggestions. The ways of business seemed to possess merit at precisely those points where municipal government failed. In contrast with the large city council or board of education with its waste of time and dissipation of energy, its log-rolling and subordination of public welfare to factional selfishness, the governing boards of large corporations evidenced an enviable singleness of purpose and a capacity to distinguish between essential policies and details of administration. Superintendents of schools were weighed down with huge boards of education and checked at every point in their administration by petty interference on the part of laymen. Boards of directors in business were small and encouraged their executives to exercise initiative and independence. Provided he served well the ends of business, a manager could exercise a free hand in his conduct of affairs. This same principle of direct responsibility extended throughout business organizations. A general manager appointed his department heads on the basis of merit, and held them responsible for results. No consideration of politics or special favoritism stood in the way of increasing output or the lowest cost of production. Divisions of functions, centralized responsibility and control, and whole-hearted concentration of each member of the organization upon realizing a clearly defined purpose seemed indeed an ideal and a method worth incorporating in the conduct of public affairs.

This explains why, in the past thirty years, authorities in

school administration have urged that school systems follow the example of big business. And their recommendations are going into effect. The large school board is being replaced by a deliberative body small enough to function as a unit. Ward representation yields to citywide representation, either by appointment or election. Within the school system the confused tangle of responsibility and overlapping of duties is straightening out along the clear lines of centralized authority and clean-cut divisions of authority. The superintendent acts as the agent of the board and is charged with supreme authority in the conduct of the business and educational affairs of the schools. Legislation protects him from outside interference, be that from members of the board or pressure groups in the community.

The following quotation from Cubberley surveys very well the area of the superintendent's operations. It applies to the first-hand activities of a superintendent in a small school system. As Cubberley remarks, when a school system increases in size, the superintendent will delegate tasks to others. But the principle remains the same. He is looked upon as the educational fountain from which proceeds the thought and the energy that gives health and life to the school system as a whole.

"At one time he must be an organizer and planner for the development of the system, often looking into the future beyond the vision of the teachers, the board, or the people. At another time he must be an expert on school organization, bringing to teachers, principals, the board, and the people the best experience of other cities. At another time he must be an expert on the making and administration of a course of study, slowly educating those associated with him up to his larger point of view. At another time he must be an expert investigator and tester of the work of the schools, and the progress of the pupils therein. At another time he must be an expert on the details of schoolhouse construction, and on the proper care and maintenance of the school plant. At another time he must be an expert on playgrounds and playground work. At another time he must be the real authority back of the attendance officer, administering the law, and protecting the educational rights of the children. At another time he must be protecting these same rights in the employment, dismissal or safeguarding from injustice of teachers. At another time he is again voicing the need of the children, or protecting them along the line of health control. At another time he is a business man, looking after purchases, budgets, and the larger problems of educational finance. At another time he is a petitioner before the board, asking for some improvement in conditions, some new grant of power, or some change in ruling, and following this he is the servant of the board, seeing that its decisions are carried out. At another time he is an administrator, looking after the hundred and one little details of daily school administration, dictating letters, meeting people, smoothing out difficulties, eliminating friction, and adding to the confidence of the people in their schools. At other times he is a supervisor of teachers, directing them, inspiring them to larger service, and extending helpful supervision to them." [16]

III

In a moment we shall examine the appropriateness of the proposal to shape our educational systems according to patterns derived from industry and business. Imitations in practice as analogies in argument are always in danger of neglecting significant differences. But before proceeding to this phase of our discussion we should like to refer briefly to several factors within our general educational situation which gave aid and comfort to the tendencies described.

First was the perpetuation of the traditional conception of education as a supplementary process in which it was thought that the school should add to the educative influences coming out of "the main business of living" certain academic information and a training in the use of intellectual tools. For centuries education has been identified with the use of books. On its lowest level it has centered upon abolishing illiteracy and upon helping people to acquire the rudiments of reading and writing.

[16] *Op. cit.*, pp. 163-164.

On the higher levels of learning it has envisaged culture as an external acquisition: as primarily an entering into those aspects of racial inheritance which are easily perpetuated in books.

This encourages administrators to oversimplify the educational process; to view the school as an organization devoted to the dispensing of ready-made knowledge, much as a wholesale establishment prepares and assorts packages for distribution, grading them according to the needs of different types of consumers. Moreover, the tools put forth by scientific education in the period under review were well adapted to reinforce this trend. Intelligence tests seemed to hold forth the possibility of classifying children in terms of their native abilities, while achievement tests revealed the extent to which children measured up to their powers. Job, activity, and functional analyses in the hands of scientifically trained curriculum experts pointed to the specific performances in which children could engage and the specific information they could acquire in order to arrive at the specific ideas and to establish the specific responses essential for effective performance in a mechanized world. Behaviorism in psychology and the scientific study of education thus seemed to confirm the suggestion that business methods of organization and management be applied to school administration and supervision.[17]

[17] In the *Twelfth Yearbook* of the National Society for the Study of Education, Part I (The Public School Publishing Company, 1913), Franklin Bobbitt proposed that scientific management, evidently so successful in business, be applied to the supervision in schools. He listed a number of principles which he thought with some modification could be applied to teachers much as they had been applied to workers in industry. A few of these principles are of interest in connection with our discussion. They are:

"Where material is acted upon by the labor processes, and passes through a number of progressive stages on its way from the raw material to the ultimate product, qualitative and quantitative standards must be determined for the product at each of these stages. . . .

"The worker must be kept supplied with detailed instructions for his kind of work during his entire service. . . .

"The worker must be kept up to standard qualifications as to the work to be done, the standards to be reached, the methods to be employed, and the appliances to be used. . . .

Second, the rapid growth of cities, with the need for rapid expansions and multiplications in school plants as well as the addition of new departments, resulted for a time in a demand for teachers far in excess of the possibilities for adequate training and preparation. The heavy turnover in teaching staffs, the low level of professional performance, and the absence of the spirit of craftsmanship on the part of teachers indicated further the necessity of an organization of education that would assure continuity and effectiveness in children's learning, and control and direction in educational programs.

And, finally, the appeal to business models as a basis for redeeming public education secured reinforcement and support from constructive elements in public opinion. Of course it carried an inherent conviction to the public-spirited business man. He was predisposed to favor suggestions derived from his own successful experience that pointed toward the attainment of clearly defined objectives. For quite different reasons social reformers supported programs of efficient school management. Their concern for child life led them to support policies that would result ultimately in the insulation of the school from outside influences, whether these influences were the plunderings of politicians, the self-seeking purposes of pressure groups, or the baneful effects of an industrial civilization upon child life. On the administrative side, the first essential, as they saw it, was to ensure an honest and efficient conduct of public education. To safeguard children for a necessary period of healthy growth, reformers fought for and secured legislation which raised steadily the age of compulsory

"Incentives must be placed before the workers so as to stimulate the output on their part of the optimum product.

"In a productive organization, the management must determine the order and sequence of all of the various processes through which the raw material or the partially developed product shall pass, in order to bring about the greatest possible effectiveness and economy; and it must see that the raw material or partially finished product is actually passed on from process to process, from worker to worker, in the manner that is most effective and most economical." (Quoted by the permission of the Society.)

school attendance and protected children in other respects from the blighting effects of their environment. Consequently, more or less unwittingly, they both fostered the isolation of the school from life and, for want of a satisfactory alternative, encouraged not merely the freeing of the administration of education from lay interference but also the conduct of education in such wise that children attend autocratically managed schools where they receive formal instruction in what is deemed essential for participation in democratic citizenship. Similarly vocational education, in order to preserve its educational purposes, has operated in the main under the roof of the school.

IV

This very hurried analysis of the conditions giving rise to the organization of education along lines analogous to those followed in business should suggest that it represents a stage in the evolution of public education rather than a form or a pattern inherently adapted to the carrying-on of the educational process. And we should expect that, as we progress toward a state of greater maturity in our comprehension and understanding of the nature, the purpose, and the function of education in society, its inadequacies will become obvious.

We have already suggested that it operates best where teaching is looked upon as the distribution of ready-made knowledge. Similarly the autocratic method of administration and supervision functions most smoothly where educational efficiency is identified with the successful teaching of the minimum essentials. We should recall that Superintendent McAndrew's administration in Chicago was most invulnerable when it concentrated upon a "one-hundred percent mastery" of the fundamentals. The shortcomings and the failures contained within the analogy from business become more apparent when the school attempts to organize its program in terms of a wider and a more flexible conception of education.

The previous chapters in this book have stressed what might be termed an organic theory of education. This conceives the growth of the individual as the outcome of an intimate interplay between the organism and its surroundings. Indeed it looks upon the self as a combination of inner and outer influences that constitute a unique product. Accordingly education is no longer viewed as a process of formation from without, the imposition upon the learner of preconceived ideas, attitudes, and dispositions which he passively absorbs; nor as a blossoming-forth from an inner nature without reference to the operations of an environment. It is rather a reconstruction and a reorganization of experience, a novel result of two groups of interpenetrating forces. Consequently, no matter how concerned the administrator or an instructor may be that the learner grow into specified ways of thinking, acting, and feeling, he must strive for self-directive behavior. The learner's ideas must be self-grown, his actions must ring true to the qualities of his own nature.

The educator desires, moreover, that these ideas and actions be charged with an expanding meaning and significance. As Professor William H. Kilpatrick states:

"From the broad point of view all life thoughtfully lived is education. To give conscious attention to what one is about, to seek and note significant meanings in what is happening, to apply these meanings as intelligently as one may to the direction of one's affairs—all this is not only the path of efficient dealings, it is equally the process of education in possibly the only full sense." [18]

Education thus extends actually or potentially to every department of one's life. It is by no means exclusively an affair of the class-room, the school, or of formal educational

[18] *Education and the Social Crisis,* p. 44. New York: Liveright, Inc., 1932.

agencies. It applies or should apply as well to the work which we do in order to earn our daily bread. When over and above its immediate vocational purpose we see in our work interesting possibilities in the way of cultural, scientific, and social relationships, it tends to lose the dull, drab appearance it might otherwise assume. On the other hand, a routine activity that fails to rise in significance above the level of the routine carries with it positive dangers from a mental hygiene point of view.

In an article written for the *Journal of Adult Education* [19] L. P. Jacks writes as follows of the educational possibilities within the vocations:

"The quality of the spiritual food that mankind gets for its soul is strictly dependent on the way it goes about the business of earning the daily bread that feeds its body. If the breadwinning part of its business contributes nothing to its spiritual nourishment, the soul of civilization will die of famine, all social reforms, political philosophies and religious revivals notwithstanding, while the drugs, stimulants, and appetizers made use of to keep it alive will only hasten the process of spiritual decay. In this article I am pleading for the continuity of things. Breadwinning and soulsaving are not two independent operations—most assuredly not when the soul of a civilization is in question. They form a single and continuous operation, called material, if we look at it from one end, spiritual if we look at it from the other. A civilization saves its soul by the way it wins its daily bread. And I have no hesitation in saying that the chief reason why the various soulsaving enterprises now in being are yielding such meager results lies in the general overlooking of this elementary and everlasting truth. . . . A type of education based on this vision of continuity is, obviously, the outstanding need of our times. Its outlook will be life-long. It will look upon the industry of civilization as the great 'continuation school' for intelligence and for character, and its object will be, not merely to fit men and women for the specialized vocations they are to follow, but also to animate the vocations themselves with ideals of excellence appropriate to each. At the risk of seeming fantastic I will venture to say that the final objective of the New Education is the gradual transformation of the industry of the world into the university of the world; in other words, the gradual bringing about

[19] February, 1929.

of a state of things in which 'breadwinning' and 'soulsaving' instead of being, as now, disconnected and often opposed operations, shall become a single and continuous operation."

If Jacks is right, the first institution to explore and to demonstrate the educational opportunities implicit within vocational performance should be the school. The applications of educational theory would thus extend to all participants and not merely to those who are technically in the position of learners. That is to say, an educational system is under obligations to strive toward that type of relationship between all engaged within it which will enable each individual to function organically with others; to encourage the performance of functions on the part of each one in full realization and with conscious recognition of their implications in the thought and the actions of others. Honesty requires that school executives who preach to teachers the doctrine of education through shared activity shall apply it in their relations with their own colleagues.

But there is more than a theoretical inconsistency between educational theory and the business plan of school administration. The growth and development of a school system always involves more than an increase in the size of what previously existed. Educational evolution is more often synonymous with creative evolution. Consequently the necessary specialization that follows is no mere subdivision of labor, analogous to what follows upon the enlargement of a business.

Progress in education has meant both the blossoming-forth of new possibilities within old processes (witness the rich and varied nature of elementary and secondary education to-day as against their exclusively bookish character a generation ago) and the acceptance of a public responsibility for the education of individuals and groups once ignored by the school. The school now ministers to the entire period of life. It adapts itself to needs as varied as those of an infant in a nursery school, a college student, a research worker in the graduate school or a research foundation, and a member of a professional or a vocational group. Nor is education any longer restricted to class-room, lecture hall, and laboratory. It follows the student to the place where he can use it most effectively. For example, as a result of the 1931 epidemic of infantile paralysis, the New York school budget carries an enlarged appropriation to be used for employing teachers who are to instruct crippled and disabled children in their own homes. Similarly one of the distinctive features of the junior college is its provision for extramural education for young people and adults on an accredited basis. Part-time education on secondary school and college levels is also on the increase.

Public education is thus reaching out into new fields. It is also growing in complexity. That is to say, with new insights operations that seemed comparatively simple are turning out to be quite the reverse. This holds true even of simple matters such as learning to read and to write and to cipher. Educational research reveals subjects for investigation and specialized attention in each which were undreamed-of a generation ago. Nor are the three R's the ends-in-themselves they once were. With the raising of the level of general education they have become more distinctly tools for the attainment of significant insights, interpretations, and appreciations and growth in fundamental attitudes and dispositions. Consequently to their early verbal and narrowly intellectual character we are adding other values and in doing so we are opening up new avenues of learning.

This is merely saying that an organic conception of learning stresses the intimate interplay between the individual and his environment hitherto little understood and scarcely at all practised. But it also carries implications for supervision and administration quite contrary to the conventional theory with its emphasis upon a central authority who formulates the plans which subordinates are to execute.

Take, as a relatively simple example, the coördination of the efforts of teachers in so far as they affect a child in the class-room.

One of the possible advantages in "units of work," as now carried on in the elementary school and to a considerable extent in the junior high school, consists in the fact that they cut across the lines that have hitherto divided subjects and the teachers of subjects. They center upon unifying the educational experiences of pupils. They distinguish between what we might term organizing ideas and the particular instruments utilized in helping children to enter into these ideas. A teacher may have in mind, for example, introducing his class to the meaning and the significance of the industrial revolution: what it has led to in the substitution of machine labor for hand labor; what revolutions it has brought about in the way people live and work and play; and how it has transformed relations between classes in society and between the people of one country and another.

Now, all of the possibilities that lie implicit within a unit on the industrial revolution are in a sense independent of any one arbitrary subject-matter or any one method. If a teacher or a child has been in China, the influence of the industrial revolution in China may serve the purpose just as well as the more conventional study of its development in England. Or, again, a class might trace the influence of the industrial revolution in its effects upon a section of the United States. The basic understandings which are the ultimate objectives are better realized when teachers realize this difference between the materials that one might use and the ends in view.

Similarly the units of work take on vitality when they employ what we might term the use of many languages. A knowledge of the significance of the industrial revolution is by no means confined to what one learns from the printed page. The arts and the crafts have an equally important part to play, but not so much as courses of study which merely *supplement* the work of class teachers. Their interpretative functions are better utilized when they are intimately interwoven with the regular class-room activities. In other words, the educational values of units of work vary with the degree to which subject-matter and departmental lines are broken down and teachers of all subjects consider that they and their special subjects are to function as resources for stimulating the educational growth of children.

It is clear that the unit method of teaching requires careful planning and a degree of preparation on the part of teachers little dreamed of in the conventional school; but a preparation and a planning that cannot be standardized and stereotyped. It calls for a sense of the relations between the factors involved in carrying it on that is quite at variance with the conventional conception of leadership. No one person can alone foresee all the possibilities within a proposed unit, since these vary with individual children, class teachers, special teachers, available materials and equipment, and local conditions. On the other hand, the educational values that emerge are conditioned upon a free and understanding coöperation on the part of all participants, instructors and children alike.

From the standpoint of staff relationships the first essential is that class-room teachers and special teachers (teachers of the fine and practical arts, music, dramatics, and the like) keep their eyes first upon the children, their needs and potentialities. Subjects thus become instrumental in the development of children's powers, and each teacher asks himself: "To what extent can I draw upon my special field in order to realize the purposes of this unit?" "What are the unusual abilities and the limitations of the group or individuals within the group which call for special attention?" "In what respects may the work of this unit require supplementation in order that values not found in it may be made accessible to the children?" "How can I modify my procedure (as regards both subject-matter and method) in the light of what others are planning?"

Not only do unique and unexpected contributions on the part of those participating evolve out of a conference of this character, but the undertaking as a whole acquires a balance and a proportion not possible under the conventional plan of departmental teaching with its divisions of responsibility for developing different areas of the child's school experience.

Our illustration is drawn from conditions that apply to class-room teaching; but the principle holds good with reference to healthy relations between the divisions within a school system and between the work of schools and the social agencies in a community. It is our contention that in each case the patterns which should determine the functioning of educational organizations are more appropriately found in valid conceptions of the nature and purpose of education than in the structure of business and industry. Always it is the special task of the administrator to center upon those conditions basic for the active participation of all functionaries; and the end he should have in view is that type of planning which enables individuals and groups to carry on their own activities with intelligent reference to others. When problems arise or new policies are called for, the administrator is charged with peculiar responsibility for seeing to it that all relevant aspects are considered. Leadership on these occasions does not consist in imposing his will upon others; it involves rather bringing about the coordinated and coöperative thinking and planning of all interests in the light of purposes that transcend petty ambitions and concerns and which direct the active energies of every one toward the realization of ends shared by all.

Leadership under these conditions is no small undertaking. It involves first of all bringing the specialists together and keeping them together until their association has brought forth good fruit. As chairman the administrator must guide and direct discussion along lines relevant for all. He must be able to see and appreciate relations possible as well as actual between two experts who are perhaps blinded by excessive preoccupation with their own specialties. He must respond sympathetically to a wide variety of interests. These he must hold constantly before the eyes of all participants so that in attaining one value others are not sacrificed. What wisdom he possesses he will contribute to the common pool, but the final decision arrived at will not flow from his superior will or depend upon his position of authority. It will evolve rather out of the group deliberations and win approval because it is the most relevant and comprehensive program possible. And as a means toward the emergence of a common program of this nature it is his special concern and responsibility to maintain and create the conditions which will elicit from each participant the very best he has to offer for the unified program. Finally, when deliberations are ended, his is the genius which must see that agreements arrived at are executed with the same intelligent and understanding appreciation of the relations between part and whole and whole and part that characterized their evolution.

We do not suggest that the principle of participation can be introduced at once or to the same degree in all school systems. We recognize that differences exist in states of readiness, local conditions, and stages in educational evolution. But nevertheless we can say that the wise administrator, as the wise teacher, will shape his actions with reference to a goal in mind as well as to immediate conditions. He will appreciate the fact that the elements which go to make up his analysis of the immediate situation as well as the suggestions which occur for dealing with it are relevant to the port toward which he wishes his ship to head.

With this word of caution regarding the need always for adapting theory to practical conditions as well as shaping practical conditions with reference to theory, we shall attempt to illustrate a few of the implications of a democratic conception of school administration.

First, as regards its application to the professional staff:

The usual organization affords an excellent starting point in that it provides a basis for functional differentiation. It is essential to see, however, that what distinguishes two individuals is a difference in performance rather than false notions of status. The essential difference between a principal of a school and a teacher, for example, consists in the former's responsibility for the smooth operation of the school as a whole. He is the servant of his colleagues in that his first concern is to provide conditions under which they can best exercise their distinctive functions. His task it is to coördinate and integrate all factors that affect the general conditions for carrying on the educational process. The teacher, on the other hand, is primarily interested with life in the class-room, his pupils, and the work in which they are engaged. Elements of general discipline, the work in other class-rooms, in grades above and below and parallel to his own, involve him in so far as they modify of necessity the plans that he wishes to carry out. Consequently the principal's activities and the teacher's concerns should supplement and reinforce one another. Each is dependent for the adequate performance of his duties upon the understanding and the coöperation of the other. The same is true of relations with the office staff, janitors, and so on. And there is every assurance that the interests of each group will receive fairly adequate recognition when facilities are provided for pooling information regarding common needs and formulating individual purposes in the light of all relevant considerations. A principal thus performs the duties of general administrator best when he brings all these functionaries into relationship with one another and by the exercise of tact and consideration stimulates the origin and development of policies which express the consensus of the best judgment of the whole group.

In a small organization all interests may secure expression in a building council that includes all workers and which may function much as does a town meeting. In the large school other plans for common participation may realize the same interchange of views and knowledge of needs and lead to similar results. If we adhere to the principle that the form or organization utilized should grow out of the peculiarities and the needs of the particular situation, no one administrative set-up will receive final approval. However, a large school or a complex school system cannot function on the town meeting plan. Consequently sound administration will promote the formation of functional groups for the purpose of realizing at least two things: (1) the discussion of problems relating to common activities so as constantly to encourage progress within the area of their own professional interests, and (2) provision for necessary interrelationship with other groups, again with a view to furthering both the intelligent performance of each group's major responsibility and the smooth administration of the system as a whole.

This implies both administrative approval and direct administrative encouragement for the organization of not only the teaching staff but all functionaries within a school system. And it implies, in the large educational centers, a union of these organizations in something akin to a guild, so that, in matters that affect all, the voices of all may be heard.

In other words, the organization of a professional staff must provide for both unification and differentiation. The teachers of a given department or grade level, for example, cannot concentrate adequately upon problems that are peculiar to them if their only association is in a building council. Consequently for purposes such as working out the more technical and narrow aspects of their own courses of study and the like they should function alone or as subcommittees of a general organization. On the other hand, in so far as their actions bear upon other groups and are but phases of a common program, provision should be made for a general pooling of thought and effort.

Our proposal involves little more than raising to the conscious level of a general principle of procedure practices that already exist in different stages of development in progressive school systems. It is fairly well recognized, for example, that a course of study or a curriculum is most successful when it evolves out of the coöperative thinking of both teachers and experts. The Denver program for curriculum revision as organized under the superintendency of Jesse H. Newlon will long remain an object lesson in this respect. When experts and teachers thus gather about a round table for the purpose of securing a joint product, the expert finds himself called upon to organize and direct his special knowledge with reference to the variations and the peculiarities of the local situation, while the staff through the help of the expert rises above the limitations of its own experience to a level of thinking and future performance higher than would otherwise be possible. Similarly the experience of progressive schools indicates that courses of study stimulate the best results when they express the agreement of participants along general lines but contain a wealth of suggestive procedures, materials, and information regarding available resources, so that each teacher may exercise initiative and originality within the common pattern of agreement. In short, where administrators have sought definitely to promote common agreements, a general pooling of individual experiences and suggestions and freedom for variation and experimentation, there we find a dynamic and vital curriculum.[20]

What we have said regarding democratic curriculum construction applies to other aspects of school planning. Only recently, for example, have school architects and progressive school administrators come to realize the advantages in the functional approach to school construction. When the school architect sits down with a school staff and evolves his plans in the light of what he finds competent teachers wish to accomplish and the types of activities they carry on in their classrooms, a new type of school building begins to evolve. Deadly uniformity and standardization give way to varied physical opportunities for learning in an environment friendly to creative activity.

Similarly the coöperation of the professional staff is needed

---

[20] Professor George W. Strayer states in an article on "Creative Administration" (*Teachers College Record*, Sept. 1925) : "A superintendent of schools in a middle western city was responsible for the development of a staff of assistant superintendents, principals, and teachers who set the pace in public education for the whole country during his administration. It was interesting to visit that school system and to discover the individuality of the separate units composing it. No two schools were alike, but in every case principals and teachers were investigating and experimenting. The superintendent of schools was vastly more concerned that teachers and principals do the work in which they were most interested and carry forward the program as they conceived it than that there should be uniformity of procedure. He was able to appreciate their endeavors even when he may have thought that he knew a better way. He brought them together for conference and discussion and they stimulated each other. His influence was felt not only among those who had the good fortune to work with him intimately, but also throughout his state and throughout the nation. His work as an administrator has borne fruit not only in the achievements of the members of his staff, but also in the lives of thousands of men and women who were fortunate enough to be enrolled in the schools under his supervision." (Pp. 1-2.)

"The one most important criterion by which to judge the work of the administrator is found in the query, 'Have those who have been associated with him grown?' It is not to be expected that all will have achieved great distinction, but the demand may well be made that all do better work and that all are ready to accept greater responsibility. In every large school system there are teachers, principals, and supervisors of unusual ability. Possibly the most severe test that we can put upon the work of the administrator is to ask in what degree these superior persons have realized their highest possibilities under his leadership." (P. 4.)

in defining and clarifying the conditions essential for the adequate performance of professional services. This applies to the physical conditions of work, matters that affect health and hygiene, necessary equipment, materials, and the like; but it holds true equally of all the complex factors involved in the adequate definition of a living wage. And when the coöperation of an educational staff is sought in determining wages and salaries and to suggest ways and means to balance teachers' wants against other needs of an institution or a school system, there results not merely a greater satisfaction with the outcome than is otherwise true, but less probability of one group pressing its interests to the detriment of others.

The financial stress under which most school systems are now operating affords opportunities to test the comparative effects upon teacher morale of the autocratic and the democratic plans of administration. In the former, fear and uncertainty prevail, and specific suggestions for economy, such as salary reductions, arouse suspicion if not actual opposition. This follows from the fact that no one knows to what extent proposals for salary reduction are based upon a thorough study of all elements in the situation. On the other hand, in other school systems quite a different spirit prevails. For example, in one school system known to the writer, the board of education requested the different functional groups, the superintendent, principals, heads of departments, supervisors, representatives of teachers, and financial officers, to study the financial problems of the schools and to suggest plans appropriate to the situation. All available information was given to this group. It soon became evident that a reduction of salaries was inevitable; but the reductions finally voted by the board of education were those recommended by the staff!

This coöperative method of coping with a financial difficulty in the school system mentioned illustrates what might constitute the permanent relations between these same functionaries. Under these circumstances, as we have previously stated, superintendents and heads of departments are no less able to exercise leadership than under an autocratic system. Indeed, the vital contact with others which the proposed relationship affords gives ample opportunity for that interplay of mind upon mind which constitutes leadership of a most vital quality.

Furthermore, programs that evolve out of a democratically organized school system are *ipso facto* more firmly grounded than are the policies of a one-man institution. In the first case, they evolve out of the coöperative thinking of the staff and thus carry with them the friendly support which ensures their passing over into action. In the latter, their claim upon life is little better than the tenure of office of the official who originates them.

Finally, we should like to remark in passing that staff participation in school administration should contribute toward an intelligent public discussion of educational questions. We have already referred to the prevailing opinion that boards of education should function primarily as legislative bodies. If this be true, they should have access to every possible source of information that bears upon educational policies. Prevailing theory excludes the professional staff from membership on boards of education. It assumes that the chief administrative officer of the schools should alone speak for the staff. If, however, it is our intention to encourage the development of a sifting and winnowing process of representation and coöperative consideration of school questions, we may conclude that even boards of education should take their character from this fact.

The implications of this conclusion we shall postpone, however, until we deal more directly with the organization of boards of education.

V

The duties of an administrator are by no means limited to the internal relations of the school. They put him as well into communication with outside social, economic, and civic agencies.

This follows inevitably, since the trend of modern education has been to adapt practice to an organic theory of learning. Courses of study in the so-called practical subjects—agriculture, home economics, industrial arts—probably broke the first ground in the attempt to integrate the school and the home experiences of the student. To-day scarcely a school system fails to identify in some way the out-of-school interests and needs of its pupils with the work of the class-room.

The most successful illustration of attempts of this character is probably to be found in those rural schools that are endeavoring consciously to exploit the possibilities of an education through shared experiences. For example, Miss Elsie Clapp of the Ballard Memorial School in Kentucky is not only helping children to appreciate better and to utilize more effectively the cultural, vocational, and esthetic possibilities within their environment, but through the impact of the school upon the homes the standards of community living in all these respects are undergoing transformation. Similarly Langford describes, in his study *Educational Service, Its Functions and Possibilities,* a large variety of educational activities in the Province of Ontario which point in the direction of a life-centered education and contrast with the usual subject-matter emphasis.[21]

The necessity of protecting children from the evil effects of a city environment render more difficult, if not impossible, any very effectual participation on the part of children in life

[21] See *Contributions to Education,* No. 509 (Teachers College, Columbia University, New York).

outside the school. Nevertheless, through excursions to social agencies, civic institutions, farms and typical industries, museums, and the like, children can derive first-hand contacts that serve as concrete starting points for an interpretation and understanding of the varied activities and concerns of a community. In secondary school and college opportunities for actual participation of students in social and civic agencies are more easily provided.

To reach out and make accessible to students and teachers opportunities of this character is an important task for the administrator. Nor is it an easy undertaking, since he must both find the occasion and see that it is used solely in the interests of education. All too frequently agencies that profess a social or a civic purpose are peculiarly tempted to violate good educational procedure. They easily become super-salesmen for the kingdom of heaven or utilize all the subtle instruments of propaganda. Counts, for example, in *School and Society in Chicago* portrays a number of reprehensible methods employed by the Association of Commerce in fostering in the high schools Civic-Industrial Clubs, Hi-School Press Associations, and Presidents' Councils. Thus in the "Clean-Up-Paint-Up-Plant-Up" campaigns the animating motive for a time was to use the schools for commercial purposes.[22] In the case of the Hi-School Press Association the commercial motive was less dominant, but the organization evidently served as an open medium for inculcating the ideals of the Association.

Not all contacts with the social and civic life of the community need be of this character. In the first place there are many agencies such as settlement houses and other philanthropic and civic organizations whose purposes are broadly social and representative of no special interest. These may serve the purposes of laboratories for study as well as afford

[22] *Op. cit.,* pp. 152-153.

some opportunities for direct service on the part of students who may wish to participate in their activities.

It must be admitted, however, that on the whole the larger community in our cities is limited at present in its socially useful and socially motivated functions, and the opportunities for children and young people to participate directly in such functions are relatively restricted. But where they exist and are utilized, it is the school that must ensure participation of an educational character. It is the responsibility of the administrator to bring about a relationship between the school and the agency such that educational values come to the fore. That is to say, he must strive to establish a relationship between teachers and outside groups of such a character that students by virtue of their participation acquire an increased knowledge and a critical understanding of social relationships, self-directive methods of procedure, and a sensitive responsiveness to conditions operating in the lives of others.

A program of this nature, when carried out with understanding, holds forth the possibility of transforming the attitude of outside groups with reference to their own responsibilities toward children. This endeavor of the administrator to help the community function more consciously with reference to the educational needs of children leads him to apply the method of coöperative functioning to relations between the school and all other instrumentalities concerned with child life. In every community there are numerous agencies that deal with children: the police department, settlement houses, social workers, welfare agencies, the health department, playground directors, and so on. All too frequently they operate in ignorance of each other. It should be the school's concern that these agencies be brought together so as to function for the city as a whole, or in separate districts in such a manner that the needs of the whole child are considered and the methods employed in dealing with him are directed toward the ends of healthy growth.

An illustration of what we have in mind is the work of the Coördinating Council established in Berkeley in 1924. The organization of this Council is described as follows in *School Life:*

"It was to foster this spirit of coöperation that representative executives of the schools, the police department, and the health department met in the year 1924 to discuss ways and means for a better coördination of work, especially with reference to salvaging maladjusted children. The group met informally several times, then effected an organization, and called itself 'The Berkeley Coördinating Council for Child Welfare.' Its aims and purposes were stated as follows:

" '1. To promote the physical, moral and mental welfare of the children in the community.

" '2. To coördinate the activities of existing agencies, preventing duplication.

" '3. To promote personal acquaintance and *esprit de corps* among executives of the various agencies.'

"Since these early beginnings six years ago, the work of the Council has developed until its membership now includes the following: the assistant superintendent of schools, who is also the director of the bureau of research and guidance, and who acts as chairman of the coördinating council; the chief of police; the director of the city health department; the superintendent of social service in the city health center; the executive secretary of the welfare society; the visiting teacher; the police woman; and the director of playgrounds. With such a staff as this working as a unit in the interests of childhood, we should be able to look for results that shall make for better guidance and happier adjustment in the lives of boys and girls throughout the city.

"The Coördinating Council meets in weekly sessions and considers the problem cases that have come to the attention of one or another of the agencies represented. All the information concerning a given child which is in the possession of any one agency is placed at the disposal of every other. Typical cases which come up for discussion are those involving educational maladjustment, behavior difficulties, social indigency, and physical inadequacy. So also the child with special ability or talent may become an object of attention, particularly through the enlistment of the aid of some public-spirited citizen or organization to help in the development of his capacity. Assignments for follow-up are made by the chairman of the council. With skilful executive leadership and with the unity of purpose which marks its program, a consistent policy of coöperative effort is followed by all its members." [23]

VI

What we have suggested in the way of relating the school and social agencies applies as well to industry. Here, too, there is a trend toward increasing coöperation. The Cincinnati and Antioch College plans for coöperative student service are seeping down into the secondary schools, and a noticeable increase in part-time employment on the alternating plan is evident.

Under these new conditions the school becomes directly responsible for guaranteeing to youth genuinely educative opportunities and for safeguarding them from unhealthy working conditions or possible exploitation.

Antioch College represents a serious attempt in this respect. Through its personnel department it not only places the students in positions that have reference to the traits and characteristics of the individual and that hold forth possibilities for vocational and professional self-discovery, but it works directly with coöperating firms so as to ensure an educational point of view on their part in dealing with student workers.

Particularly is this essential when secondary school pupils enter business and industry, as they are doing under the part-time plan of education. The nature of these contacts will vary with the nature of the occupation and with the age and preparation of students, but the task of the administrator in each case is clear: to establish that type of coöperative arrangement which will bring to the surface the richest possible educative effects upon all concerned.

[23] *School Life,* Vol. XVI, No. 2 (October, 1930), p. 24. Washington: Department of the Interior, Office of Education.

That the school will profit in its technical work from this close relationship is obvious. But technical improvement is not necessarily the most important outcome of the interrelationship. It is equally possible for the school through the organization of advisory groups in business and industry to test out its program of general education by reference to the criticism and advice of men and women in industry and business. For example, it was President Davis's close contact with the experience of practising engineers that confirmed him several years ago in his decision to reintroduce at Stevens Institute a general engineering course and to insist that students receive a basic and fundamental training in subjects that cut through the specialized types of engineering. Similarly in organizing courses for a preprofessional course in business at the Fieldston School in New York the educational authorities are utilizing the advice and assistance of business men both in organizing the content of foundational courses such as economics, accounting, and orientation in the field of business and in the selection of material that will serve as a basis for a critical analysis and appraisal of contemporary practices.

It is true that the school's approach to industry will have first in mind the bettering of educational opportunities for its students. We may venture the hope that results will go much further. By encouraging the organization of vocational and professional groups for the purpose of vitalizing and broadening educational opportunities for young people, it is inevitable that the thinking of these groups will be turned upon an analysis of the educational possibilities implicit within their own fields of interest. Consequently in searching for genuinely educative opportunities for the novice or the apprentice they may at times move on to a still broader conception and become sensitive to a reorganization of industry with reference to its effects upon its own participants. They may come to see that conditions which harm the young also impede the old; or that advantages which are created for the benefit of the novice and the apprentice can be profitably extended to the more mature worker. And, in so far as the administrator fosters affiliations of this character, he will be proceeding along lines that are in harmony with his distinctive function, namely, the creation and fostering of relationships out of which will blossom new and vital educative forces.

VII

The understanding and coöperation that we have suggested should obtain between the school on the one hand and industry and social agencies on the other have become of added necessity because of the transformations under way in the home. The home no longer furnishes to children the opportunities it once did for engaging with adults in the serious undertakings of life out of which came common ideals and an identity of purposes. Nor do young people participate with adults as they once did in the play and recreation which generate a community of standards. The child of poor parents, as well as the child of the well-to-do, encounters to-day conflicting tendencies in all of his relations. If he plays on the street or with the children of neighbors of whom his parents know little, he grows into ways of thinking with which his family finds it difficult to cope. If he joins a recreational group, the methods of discipline and association, the settling of difficulties and working out of joint undertakings, contrast frequently with those adopted in his home. As he grows older his associations are less with his parents and increasingly with young people of his own age. He is thus again led into ways of looking at life which are all too often out of harmony with the convictions of his parents. Both the complexity of the workaday world and the injurious effects of early participation in economic activity deprive him of a first-hand acquaintance with economic life, while the same specialization of labor characteristic of an industrial civilization takes the father and often the mother as well away from the home and out of shared concerns with the child. Add to this the general lack of preparation on the part of parents for the rearing of children and we have a condition fraught with danger for the child as well as with unhappiness, disappointment, and frustration for adults.

It is this situation that sets the problem for parent education and parent participation in the school. The best nursery and primary schools recognize to-day that effective work with children in school involves helping parents to solve problems of child care in the home. Frequently parents are brought into the school for direct instruction and guidance in connection with the behavior problems of their children. Consequently the education of parents has become an integral part of the program in many schools. The parents are now receiving assistance according to their individual needs in matters affecting the health and hygiene and physical care of their children; they are being guided in planning and providing for constructive work and play activities in the home; and they are receiving courses in the applied psychology of childhood, as well as essential information bearing upon the school's plans and purposes for the more distinctly academic and technical aspects of the child's education.

To provide adequately for this growing field of parent education many schools are now establishing special departments which work in conjunction with parents, class-room teachers, and administrative officers. What thus began as a helping hand in the nursery school and kindergarten extends to-day through the elementary and secondary school periods, and here and there we find indications that even the college will shortly include parents in its educational program.

But parent participation is one-sided if it is restricted solely to the instruction and help which the school can give the home. The school in turn requires for its effective dealing with the child an interpretation of the home and the broad point of view regarding child development to which the wise parent is sensitive and the teacher frequently indifferent. Furthermore the school carries on many activities in which the criticism and coöperation of parents are needed.

So here again the administrator must enter to create conditions that will meet all of the needs involved. By bringing together teachers, parents, and experts who represent all aspects of child development, he will both provide a necessary clearinghouse for information and lay the basis for intelligent programs of action.

We thus lay down as a major premise the increasing participation of parents in the school. It is inevitable if the school, in harmony with an organic conception of learning, is to provide for the integrated development of the child's personality. The new education cannot sanction an exclusive and partial attention to one phase of the individual's growth.

It is true, however, that many administrators and teachers oppose this development. This opposition proceeds from different motives. If it is not a lack of sympathy with the assumption of a responsibility that goes beyond traditional provisions for education, it proceeds from a genuine fear of parental interference in the conduct of the school. Nor can we deny that parents and teacher associations have often given just cause for this fear. Nevertheless the trend is both inevitable and wise. The essential procedure, therefore, is to clarify in the minds of school people and parents alike the principles that are to guide and direct parent participation. These are but special applications of the general policy of administration for which we are contending, namely, that the administrator is to stimulate the participation of all groups involved in an educational system along lines that will assist them the better to perform their distinctive functions and to react in helpful ways upon other functionaries. As applied to parents, this means an encouragement of a participation that leads to more intelligent attention to their duties as parents, and to the school it means deriving from responsible contacts with parents every possible suggestion for the better instruction and guidance of children. In short, it means the evolution of plans and policies in the light of a shared study in which each one can contribute and each can derive assistance from the others. In neither case, then, is it a matter of the imposition of one's will upon others or putting into operation a program conceived in isolation. It is true that an administrator faces a serious problem when officious parents attempt to use a parents' organization as a tool for imposing their will upon the school. The results are similar to the operation of Gresham's Law in the field of finance: the wisest and best parents tend to leave the organization. The cure for the situation, however, is not found in abandoning work with parents. This will result merely in injury to the school, the child, and parents. It consists rather in seeking for ways and means of redirecting parent activities along more vital and significant lines. It is nothing less than a challenge to the administrator to exercise his unique function of seeking and finding and perpetuating those conditions of vital interrelationships between groups and individuals which lead progressively to growth and development in the effective performance of unique tasks.

We might continue with further illustrations and applications of our conception of the distinctive functions of school administration. We trust that we have said enough, however, to indicate its basic nature. A more adequate analysis would have dealt at some length with the pupil-school relationship. In this connection we should have stressed the need for breaking down the departmental barriers that tend to grow up in direct response to attempts to provide for new educational needs. We should have stressed also in this connection the necessity for organizing the life of the school so that the learner may engage in ways of living that are designed to develop the attitudes and dispositions necessary in a more adequate social order. For example, suppose we believe, as the analysis of the second chapter in this book suggests, that society suffers to-day because it is unfriendly to calling out and giving direction to the latent possibilities of people. In so far as this is true it is undemocratic and uneducational, and it becomes therefore an obligation on the part of the school not merely to introduce children to this traditional American ideal, but to examine the difficulties that beset its realization under present conditions, and to organize life within the class-room and the school as a whole so as to develop the appropriate attitudes and dispositions through participating with others in activities of intimate and vital concern to themselves. This calls for an interrelationship between departments in the school and specific planning in which children as well as adults genuinely participate. Similarly a more complete discussion would take us into the problems of administering adult education.

All this the limitations of space require us to neglect. We can only remark that in each case we should merely apply to the peculiar circumstances the same general principle of administration: seek always to bring about and to foster relations between the participants in a situation so that they perform their functions better and with intelligent appreciation of the significance and the meaning of their activity for the activity of others.

We shall conclude with a brief reference to the organization and functioning of boards of education.

As we have seen, the present tendency in theory and practice is favorable to a small board that exercises only legislative powers. The purpose is to secure a non-partisan and a public-minded group of individuals free from all commitments except that of single-minded devotion to the best interests of the schools. It is hoped that a board of education thus constituted will both safeguard school systems from outside influences on the part of selfish interests and adopt educational policies in the light of broad and generous points of view.

There is some cause to doubt the success of this theory in practice. Counts's study of the Chicago situation is a fair example. Here a small board of eleven members became easy victims of outside pressure groups and were captured without difficulty by the mayor, when he so willed. Counts concludes,[24] after reviewing the influence brought to bear on school affairs by organizations such as the Association of Commerce, the Federation of Labor, the women's clubs, the churches, and teachers' organizations, that schools cannot be divorced from their surrounding medium; that education in an industrial society carries with it of necessity an intimate interplay between the school and forces within society; and that what we need to do is to provide opportunities for each major interest in the city to make itself heard. This requires, he states, an organization of educational machinery of such a character as

"to insure to each major legitimate interest in the city an opportunity to make itself heard. Thus the play of social forces upon the school which today is constantly disrupting the program of instruction, might be turned to a useful purpose and be made to contribute to the formulation of a stable but ever-growing policy of public education." [25]

[24] *School and Society in Chicago,* Chapter XV. New York: Harcourt, Brace and Company, 1928.
[25] *Ibid.,* p. 358. Counts also believes that present methods of selecting boards of education tend to load them with representatives from one class in society. Thus, in *Social Composition of Boards of Education* (Chicago: Department of Education, University of Chicago, 1927), he writes: "A major obstacle to the direct representation of these conflicting interests on the board is found in the method employed in the selecting of board members. Through these methods the dominant forces in the community win practically all the seats on the board. If they are able to win one, they are able to win all. Thus, board members, though varying greatly with respect to personal traits, such as intelligence and probity, are fundamentally alike in point of view. The educational issues which divide them are minor

To counteract the influence of this plural representation of interests on boards of education Counts favors the "thorough organization of the teaching staff in a city," which would thus "present a united front to those who knowingly would despoil the schools, or in ignorance would enforce a special point of view." [26]

But what steps can we take so as to make certain that by the extension "of a direct voice in the control of education to the most powerful interests and the more significant points of view" we go no further than to sow seeds of discord? Will this policy result in anything more than a neutralizing of the forces operating within boards of education or a mutual slaughtering of special interests? If not, we have indeed made inadequate provision for the development of positive educational policies.

Clearly, a further step is essential. When we accept the principle of representation of differing interests on boards of education, we must also seek ways and means for giving an educational character to this relationship. This suggests that an analysis of a community in terms of conventional political or social or economic groupings may not serve the purposes of public education. Here again we should realize that an analysis must always take its character from the end it is to serve. As applied to education, this means that the groups represented on boards of education should have some functional interest in the processes of education. The criterion for representation should be an actual stake in the enterprise. This suggests a functional organization of boards that would include at least the professional staff, parents, the community at large, and those outside agencies with which the educational system is in intimate contact. To these should perhaps be added

rather than major issues. They look out upon the world through the same eyes. As a consequence they fall an easy prey to the temptation to use the schools as an instrument of indoctrination." (P. 95.)

[26] *Ibid.*, p. 359.

a representative of the city financial administration. The principle we have in mind is a functional grouping that will ensure a hearing for all legitimate interests in education and a basis for mutual understanding and a necessary give-and-take, as between these groupings, on behalf of larger common concerns. Where the activities of the school are administered with the educational emphasis stressed in our previous discussion, we may hope that representation of diverse interests on the board of education will serve the necessary purpose of interpreting society to the school.

We thus conclude that it is not solely in its relation to the learner that the school should observe the precepts of education. In all of its dealings it should bear witness to its major function. This implies the fostering and creation of living arrangements which permit of an intelligent sharing of experiences. It means an organization of such character that each one participating performs his own special work with a full realization of its implications and effects upon his associates and the larger aims of which he is a means. In short, a school system should typify and exemplify in its operations as a whole and in the functioning of its parts the process which is the be-all and the end-all of its existence. It should stand forth clearly as an educational institution. And to make these purposes manifest is the distinctive function of school administration.

Chapter VIII

PROFESSIONAL EDUCATION FROM THE SOCIAL
POINT OF VIEW

IF conscious education is to go forward under a new social
vision, a new social emphasis will be necessary in the professional preparation of teachers and other educators.
This becomes even the more necessary because for some two
decades now the dominant stress in study and research has
been laid upon the scientific and impersonal aspects of education, with a resulting accumulation of techniques and procedures which largely ignore any social outlook and bearing.
Indeed the net effect has often been anti-social in that many
have been led to believe that a scientific and statistical treatment of facts as such would supply all needed direction and
aim. The inadequacy and impossibility of such a position is
elsewhere herein discussed.[1] It must suffice at this point to say
that an adequate stress upon general and social considerations
is now long overdue. The new social situation thus gives re-
newed emphasis and adds besides its own peculiar demands.

I

How the recent great development in the university study
of education has brought one-sided stress in the preparation
for education is not difficult to understand. Never before has
so much study been given to education either in so many of
its phases or in so intensive treatment of detail; and nowhere
else so much as in this country. In quantity the new materials
growing from this study have accumulated even to vastness.

[1] See pp. 289-290.

Many students and educators seem bewildered, losing the town for the houses.

Among these accumulating materials specialized techniques and specific procedures have loomed largest. The dominant psychology underlying this study has reasoned uncritically that the whole, whether of life or of character, is one constructed of separate small parts added together. It has accordingly stressed the building of specific items of habit and skill, and in order to effect these has devised the specialized techniques and procedures above referred to. Measurement, which is most at home in dealing with specific items, has reinforced the tendency; and science, in whose name this kind of work has been done, has added its approving prestige. Since one effort has been to devise such techniques and procedures as minimize the need for thinking, the appeal has, from this and other causes, met a wide response. If thinking could be done once and for all by a few experts and the results embodied in easily managed techniques, then, so the advocates of this position have thought, there need be no worry if teachers do not think. These expert results would supply any lack along this line, so that now at length could an inclusive businesslike centralization of authority be effected. If a curriculum could be made at the top and thus handed down, and if standardized tests could measure the output, then managerial "efficiency" would become as available for the school system as for any business organization.[2]

If expert thinking on the part of the few could in this manner suffice for all the rest, then could the professional preparation of mere teachers be restricted largely to the specific acquisition of these expert-made materials. Seldom perhaps do explicit statements of theory make this conclusion quite so obvious, but the effect has been the same. A general outlook with individual thinking for the rank and file of teachers had

[2] For a fuller discussion of this general position see pp. 217 ff.

thus become, on the one hand, impossible—they couldn't think —and on the other hand, needless and futile. On such a basis professional preparation could become "training" not simply in name but now also in fact. The traditional conception as embodied in this term received a new lease on life, blest it was thought by the new science of education.

To back up this point of view—for it is a point of view, a philosophy in fact, and as such must stand or fall on its merits in comparison with other points of view—necessity arose to claim for such procedure an entire sufficiency. It became then common to say that this new way, this science of education, begins where there can be no doubt, namely with "the facts" themselves. Upon such a sure beginning scientific procedures could, it was claimed, in time advance to the unquestioned settlement of all our problems, and on this theory a whole educational program has been based. Here we need simply say that no such claim has been justified, that the claim itself is less and less clearly made, and that its direct opposite is increasingly accepted.

The need for thoughtful general orientation toward life and toward education becomes daily more obvious. Without it intelligent direction is impossible. The choice is, however, not between a general orientating outlook and no such outlook; the choice is between a criticized orientating outlook and one that Topsy-like has just "growed." Early life, the accident of family and community bias, traditional ways of thinking about one's own haphazard experiences—all these, unsubjected to criticism, will give to the teacher or other educator an undigested, inconsistent outlook and orientation or, perhaps better, a chance collection of conflicting outlooks. In particular at the present time, as this book has already several times stressed, our traditional standards and ideals are no longer equally applicable to the changed industrial condition. The ordinary citizen lives in conflict with himself. Broad demands call for one kind of moral behavior, actual conditions of business and social success make quite other demands. As American social life is a maze of conflicting demands, so is the typical American personal outlook. Until clarification and consistency can be had, neither ordered life nor internal peace can be expected. Criticism—conscious, definite effort to see our inconsistencies—and evaluation are necessary. Otherwise there remain conflict and confusion within and without.

If these things be true for each one as a person, doubly are they true for the educator. Not only has he to order his own life, he must besides help those under his care to order their lives. Their growth and outlook must be considered in all that he does. The atomistic psychologic outlook criticized above seems to consider that we can teach arithmetic skills, for example, as if nothing else were going on at that time. Such an idea is false, tragically false. Children cannot learn simply arithmetic, they are also at the same time—always and of necessity—building significant attitudes and interests with reference to the subject, to the school, to themselves, to their fellows, to the teacher, to all the teacher stands for to them, to school government, to courtesy, to truthfulness. In short, the pupils are during each class-period building attitudes with reference to any and everything that enters significantly to them in whatever is then going on. Out of these attitudes grow interests and repulsions, and out of these in turn come life's decisions. It is a hard saying, but the teacher, so far as taking thought can affect results, is properly responsible for all these attendant attitudes just as truly as for the arithmetic—more so, if there be any difference, in the degree that the attitudes enter more significantly than do skills into the learner's life to direct it and give content to its decisions.

But the teacher cannot give due consideration to these child attitudes and how they build the child's life outlook except

as the teacher himself or herself has thought upon such things.
And mere knowledge of such will not suffice. Mental hygiene
makes us seriously, even tragically, aware that the maladjusted
teacher means, in tendency, at least, maladjusted children. Only
as the teacher has brought order and clarity and integration
into his own or her own grasp of life can we expect the children to profit by the teacher's leadership. To trust vital matters
to chance is a cruelty to tender youth of which we cannot be
guilty. The teacher must have a balanced and integrated outlook, so criticized to conscious consistency that intelligent
direction can be given to inclusive child growth.

That the teacher of children has been used as an illustration
does not mean that these demands are not equally binding
upon supervisor and superintendent. All who have to do with
youth—with human growing, in fact, at whatever age level
and under whatever condition—are under the same correlative
obligation. More than anything else, so far as importance goes,
does education mean the building of the life outlook, for when
put to work the life outlook includes and orders everything
else. This means that all educational steps and procedures must
be criticized and finally judged just as much—if not more—
by their general educative effects upon character and social
outlook as by the specific ends and aims for which they have
been devised. Techniques and procedures become then subordinate, *always so,* to the general aims we set up for life and
education. And all who have to do with such techniques and
procedures, those who devise them, those who responsibly
accept and perhaps order them, as well as those who concretely
apply them—all must ask as to these wider educative effects,
and judge them, each to guide his own steps, in the light of the
best attainable educational philosophy.

All techniques and procedures—whether of teaching and
measuring or of supervising and administering—must then be
learned, as they must be applied, in conscious subordination

to the values affected by them. Professional education must thus hold as its central and dominating feature the building of an inclusive and criticized outlook upon life and education. No step in the educative process can be weighed or judged except in the light of such a point of view, itself always growing as each new problem is most thoughtfully faced. The building and use of a philosophy of education thus becomes the key aim in professional education.

In building such a general outlook as a philosophy of life, the social element becomes the orientating essential. The individual life process must be seen in its relations with the surrounding social process. Otherwise criticism is blind. As the individual grows, with wider outlooks and deeper insights increasingly possible, each new situation met should be the means for relating one's individual conduct more and more adequately with the larger whole. In this way does true individuality, as opposed to mere oddity, become a possibility. To hold to a position in advance of thought or in spite of thought is but ignorance or stupidity or obstinacy. To hold out against others after thought and because thought demands it—this is true individuality. One guiding aim, then, in preparing the educator for his work is that he build an ever more inclusive and adequate social outlook. Inclusive criticism with reference to ever more adequate social action—this is our guide.

Since the heart of the work of the profession of education is to guide the educative process, the preparation of the educator proceeds along two correlative lines. He must understand, on the one hand, the individual life process and how learning is essential in it to its continuous upbuilding; and, on the other hand, the social process and how education is essential in it also to its continuous up-building. And the educator must be devoted to his work. No mere hireling will suffice. He must love to work with others and help them grow, he must have the social outlook and wish to give himself, as to the one great cause, to bring a better world in which we all may live.

We must now close this introductory section as we began it. A new social-moral situation confronts us with its new demands. The considerations brought out above are general. The actual situation confronting us is specific. It is the latter which must translate our general discussion into concrete steps. For our task is to meet our situation. Judging from the best insight that we of this book can get, the traditional forms and institutions of society and underlying theories no longer fit our technologic society. Even radical reconstruction seems necessary. This situation, we believe, defines the moral obligation of to-day. Education as the social process intelligently directing itself cannot be true to itself, cannot be intelligent or act so, except as it knows the social situation and acts accordingly.

II

As we think of the preparation of prospective teachers for their work, a word at the outset about terms may not be out of place. The verb *to train* is customarily used in connection with the preparation of teachers. It is probably correct to say that this term was chosen when the process, like most education of that day, was conceived in rather a narrow training sense. Those in charge had ideas and procedures which they wished the novices to acquire and use. The processes of memorization and drill were chiefly relied on to give the desired command and facility. While *education* and *training* thus formerly meant about the same thing, later developments have carried the two terms, at least for some of us, in quite different directions. For these, *training* has become more precisely a process of habituation in the facile use of responses previously chosen by the instructor,[3] while *education* is increasingly used

[3] We seldom or never call the instructor of teachers a trainer. This noun everybody reserves for one who deals with the lower animals.

in a more desirable sense to designate the process of helping another to become intelligently capable and independent in his thinking and action. Whether the two terms do carry this contrast to most readers may be argued; but the distinction of fact, without reference now to name, is certainly a proper one to be made, and in what follows the terms will be used to designate the distinction. Accordingly the term *training* will not be used to describe the preparation of teachers.

In the theory of education upheld in this book the teacher is the key to the actual educative process so far as we properly rely on the school to guide it. It was not so in the older point of view. There tradition or the textbook or the course of study dominated teacher and pupil alike. Under the lead of many who affect to speak in the name of science this domination is continued under scientifically determined techniques and procedures. But with us the teacher stands forth in new importance. This makes far-reaching demands: on the selection of prospective candidates, on the early education which they should have, but most of all on the education which they are to have in preparation for teaching.

As to the selection of candidates, there is at the present time an oversupply of available teachers. As unfortunate as this is for those not chosen for appointment and as indicative as the oversupply is of bad social planning, these things still mean that by taking thought we can at this point begin upon an improvement of the profession. Stating the factors separately—though in each concrete case all must of course be weighed together— we can choose those of better native ability, those of better cultural background, and those of better emotional balance. Native ability needs no explanation. We wish as much as we can get. There is no upper limit to its use. The better cultural background, in spite of a certain apparent undemocratic aspect, cannot be disregarded. Early contacts are very pervasive. In our country the school must in very many cases be our chief reliance for giving the children the best chance for at least an introduction to the finer things of life. This becomes, then, one important factor in the choice of prospective teachers. Sound emotional balance in the teacher is, as has already been suggested, almost a precondition to emotional health in the children. In the past this factor has not been sufficiently considered.

The prior education of the candidate coming to the school of professional preparation will perhaps lie mostly beyond our control. We must, however, prefer that the prospective teachers shall have had as much as possible of the kind of schooling advocated in Chapters V and VI. How one has been taught gives at least an initial bias to how one will teach. The kind of school we here wish will not come all at once simply out of the normal school itself. The continuing process must facilitate its own becoming.

A remark in this connection upon the length of period of professional preparation may not be out of place. Until recently two years was the rule for elementary teachers. Now the rule lengthens toward four years, and we must approve the tendency. There would seem no sufficient reason why teaching should not ultimately expect as long and rigorous preparation as is required in law or medicine. Why those who care for the child as a whole personality in his ever-growing social relationships should not be as well prepared as those who care for the body is certainly not evident. Probably the chief reason why our people have not already demanded more adequate preparation in the teachers of their children has been the lack of any very clearly observed connection between extent of teacher preparation and the educative results in the children. Of course, at the moment the depression works for reduction rather than increase of expense of preparation, but this may be counted as temporary. Now that the study of education has more to offer to the prospective teacher, we may expect returning prosperity to demand more extended preparation. Fifty years ago the usual medical course in this country consisted of two years of six months each, the identical lectures being repeated both years. Possibly the next fifty years will see an analogous increase in the preparation expected of educators.

In the education of teachers probably no one factor is more important than the social attitude of the faculty of the professional institution. In general social outlook and attitude, as considered in this book, the staff of our ordinary normal school or teachers' college is only too often severely lacking. A more adequate social outlook is an absolute necessity if prospective teachers are to catch the social vision. The socially unenlightened teaching too often found in the ordinary college or normal school can hardly have any other result than turning out teachers ignorant of our social situation and with no intelligent concern about it. We must, then, as fast and as far as is humanly possible bring it about that all the members of the professional staff hold an intelligent and positive social outlook. And this demand holds for all, no matter how technical the specialty. Here as always is it "like teacher, like student." Beginning teachers almost inevitably teach in the way they themselves have been taught. If the staff under whom the young teachers have done their highest study are indifferent to social life and outlook, so as teachers will they probably teach.

The American tradition is against us in this matter of building up a better social attitude in the staff. With a proper wish to avoid partisan bias state school authorities have at practically all levels fallen into the opposite error of disregarding all live current problems. Moreover, specialization, good within limits, has increased the tendency to leave social matters to the social science group. Sheer inertia and present indifference count also for a good deal in connection. Still further, the sheltered life of the school has tended to attract the retiring and timid. And finally, the stress of the modern situation has not yet had time to make itself significantly felt in academic procedures and outlook. Thus in many ways the existing school tradition puts serious obstacles in the way of our proposed new social emphasis, possibly all along the line, certainly in the normal schools and in the lesser teachers' colleges.

How to effect a new attitude within the professional school staff is no simple matter. One chief hope must lie in the work of the greater schools where the staff members of the lesser professional schools are prepared. These should be somewhat freer from mere tradition and so more open to see the new need and work to create the demand for it. One resource at least is within reach of any who will try it, and that is the discussion group procedure. Even one determined staff member can enlist at least a small group of colleagues for a trial at study. If the general idea herein discussed is, as we believe, well founded, we can with considerable confidence believe that fair study will spread an interest in further study. Summer session work at the larger centers may help. All who already have any measure of insight must work in every possible way for the general increase of intelligent interest. One attendant possibility in connection should not be overlooked. Each staff member should be encouraged to know at first hand how the less-favored among us live and feel. First-hand contacts carry great potency. We easily disregard the needs of those we do not know. In every possible way we must work for the more intelligently social outlook within the staff of our teacher-preparing institutions. Without this, we can hardly hope for socially prepared teachers.

Not much perhaps needs to be added regarding the actual curriculum for the preparation of teachers. For the purposes immediately at hand the theory of education is probably our chief concern. Psychologically, this should show how life is an active process, grappling always with precariousness and unpredictability; how learning is inherent in such life amid such conditions; how learning builds the very structure of the organism, the whole organism coöperating in each learning act and sharing accordingly throughout in the learning effects; how the individual must always be studied in the larger inherent unity of organism and environment; how thinking is the intelligent interactive adaptation between the novelly growing organism and the novelly developing environment; how living and learning utilize the surrounding social forms and so build these into the very being of each member of the oncoming generation. No system of psychology inadequate to these possibilities can, it would seem, be counted adequate to deal with life or education satisfactorily from the social point of view.

On the social side, the theory of education should show how the individual alone is but an abstraction, impossible either to be or be conceived (except partially); how the individual life process involves and is involved in the surrounding social process and itself grows properly only as it reaches out ever more effectually into the social process; how the accumulated results of the evolving social process more make the oncoming generation of mankind than are themselves in turn remade by that generation; how public education as a social agency becomes then charged with the responsibility of making the social culture, the accumulations of the social process, ever more fit to form the successive oncoming generations; how the institutional forms of our culture are to be conceived as properly but the best available ways of coöperative living; how unequal social growth may leave a hurtful lag in some parts of our culture; how from all such considerations our culture and institutional life call for continual criticism and appropriate remaking; how public education is vitally concerned in all these matters, in fact how public education in any full sense is the social process intelligently directing itself; and how, finally, the profession of education in all the foregoing ways accepts high social duties and obligations.

In closest connection with the foregoing, as has already been more than implied, a positive social attitude and disposition becomes an essential in prospective teachers. No mere intellectual understanding—if such in fact can stand thus alone—will here suffice. Appropriate attitude and disposition must be positively united. The building of such an attitude and disposition in inherent connection with all their education becomes a chief concern in the preparation of teachers. To this as end the intelligent criticism of our institutional life with intent to improve it becomes one important means. The discussion of "controversial issues" becomes accordingly a necessary part of the curriculum. Actual varied social contacts as full and fruitful as possible become a further necessary means. In fact any education, to be satisfactory, ought to be part and parcel of the actual community life. On no other basis can education get its true meaning and place. In no other way can the learner find adequate stimulation, or acquire adequate content to thought and feeling and act or receive adequate testing of his thought and act. Unfortunately our tradition and present social arrangements forbid this necessary merging of education in life. The existing set-up is all the other way. In political activities, in industrial activities, in civic affairs, the rising generation is always out of place, except as they may be hired to work, and with that the conditions of work are generally so non-educative that legislation has been compelled to interfere. One of our social aims, even though its full realization be remote, will be so to place the various necessary activities of social life on a thinking basis that the young may participate therein with mutual advantage to themselves and to the work. Except as this can be done, educational endeavor can but feebly play its possible rôle in individual and social life.

Meanwhile we must do the best we can to put education into

life. Social contacts and socially imbedded activities must be sought in every way possible. Excursions, while in danger of giving no more than surface acquaintance, will, for want of better, help materially. More significant is it that what the Russians have named "socially useful labor" should find definite place in the school work. That is, the student-teachers should study the social situation immediately at hand in school, in community, in the larger relationship, and find continued opportunities through which they can here and now make social life actually better. Such efforts should grow out of all their other social study and feed back into it. In season and out the teachers' college must work to build in its students an intelligent zeal for the bettering of our common civilization.

At this point enters the matter of personal integration in the face of the conflicting demands of social life. It has already been brought out that no one can live successfully either in respect of his own personality or in social relationships who has not effected a satisfactory unified criticized outlook on life. And we saw in connection that a double obligation rests here on teachers and accordingly on teacher-preparation institutions. One essential part of a social disposition and outlook becomes, then, that the individual student shall come to defensibly satisfying terms with himself as he faces the various conflicts, within and without, that beset him. The conflicting demands within the social life should be brought to clear consciousness in the consideration of controversial issues, and every effort should be made to help the student form an adequate social philosophy. The more personal life of the students has also its many conflicts, most born perhaps of our inherent social conflicts. The school must find adequate opportunity to consider all such personal conflicts, with conscious care again to help each gain the integrated outlook and poise needed if one is to face life happily and helpfully. These two regions of maladjustment—the more social and the more personal—

interact probably more than is commonly thought. The two must probably be considered together or we cannot expect of our teachers an adequate social outlook and disposition.

To us here interested in educating teachers from the social point of view the problem of "subject-matter requirements" makes not only the usual demands but many besides. Here as elsewhere we cannot approve the traditional treatment of subject-matter, still strong in most teacher-preparation institutions. In this ordinary way of teaching, the probability is great that even as "subject-matter" what is learned will not function in the life of the learner and even more that the learner's self is not being intelligently nourished for growth. It seems, on the contrary, clear that what is learned should be learned as and because it is in fact then and there demanded by the activity under way as the learner gives himself zealously and intelligently to carrying this forward.

To ask, as some do, what opposed line should be followed if these learning conditions of zeal and thought be not met seems to miss the meaning of education and to disregard the character of the educative process. If the student does not now have worthy purposes which appropriately call out what is in him, this state of lack and deficiency exactly defines the educator's immediate task as regards that student. Such a lack is sign and evidence that the preceding life of the student has therein and in so far educatively failed. Study must then be made of the particular case and situation to see how the failure has come about and thus to find suggestions for getting the educative process going once more satisfactorily. If students disappoint us, resort then is to be had not to extrinsic incentives or other less adequate alternative conception of the educative process but rather to such steps as will allow our fullest conception of the process to function more adequately.

As far, then, as possible the specific preparation of the prospective teacher, both broadly and narrowly conceived, should be carried on through the process of helping him educatively to raise to more adequate self-directive efforts his own life and work. As previously brought out, this life and work of the student-teacher—again in both its broad and its specific aspects—should, as far as we can effect it, be part and parcel of the surrounding existing social life. We wish this from several considerations: one, so that each thing undertaken can be studied in the light of its general setting and bearings and so be decided upon in full view of its criticized probable consequences; another, so that, further, each such undertaking, each such instance of study, choice, and act, can later be criticized in the actual resulting consequences. On this basis can study and learning become the inherent functions of the life process which they properly are, themselves to be directed and judged by the ways in which they intelligently further that process. In the degree that this is done will study and learning become real and effectual. In like degree will each thing learned be related vitally with other things already known, and the individual student himself through it all be made a more intelligent and effectual participant in the social process. This becomes thus a very significant and urgent ideal in the education of prospective teachers.

Learning to teach is an immediate application of the considerations just presented. Here it would seem clear that the student-teacher should increasingly participate in the actual teaching of children and that much if not most of all that he learns in the teachers' college should be learned in connection. That we have not yet worked out satisfactory ways for doing this is no sufficient reason against it. There has been but little consistent effort in this direction. Extended trial and study are necessary. The considerations of the preceding paragraph apply both to the children taught and to the student-teachers. The children in the practice school should be studying and choosing and acting as far as feasible (all things considered) in actual life situations which are themselves in turn as inherent parts of the surrounding social process as can feasibly be managed. Then as the student-teachers work with these children and help them with their problems, so does their own professional work come inherently to call for a consideration of the varied ways in which the children's education and their own education inevitably include the fullest social bearings they can manage. All the richness of child life with all its possibilities becomes thus potential subject-matter to the student-teacher. And their study and learning can thus go on with such clearly seen purpose and in such a natural setting as to constitute ideal learning conditions.

Many considerations seem to concur that this kind of student-teacher participation in such actual socially connected pupil teaching should constitute the crux of the work of the teacher-preparation institution. Theory and practice and pertinent subject-matter can and should be learned as and because they are needed in carrying on the participation. So far as appears, the work of the whole institution should turn about this dominating center.

To say these things is not to deny that the student-teacher will need to study our accumulated culture in all its pertinent aspects, or that the best professors as helpers will not be necessary. The exact contrary is true. But it does call in question the usual custom of giving courses in such separated aspects of culture to prospective teachers in advance of and independently of some felt need of them. It is of course true, pitiably true, that much current teaching in this country fails of what it might be because the teacher, whether teacher of children or instructor of student-teachers, lacks "the subject-matter" appropriate to the matter at hand. This fact, however, is, we submit, no sufficient justification for requiring prospective teachers to repeat the deadening academic error of learning "subject-matter" in its traditional independence of living connections. Proper effort must find a better way.

Lest some mistake the emphasis just made to mean a lack of appreciation of learning, or knowledge—"subject-matter," as some call it—let the contrary be stated with equal emphasis. Neither instructor in a professional school for teachers nor a teacher of young people can expect really to succeed without a knowledge of what he is teaching far in advance of what most teachers can now show. No amount of educational theory or skill can take the place of full and exact knowledge. But, on the other hand, it is equally true that no mere subject-matter acquisition as such can hope to succeed in the long run apart from the general educational preparation discussed above. The two components are much like the length and breadth of a rectangle: both must be of appreciable size for the results to be considerable.

In this connection it is greatly to be feared that many teachers' colleges have, in spite of the earnest intent of its proponents, taken the term *professionalized subject-matter* as simply a modern excuse for more of the same old thing, acquiring separated subject-matter in advance of seen need or pertinence, only now dressed up with pictures or "made interesting" with anecdotes or biographical data. Whenever the idea is so degraded and "subject-matter" is so learned apart from sensed pertinence and not because it is seen to be needed in some vital connection for the learner, we can have no just basis to expect that it will be either intelligently learned or appropriately applied. It is, of course, true that a student may build a vital interest within a specific "subject-matter field," and if so the pursuit of this interest will of itself make its appropriate demands for subject-matter. It is further probable that scholarly interests of this kind are essential to good teaching. But the chief and dominating demand seems clear: that prospective teachers should begin with the work of teaching and broaden out their interest and knowledge in connection with that. In the degree that this is done, in like degree will variety and depth of subject-matter be called for.

For many there arises here an urgent question. Will such a conception as that advanced in the preceding paragraphs result in the proper well-rounded choice and organization of knowledge to the learner? Is there not danger that this principle of learning only as and when needed will result in a scrappy choice of subject-matter and a haphazard organization? No full discussion can here be undertaken, but a few words may help clear the matter. First, as regards range and extent of knowledge, we can have no thought that we shall give the student-teacher all that he will later need. It is impossible. We hope he will get a goodly stock (and he will get more in the way outlined above than is now usual). We hope even more that he will form ideals and standards of conduct for himself which will make him seek the more as it is needed and that he will build meanwhile interests which invite him always to note and study as he goes, learning ever better where to seek and find. Second, as regards organization, we believe it is a mistake to think that materials acquired in a form organized by another mean organization for the learner. Organization seems better conceived as the way of holding materials in such perceived relationships as facilitate appropriate use. The crux here is perceived relationships. To acquire what some one else has put together need not mean perceived relationships; it may very likely mean vaccination against the desired perceiving. While the experience of others may be of great help in the matter, organization for effectual intelligent use becomes thus almost the same thing as personally made organization. Certainly, unless it is so personally made and in answer to personally felt needs, we can have little if any faith that organization made simply by another will greatly facilitate intelligent use. To speak, then, of our organizing subject-matter for others to acquire comes dangerously close to treating subject-matter so that in the end it will probably not be organized for the learner. The best hope seems to lie in well-guided treatment of adequately varied problems.

If the work of the teachers' college be carried on as above suggested, several matters will be cared for that are now too much overlooked. One is the consideration of opposed educational outlooks and theories. As the student-teachers study how best to deal with the children—and why—they will naturally read opposed suggestions. Also the master teachers with whom they work will offer contrasts with the ways in which they themselves had been taught as children. Still further, the demands of prospective employers will raise questions as to how they will be allowed to teach when they have graduated and gone to work. It is exactly in the consideration of such matters that we should hope to have our student-teachers learn their educational theory. Opposed possibilities and dangers must be examined and weighed, and the whole studied in the light of the best criticized social consequences. It would be hard to conceive of a better way for building a philosophy of the educative process, as this in its turn must contemplate the philosophy of the social process. Both must come, and they come best together.

A second matter often not sufficiently stressed is the building in the student-teacher of new instruments of appreciation of the various aspects of life. If the instructors of the student-teachers will but capitalize the opportunities disclosed by the work with the children, there is literally no limit to the demand for the enrichment of the personalities of the student-teachers. Some six or eight years ago "friendship dolls" were exchanged between American school-children and those of Japan. What the dolls did in fact mean in Japan—as the writer well knows —can only be equalled by what the preparation for sending them could and should have meant in this country. Imagine the children of a practice school working on such a project: what correspondence might go on between the two sets of children? What must the student-teachers who were helping the children themselves learn about Japan? What dolls mean in Japan, the doll festival, the exquisite taste of Japan in all such matters, the place of art in Japanese life—all these suggest just one possibility of enriching the personality of prospective teachers. Or consider an historical pageant which the children of a school might give. Any teacher who has ever helped children with such will know the unlimited possibilities. Moreover, if these things are studied always also with their lessons for us now, for the criticism of our own American life, of our own personal lives, the possibilities are simply infinite.

A third thing which should come from treating prospective teachers as herein proposed is the education in scientific thinking thereby made possible. Since this book contains suggested criticism of certain scientific attitudes often found in the study of education, it may not be out of place to make our position clear. Not only do we not wish to disparage science: we reckon on the contrary that the conceptions and processes of modern science are probably the greatest achievement of the mind of man to date. We wish to spread the spirit and method of science as broadly as possible, particularly for our purposes into the work of education. Possibly we can make clearer what we mean and how we wish prospective teachers to learn to think scientifically if we analyze the teaching process in such a way as to show how science can help.

The teacher undertakes to deal with the experience of young people so that they do not simply live but live well, and that this shall leave also such abiding effects in character and disposition as promise best for future living. If this living well and the desired abiding effects be interpreted broadly enough, no aspect of life either actual or desirably possible is properly omitted from consideration. So much for the teacher's aim as stated in general. But this general aim is vain and futile except as it is translated into particularities of this child with his present state and potentialities, of this social situation now confronting us with its characteristics, its demands, and its possibilities, and of the interaction of the two in terms of specific resulting experiences and how to direct them as educatively as possible. These things when they are analyzed for actual guidance of the child's continuing experience give some indication of what the teacher must know and be able to do if the child's education is to go on best.

As now the prospective teacher under the instructor's guidance undertakes to make these needed analyses and gain these needed knowledges for help in actual class-room work, the possibility that the analyses be good and the knowledge reliable will depend in largest measure on the ability of the student-teacher to bring to his service the best available methods of analysis and of knowing that past thinkers and workers have devised. We call it science if there are available for use such methods of analysis and knowing as allow the user to rise above mere habit and bring a freeing and creative intelligence to bear on his particular situation. The student-teacher will need to use the best available methods of observation, knowing what to look for, how to state what is seen—if the matter be measurable, how to measure it—all to the end of getting accurate and reliable data in terms of which to project steps to be taken as the teacher undertakes to help the child. The projecting of those steps—what the teacher is to do—clearly calls for creative imagination on the part of the student-teacher, but the imagination itself is directed in terms of criticized conceptions gained from past experience (the criticism here should again be scientific in quality) and should make conscious use of the data scientifically validated as above described. Next will come the criticism of the results of the steps after they have been taken. Again will data be required, the data as to the changes effected by the experience, and again will scientific care be needed. The criticism of these results must go on with all the care that criticized past experience will allow us to bring to bear.

Enough has been said to make clear two things. First, the kind of intelligent "practice" teaching expected of our student-teachers involves at each stage and aspect as much scientific care and procedure as is reasonably available for use by such as these student-teachers now are. Granted proper supervision, better conditions for learning such could hardly be imagined. Second, science as here conceived is a more vital matter of intelligent thinking than most who claim to represent science in education seem to wish or expect; these, in fact, often seem to uphold the idea that science will itself so embody the expert thinking of others that the rank and file can use its results without themselves thinking. This, we believe, is a virtual denial of the essence of science. It is in the light of these two conclusions that the writers of this book make clear their allegiance to science in education and justify their claim that the teaching procedure herein advocated will involve in high degree the learning of scientific method.

When all these things are intelligently cared for, then will our now-dominating techniques and procedures, deadly if they dominate, be reduced to their proper subjection as available means to be used when the larger purposes of life and education call for them. As the larger and finer ideals discussed in this book are developed and made dominant, so may we hope that each student-teacher will go forth as an open-minded proponent of the public good, tied to no prior chosen plan, but intelligently aware of life's problems and difficulties, and tremendously concerned to help in their solution; able, in interest at least, to take hold in any community, however backward or however complacent; determined as far as in him lies not only to work with the children of the school but also to help the community study its own problems, in the light of the best he knows or can come to know, first on the community's own terms and then to move on as far and as fast as the argument may lead. Such is the social vision we hold for the preparation of teachers.

III

Somewhat different from the preparation of prospective teachers is the education of teachers in service. Teachers at work have, we may say, each two interrelated sets of duties, a dominant one as the teachers of children, and a still very real one as citizens.

As citizen, the teacher should be deeply interested in all matters of public concern. Depending of course upon a wise division of labor, and with due regard to the first duty in the school, the teacher may be called upon to act in some measure or respect as leader in his or her community. In discussion groups along with other citizens he may find a real opportunity to get into the thinking of the community. In such contacts the teacher may at times expect most to learn, but still also to help others to learn. Even while citizen the teacher is still an educator, and as such the teacher will be especially charged to see that the educative bearings of life are considered in the face of opposed demands. As citizen, the teacher will coöperate with other citizens in worthy community projects, the appropriate outcomes perhaps of the preceding group discussion. In all of this the citizen-teacher should take great pains to know all sides of life, especially perhaps the lowest, "lest we forget" how our social life as now managed cruelly denies to some what it lavishes upon others.

As a human individual, basic foundation both for teacher and for citizen, the teacher must live a full, rich life. Society must make this possible and expect it. Often now it is denied, most perhaps by unintelligent social standards. For women teachers to be forbidden to marry, for example, should be seen as the social crime it is, and itself forbidden by law. American men would never have tolerated it for themselves: they ought not to tolerate it for women. Only the well-rounded life can do for our children what is needed. Justice to pupil and to teacher alike demand that the teacher be as fully developed as we can effect in all the possibilities of life.

Teachers as such in relation to other groups of citizens have duties which partake of both relationships. Where social institutions affect adversely the welfare of the young, teachers should be their recognized spokesmen. If slums breed young criminals, teachers in their professional capacity must be concerned and take positive steps in coöperation with others to effect the needed changed conditions. If children's teeth suffer for lack of attention, teachers are concerned until appropriate effectual measures of relief have been achieved. The time was when the teacher's admitted duty was confined to school-keeping, in order to teach a restricted curriculum. Now the duty broadens to take in the whole child. Nothing pertaining to the welfare of the child is foreign to the teacher. If other social agencies do not suffice, either the school must take the matter on or the teachers must help society to make other more satisfactory arrangements. Such a broadening of duty entails of course many problems of adjustment within the social process. The main lines of advance seem, however, clear, and teachers must in their organized capacity study and act in the discharge of the new duties.

Within the schools a socialized outlook must bring a more socialized school work, and the responsibility for effecting this should lie principally with the teachers. Existing outlooks and procedures need to be remade in consistence with a more adequate social outlook. Various types of conference groups will be needed, some to see better the school work as a whole and the relation of earlier with later parts. Others will be more specific: to study, for example, the fifth-grade work. Still others will take up some specialized line of congenial interest. For the growing teacher the curriculum will ever be in the making. Underlying principles must from time to time be reconsidered. What is done elsewhere must be studied. All that the best available social outlook may show must be appropriately and effectually put to work within every part and aspect of the school system.

The teachers must consciously mean to build and maintain the highest type of professional interest and efficiency. The education we here seek means a sharing of decision by all concerned in the consequences. This means a new place for teachers in the management of education. As matters now stand, teachers are but little used to such responsibilities and but ill prepared to carry them. Democracy must be conceived as the greatest of all educational agencies.

The broadened conception of the profession of education receives treatment elsewhere in this book, particularly in Chapters III and IV. The discharge of all these broadened social duties means just so much continuing professional education. The work is never done. New problems continually arise, study is always necessary. The new social outlook means ever new social duties.

IV

The professional education of administrators is of very great importance, especially so wherever, as now holds in this country, such great power is lodged in their hands. The full discussion of education appropriate to them would, however, so greatly repeat what has been said above on the education of teachers and what is clearly to be inferred from the discussion on administration in the preceding chapter that we need here only add a few words to make some of these things perhaps more explicit.

The need of a general point of view, a well-criticized and well-integrated philosophy, is as essential to administrators as to teachers. In fact, under existing conditions, even more so since the superintendent's philosophy is by a widely accepted expectation—herein rejected—supposed to dominate the school system. The writer has even heard in his class, from women students, that it is the teacher's duty to hold her thinking in abeyance until she has learned the superintendent's philosophy, so much do we in America repeat the *cujus regio ejus religio* of the German reformation period. The kind of philosophy of administration we here wish would exalt the teaching function as this in turn faces the social situation. It would therefore expect administration to find its reason for being in serving the educative process as the whole school endeavor seeks to foster a more adequate social functioning.

These principles, we hold, should orientate the education of prospective administrators. These would need to study the social situation and build dominating social attitudes just as we saw with prospective teachers. The same demand would hold for studying their professional functions in the full light of their social bearing and significance; and, as far as possible, the learning of these functions should go on in and through dealing with actual situations where the student-administrator should share social responsibility for results. It were greatly to be wished that feasible conditions for effecting this responsibility were easier to find; but even so the demand remains, we must do what we can.

Through such study of the social bearing of what the superintendent does it may be possible to build a higher conception than frequently obtains of administrative efficiency. The efficiency of a school system lies of course primarily in its social-educational effects. To this all else is subordinate. Business efficiency is, to be sure, necessary in all matters pertaining to the expending of money, but the ultimate question is as to how well the social-educational aims of the system are fostered, and similarly with the management of teachers and the accounting of pupils. Success is ultimately to be judged by the social-educative results, to the teachers themselves, to the pupils, to the community. To misconceive efficiency is made easier by the current inadequate psychology. A piece-by-piece conception of the human mind and character lends itself to a bookkeeping and business type of school management. A proper social outlook makes such a psychology and such an administration alike undesirable and ultimately impossible.

Similarly may we hope as the proper social outlook and attitude are built that superintendents will be less satisfied with success from the mere administrative point of view. We must be sympathetic in our judging here, for in a sense administrative success as such does underlie all else. Moreover, the general surrounding situation is very powerful. As matters now stand in this country, the common worship of business success leads many administrators to the exaltation of the business model of management. "Hiring and firing" comes all too easily. The payment of highest salaries to executives follows to be sure an older rule; but once it is seriously considered, this seems somehow not so inevitable as hitherto thought. Undertaking to think for teachers follows a more direct lead from business, with the course of study handed down, methods of teaching prescribed, and the results tested by the "research bureau." A better educational theory, both social and psychological, will help to show the wrongness of such management. To think for teachers so that they do not think for themselves is to cut the tap-root of education. Only those who themselves think responsibly can be expected to guide the learning process with full-rounded social-educative results. Again is a bad psychology at work and again may we hope that a better social theory and positive social attitude will serve to correct.

As we speak thus of hopes for more social results from more socialized teachings, we must not forget to be realistic. These all too common faults are largely the inherent results of our present economic-social system. Superintendents are, like the rest of us, caught up in one inclusive miseducative state of affairs. Possibly their work leads them more easily to the common "big business" attitudes than others of us who work in more retired positions. We cannot, then, realistically hope to cure these faults as long as the surrounding business-economic system holds sway, but we can at least work for an intelligent understanding of what is happening to us that we may the better join with others in combating it. It is this consideration which must justify the emphases here being put on a more socializing professional education.

One further failing which we shall hope our more social education will help to remedy is the all too common tendency among administrators to disparage democracy. Success in managing easily selects those who like to control and may strengthen the tendency. The current business model is of course anti-democratic, as is perhaps bound to happen wherever the output is not conceived in terms of resulting personalities. In fact, almost the whole of our management tradition, including in spite of lip-service our political democracy, has never yet given serious trial to the principle of sharing decisions. We need not be surprised if school administration has too much followed the available models. But new times demand new ways. If a better social order is to come, the school system ought to help bring it and begin with its teachers. To foster this becomes one aim of a better socialized school of education.

A further common fault with administrators is obviously chargeable to our competitive *laissez-faire* system: the tendency to "play safe" in the matter of controversial issues. To administer at all one must first be elected, and similarly with continuance in office. So the many, answering to outside pressure, discourage controversial issues, devising a course of study and choosing textbooks so colorless as to raise no ugly questions. Teachers too are encouraged, if not required, to avoid live questions lest public opposition be aroused. That there are problems here need not be denied, nor that wisdom requires a just consideration of community feelings. But after all we must face the question as to why the school system exists.

When we put together all the foregoing, we see somewhat or the social duty that faces the preparation of administrators. With them as with teachers the essential thing underlying all else is the social outlook and attitude. They must understand what education is properly trying to do and feel themselves bound before all else to these ends. All else must be conceived as subordinate and ancillary. From top to bottom the social outlook must permeate and dominate the school system. In the light of this must everything else proceed. We must educate accordingly.

Chapter IX

THE UNDERLYING PHILOSOPHY OF EDUCATION

IN previous chapters a philosophy of education has been presented. The presentation has been in terms of application and operation, not in the abstract. In this concluding chapter we wish to draw out the distinctively theoretical implications of the discussion and give them definite formulation. In so doing we shall try neither to present new material nor yet merely to summarize what has already been said. We shall endeavor to make explicit the ideas and principles which implicitly form the framework of our entire discussion.

In the first place there is not implied any pretension to offer *the* philosophy of education. We do not believe that there is any such thing—not in a world in which men act for opposed ends and follow divergent paths. We believe that a treatment which claims to be the exclusive and all comprehensive theory of education leads unconsciously but necessarily to a kind of insincerity; for it tends to cover up the conflicts that are highly important in practice. The statements thus far are negative. But they rest upon a positive basis.

For all education is an affair of action. Call before your mental eye any schoolroom and you see in imagination something going on, something being done. Even the schoolrooms in which silence and physical immobility are most insisted upon are still doing something. They are imposing these things as parts of a policy of action adapted to reach the ends which are prized. Instruction and discipline are modes of action. Now all truly human action involves preference. It signifies working for one end rather than for another in situations where alternatives exist. The chosen policy may be adopted on the basis of imitation and obedience to tradition, or it may be thought through and adopted on the basis of a clear view and decided choice of the ends and consequences which the policy serves. But preference for one kind of end and value is always there, because one kind of outcome rather than another is brought about as a consequence of action.

It is the business of a philosophy of education to make clear what is involved in the action which is carried on within the educational field, to transform a preference which is blind, based on custom rather than thought, into an intelligent choice —one made, that is, with consciousness of what is aimed at, the reasons why it is preferred, and the fitness of the means used. Nevertheless intelligent choice is still choice. It still involves preference for one kind of end rather than another one which might have been worked for. It involves a conviction that such and such an end is valuable, worth while, rather than another. Sincerity demands a maximum of impartiality in seeking and stating the reasons for the aims and the values which are chosen and rejected. But the scheme of education itself cannot be impartial in the sense of not involving a preference for some values over others. The obligation to be impartial is the obligation to state as clearly as possible what is chosen and why it is chosen. We have attempted to meet this obligation. We have set forth the values we believe education should strive to achieve in our own day in our own country, and we have stated the grounds of our choice. We believe that it will be helpful if those who disagree in practice, in the courses of action they are following, will also clarify and expose the grounds for their policies: in short, develop and formulate *their* philosophies of education.

So much in general. The point which most specifically follows is that some philosophy is implied in every educational measure and recommendation made as to every method of

teaching and discipline. There is no possible opposition therefore between that which is termed "science" and that which
is termed "philosophy" in education. For as soon as a science
is actually *used,* as soon as action based upon it occurs, then
values, consequences, enter in. Choice operates and produces
consequences. There are, then, philosophical implications, since
philosophy is a theory of values to be achieved and to be
rejected. But a conflict of *philosophies,* between a philosophy
and what purports to be a science, is both possible and actual.
For example, the presupposition of much of the work done in
the name of science is that there is no need for philosophy
itself. This view itself involves a decided philosophy. It does
so in at least three ways and directions. In the first place, since
the only thing to which factual science *can* be applied is something already in existence, there is a virtual assumption that
educational direction and progress rest upon analysis of existing practices with a view to rendering them more efficient.
The underlying philosophy is that it is the function of education to transmit and reproduce existing institutions—only
making them more efficient. This philosophy we deny.

In the second place, the assumption implicit in the method of
much of the work referred to is that processes and functions
with which education deals are isolable, because they are independent of one another. This involves the philosophical
notion that character, mental life, experience, and the methods
of dealing with them, are composed of separable parts and that
there is no whole, no integralness in them; that what seems
to be a unity is in reality nothing but an aggregate of parts.
This philosophy once dominated physical science. In physics
and biology its inadequacy from a scientific point of view is
now realized. Yet it has been taken over by that school of educational "science" which denies the importance of a philosophy
in conducting education. The ends and values which we regard
as the proper ends of choice in action are consistent only with

a philosophy which recognizes the basic importance of organization and patterns of integration.

The work done in the name of science (in the third place) during the recent period has been largely in connection with the *impersonal* phase of education, and has reduced personality as far as possible to impersonal terms. These terms do lend themselves most readily to factual and statistical treatment—but a non-social philosophy is implied. When it is acted upon, the implication becomes practically anti-social. It takes the individual out of the medium of associations and contexts in which he lives. It ignores social connections and bearings, and, in ignoring them, it invites that kind of educational policy which is in line with an outworn philosophy of individualism. Our philosophy, while accepting the results of authenticated scientific work, builds upon the idea that organisms, selves, characters, minds, are so intimately connected with their environments, that they can be studied and understood only in relation to them. The emphasis which is found in the previous pages upon the culture of a time and a community is, for example, one phase of this general philosophy.

We now come to the main content of our philosophy as far as that can be set forth in a brief number of explicit propositions.

I

Our position implies that a philosophy of education is a branch of social philosophy and, like every social philosophy, since it requires a choice of one type of character, experience, and social institutions, involves a *moral* outlook. Education, as we conceive it, is a process of social interaction carried on in behalf of consequences which are themselves social—that is, it involves interactions between persons and includes shared values. A frequent objection to this view rests upon a misunderstanding. It asserts that this conception fails to grasp the basic value of individuality. The reverse is the case. *Social* cannot be opposed in fact or in idea to *individual*. Society *is* individuals-in-their-relations. An individual apart from social relations is a myth—or a monstrosity. If we deal with actual individuals, and not with a conceptual abstraction, our position can be also formulated in these terms: Education is the process of realization of integrated individualities. For integration can occur only in and through a medium of association. Associations are many and diverse, and some of them are hostile to the realization of a full personality, they interfere with it and prevent it. Hence *for the sake of individual development,* education must promote some forms of association and community life and must work against others. Admit that education is concerned with a development of individual potentialities and you are committed to the conclusion that education cannot be neutral and indifferent as to the kind of social organization which exists. Individuals develop not in a remote entity called "society" at large but in connection *with one another.* The conditions of their association with one another, of their participation and communication, of their coöperation and competition, are set by legal, political, and economic arrangements. In the interest, therefore, of education—not of any preconceived "ism" or code—the fact is emphasized that education must operate in view of a deliberately preferred social order.

The criticisms made in previous pages of an individualistic philosophy do not imply depreciation of the value of individuality. On the contrary they assert that the form which the historic individualism of the eighteenth and the nineteenth centuries took is now adverse to the realization of individuality in and for *all.* It favors and supports legal and economic institutions which encourage an exaggerated and one-sided development of egoistic individuality in a privileged few, while militating against a full and fair opportunity for a normal individuality in the many.

It was implied in our introductory survey of the social demands made upon education to-day that the democratic way of life is that in which the identity of interest of the individual and the social is best realized. The democratic faith is individual in that it asserts the claims of every individual to the opportunity for realization of potentialities unhampered by birth, family status, unequal legal restrictions, and external authority. By the same token it has been social in character. It has recognized that this end for individuals cannot be attained save through a particular type of political and legal institutions. Historically, conditions emphasized at first the negative phase of this principle: the overthrow of institutions that were autocratic. It is now seen that the positive side of the principle needs attention: namely, the extension of democracy to the creation of the kind of institutions that will effectively and constructively serve the development of *all* individuals. It is at once obvious that this extension affects economic, as well as legal and political, institutions.

Social arrangements are to be judged ultimately by their educative effect, by what they do in the way of liberating, organizing, integrating the capacities of men and women, boys and girls. These capacities include esthetic factors, those which lie at the basis of music, literature, painting, architecture in both production and appreciation; intellectual and scientific power and taste; capacities for friendship; and capacities for appropriation and control of natural materials and energies. It is the function of education to see to it that individuals are so trained as to be capable of entering into the heritage of these values which already exist, trained also in sensitiveness to the defects of what already exists and in ability to recreate and improve. But neither of these ends can be adequately accomplished unless people are trained to grasp and be concerned about the effect of social institutions upon individual capacities, and this not just in general but in discriminating detail.

Philosophy has two definite factual bases, one individual, the other institutional. Each base is susceptible of scientific study. Psychology can study the matter from the side of the individual, asking how this and that environmental condition, especially in the human environment, affects the powers of this and that person; how it calls out, strengthens, furthers, or weakens and retards this and that potentiality. Since education is a process of human interactions, while physiology and other subjects may supply material, adequate educational psychology must be a *social* psychology, not an impersonal one. Also are institutions and social arrangements to be studied factually and scientifically. The study becomes *educationally* significant only when it is extended to include how this and that social condition works causally to modify the experience and affect the character and capacity of individuals who come under its influence.

II

While choice cannot be eliminated nor preference reduced to intellectual and logical entities, nevertheless concrete, positive material of experience affords the basis for making choice intelligent. The difference between intelligent and arbitrary choice is between a preference which does not know what it is about, which has not considered the meaning of what it prefers, namely, the consequences which will result from action, and one based on the preference which surveys conditions and probable results of the choice made. The social analyses and interpretations which are included in previous chapters set forth the rationale of the choice which determines our educational philosophy. We believe the reasonableness and validity of a choice can be judged by such tests as the following:

(1) Does the choice depend upon a survey and interpretation which discloses existing social conditions and trends? Does it, in short, rest upon genuine and thorough observation of the moving forces of a given state of social culture? (2) Does it sense and formulate the deeper and more intangible aspira-tions, purposes and values, for our own educational philosophy, in our own American scene and life? [1]

In holding that the values which should determine the direc-tion of education can be dug out of life-experience itself, we are denying by implication the position taken by some opposed types of philosophical theory. We affirm that genuine values and tenable ends and ideals are to be derived from what is found within the movement of experience. Hence we deny the views which assert that philosophy can derive them out of itself by excogitation, or that they can be derived from au-thority, human or supernatural, or from any transcendent source. Our analyses of social forces are made because of the bearing of these forces upon the choice of values and the insti-tution of purposes.

The position we take can be maintained only by recognizing that any existing society is marked by both negative and posi-tive values. Were there no values already experienced, there would be no material out of which to frame ends and ideals. But an end and ideal also imply something to be striven for, something therefore which is as yet non-existent. The aspect of an end which goes contrary to what exists does not come however out of the blue, or out of anything remote from actual experience. A man makes health an end because he has enjoyed it enough to know what it means and what it is to enjoy it. But he also has experienced lack of health and is aware that health is not automatic, that it has foes, and that

---

[1] Criticism of the philosophy we advance is likely, therefore, to be effective according as it centers upon, first, the criteria we employ, and, second, the correctness and adequacy of the use we have made of them in interpreting and recording the social situation in which we live.

it must therefore be pursued and cultivated. Values as they exist are often both obscure and conflicting. They neither lie on the surface nor constitute a self-coherent whole. If they did, education would be infinitely simpler than it is. The most urgent problems of current educational theory and practice grow out of the extraordinarily confused and conflicting state of values at the present time.

The conflict is practical; it involves clashes of individuals, of groups and classes. It can be resolved only where it exists, namely, in action. But action needs to be intelligent as to the values concerned, values negative and positive. Otherwise it will be more wasteful and destructive than it needs to be. Philosophy is the operation of studying the values at stake, of clearing up the understanding of them, of forming them in idea into a new integration, in which social forces will realize values in individual lives more broadly and equitably than at present. The formation of such a philosophy is instrumental rather than final. That is to say, it observes, criticizes, and integrates values in thought in order to determine and guide the action which will integrate them in fact.[2] A philosophy based upon actual experience is so framed, in other words, as to react, through the plan of action which it projects, back into an experience which is directly realized and not merely conceived. Moreover, it is not implied that philosophy comes to completion as a preliminary and that then action takes place afterwards. There is a continuing interaction. The intellectual formulation develops from the vague to the definite through the action which it suggests and directs, and there is no end to this process. Philosophy develops as society does. It does not provide a substitute for the values which life contributes, but it does enter—vitally, if it performs its proper function— into the very social process in which values are generated and

[2] The relation between thought and action receives explicit attention below.

realized. A philosophy of education may thus be truly said to be general philosophy formulated with particular reference to its social office.

III

A goal cannot be intelligently set forth apart from the path which leads to it. Ends cannot be conceived as operative ends, as directors of action, apart from consideration of conditions which obstruct and means which promote them. If stated at large, apart from means, ends are empty. Ends may begin as the plan and purpose in the rough. This is useful if it leads to search for and discovery of means. So the otherwise bare idea of building a house may be the first stage in thinking out detailed plans and specifications for its erection, and thus be translated over into a statement of means.

The necessary relation between means and ends explains the attention we have given to the economic phase of society. Our emphasis does not imply that economic values are superior as *values*. But economic forces are at the present time superior to others in causal power. They condition what people can do and how they can develop more than do other forces. Moreover, the habit of separating economic interests from ideal interests affords a typical instance of the too common separation of means and ends, with the result that ideals become empty and impotent, while means, left to themselves in isolation from service to ends, produce brutal and unjust consequences. The emphasis laid upon the economic is not due therefore to any *a priori* theory of its necessary importance but is due to the power of economic factors in contemporary culture. Because of the organic relation of ends and means and because the economic is so potent both as potential means for values and as a retarding and distorting force, and because it is the means most susceptible of modification by concerted effort, it is, strategically, the key at present to other values.

There are many grounds on which people associate together and there are many ends for which they associate. We do not imply in our emphasis upon the economic side of present social life that economic ends are the only things which bring people together. More particularly the American people have shown that they are peculiarly apt at entering into association; they are given to organizing and joining social groups, quite independent of direct economic aims. But we find that this ability is arrested and deflected into wrong channels by an economy in which a system of mass production and distribution is subordinated to gaining pecuniary profit. This particular example may serve as an illustration of a whole group of cases in which forms of social coöperation and participation are shunted aside and deformed by a predominant economic force.

One case is, however, so striking that it will be singled out for especial remark. Attention was called earlier to the way in which scientific values are restricted and kept down by subordination to pecuniary values. The case of art and esthetic value is even more significant. No one can doubt that art and appreciation are among the values which preëminently enrich experience and make life worth living. So true is this that no question probes deeper into any culture than inquiry as to how it stands with reference to the creative arts and esthetic enjoyment. But here again values are vacuous and impotent as ends in the degree in which they lack means for expansion.

It is customary, for example, to refer the relatively low level of esthetic use of leisure time in this country, as reflected in the movie, radio, and amusement generally, to an inherently low grade of taste. This explanation leaves out of account the commercialization which uses these things to make money instead of to serve the values involved. As long as the conditioning means remain unchanged, there is little benefit likely to accrue from eulogizing fine art no matter how ecstatic the admiration. When conditions confine the development of taste to a privileged few, its status in the community will be that of a contrast effect with the things of ordinary life. Popular art will then be a rebound to stimulation and excitement from those activities of working hours which lack freedom and meaning. Art will be a widespread enhancement of the joy and significance of living only when economic barriers do not switch it off to the esoteric for the few and the sensational for the many. The humanizing of the economic system will detract from the power of the acquisitive and add to that of the creative aspect of life. It will surely prove more efficacious in extending the scope of the arts than any amount of praise of them uttered in the face of forces which keep persons aloof from their enjoyment, and which induce disregard of the ugly as long as it is not shown to be pecuniarily unprofitable. Thus in the case of two things as far apart seemingly as the poles, material economy and ideal art, the connection of means with values that are ends is strikingly demonstrated. The liberation of individual creative activity and elevation of esthetic taste which would follow the reconstruction of the economic system is moreover an illustration of the position we have taken as to the relation of individual and social.

IV

The problem of the relation of knowledge and action equals in importance that of the individual and the social. For we live in a world wherein we have to act, where action is imperative and unescapable but where knowledge is conditional, dependent upon ourselves. And the consequences of action, that is, what comes from it and remains as a permanent deposit, depend—within limits at least—upon whether or not action is informed with knowledge and is guided by adequate intelligence. Even the will to refrain from acting, to withdraw from the scene of action, is itself, in the end, but one policy and mode of action.

Because the necessity for action is unescapable, there is one question of supreme importance: What is its dominating method and spirit? A survey of the field shows that in fact there are many methods used to regulate action. There is the method of external authority dictating conformity to its requirements under penalty of suffering. There is the method of custom, of walking by precedents of the past. There is the method of routine, of persisting automatically, without asking for a reason, in paths worn deep, smooth, and easy by long repetition. There is the method of self-interest of individuals or of a class dressed up to look like public service. There is the method of trial by force to see which is stronger in cannon and gunpowder, or in command of money and credit.

History shows that all of these methods have been more widely used and more influential in the life of humanity than has the method of knowledge and intelligence. Speaking in general terms, life is characterized by a gap between knowledge and conduct, by separation between theory and practice. This divorce between the two is "rationalized" in the philosophies which have hitherto been most influential in thought. These have glorified knowledge as an end in itself, something divine, superior to the vicissitudes of experience, while at the same time they have depreciated the importance of action, connecting it with a realm of existence which is transitory, related to the body and material interests rather than to mind and ideal things, connected with mundane affairs instead of with pure truth. On the other hand, a so-called practical people have condemned theory as an idle and impotent luxury. They have put their trust in superior force and covert stratagem.

Some separation between intelligence and action is unavoidable in a world wherein action often cannot wait, and where it plunges ahead into the novel. But professed theorist and professed practical man have deliberately widened the gap. Thinkers have not seen channels by which their ideas could be translated into effective action. They have, by way of compensation, proclaimed that ideas are too fine and pure to be sullied by contact with the baser conditions of practice. "Practical" people have been content to take thinkers at their word. They have borrowed what they wanted of what thinkers have found out, and turned it to their own account in managing affairs to their own advantage.

The gulf between thought and conduct, knowledge and action, was not originated by philosophers, though they have celebrated it hitherto as a good. It began in primitive days when there was no knowledge in existence competent to control affairs outside a small area of immediate necessities. Methods which grew up under those conditions, compounded of magic, authority backed by force, and a rule-of-thumb empiricism, persisted because of the inertia of custom and because these methods could be laid hold of to maintain privilege and vested interest. They subtly displayed their power by patronizing philosophy, art, science, and religion as long as these remained practically innocuous.

The schools as special instrumentalities of education have upon the whole adopted the principle of the divorce of knowledge and practice and have conformed to it. In so doing they have maintained the division and widened the rift. "Practice" has consisted in repetition of actions in which more emphasis is placed on mechanical accuracy than on understanding. Acquisition of automatic skill has been aimed at apart from conscious purpose in the minds of those performing the exercises. It was supposed that skill would then be ready for use when some reason for its use developed later in life. "Efficiency" in doing has been made a goal irrespective of *what* efficiency is for.

Knowledge, on the other hand, has been treated as accumulation of information with little reference to perceived bearing of what is acquired. The criterion for the selection of particular bodies of information taught has been some standard of the past regarding culture or utility, rather than connection with the values of the active present. The emphasis on information apart from purposed bearing and application has affected the governing concepts of learning and its methods. The former has been thought of as something stored in books and the heads of learned men, and the latter as transmission by a kind of scholastic pipe-line into the minds of pupils whose business is to absorb what is transmitted.

Aside from being a definite illustration in a particular case of what is involved in the separation of theory and practice, the instance cited is of importance because of its social effect. Many of those who have had their habits formed on the basis of repetitions designed to give specific skills, carry away a permanent division in their make-up. They are habituated on one side to routine activity; they fall into lines of conduct the reason for which they do not see and the purpose of which is fixed by others. They are not used to judging for themselves and forming purposes on their own account. They thus readily become later in life passive instruments in execution of the plans and desires of others, perpetuating one of the evil features of our economic system. They become factory-fodder, as in militaristic autocracies individuals are trained to be cannon-fodder. Mass production of this type of mentality compromises in advance the success of political democracy.

On the other side, the important phases of conduct cannot be reduced to acquisition of specific skills. The most significant factors in conduct are general patterns of desire and appreciation. These are not touched by routine exercises. Here too comes into play the fallacy of psychologies which try to build a whole out of an aggregation of specific but isolated parts.

Basic appetites are left undisciplined even though the motto of this type of school practice is "discipline." The deeper and more inclusive drives and moving forces are not cultivated and hence find accidental and unregulated outlet. The social effect is that youth having an unusual amount of untrained energy to dispose of fall readily into careers of revolt and potential crime; those with more moderate equipment become a ready prey to external stimulations. They grow into seekers after dissipation and excitement in order to obtain a simulation of a fulfilment of themselves which is denied them in the monotony of routine occupations.

From many angles, the separation of intelligence and practice tends to maintain the *status quo*. Change which is inevitable in any case is left to accident and external pressure. Instead of having a process of continuous self-repair on the part of society, corresponding to a continuous reconstruction of experience in the individual, we have periods of undue conservatism alternating with shorter periods of unregulated change. Only the acknowledgment, first in idea and then in practical fact, of the intimate union of theory and practice, knowledge and action, can create a society having foresight and the capacity to plan so as to regulate the inevitable processes of change.

The significant fact is that it is now possible, perhaps for the first time in human history, honestly to develop and act upon the conception of the union, instead of the separation, of thought and practice. So far as the past is concerned, the philosophies that assumed a separation were honest intellectual reports of the actual situation. Social institutions were so governed by authority, tradition, and precedent, along with possession of power by a small class, that such an ideal (as Plato for example advanced) of control of social action by understanding and insight was purely utopian. Nor did the fault lie exclusively on the side of practical conditions. The

pursuit of knowledge and the state of thought did not permit
the development of techniques for their effective operation in
action. Intellectual activity was so driven back upon itself that
it is not surprising that thinkers who were preëminently occupied with it produced by way of compensation the theory of
its intrinsic superiority to practice and the need for keeping it
"pure"—that is, aloof—in order that its superior value might
not be tarnished and diluted.

For reasons which will be stated below, this situation has
now changed both from the side of social conditions and from
the side of the pursuit of knowledge. On the economic side, an
advanced industrial country such as the United States is passing from a deficit to a surplus economy. So intellectually we
are passing from an epoch in which knowledge and understanding were the precarious possession of a small class, and
had to be guarded and cherished lest the flame die out, into an
era in which scientific knowledge breaks through into control
of actual conditions in the technological field, while there are
at hand techniques by which a similar control can be developed
and applied in other and broader fields.

A small class devoted to distinctively intellectual pursuits—
in science and philosophy—have always found the cultivation
of thought and extension of knowledge of priceless value. To
those who enjoy these things, no other enjoyments offer comparable values. To them, thought and learning are in a very
genuine sense ends in themselves. No theory of the intimate
connection of thought and action can deprive such persons of
this legitimate and precious good. But a value cannot be converted on the ground of private appreciation into a theory of
the structure, nature, and function of thought and knowledge.
Logically, such a conversion is on a par with the conduct of
those who enjoying lower, more sensual goods make their personal satisfaction in these things a measure of the status and
purpose of values in the structure of the universe. The in-

trinsic structure and function of knowledge cannot be fixed from the side of personal appreciation, but only from an examination of thought and knowledge themselves. Moreover, in the past only a few have been so constituted by temperament and so placed by circumstances that they could enjoy distinctively intellectual values. Even from the side of personal appreciation, then, there is responsibility for a change of conditions that will enable many more to share in the enjoyment.

Action, we repeat, goes on anyway. It will continue as long as life endures. The only way to arrest it is to destroy human life itself. Upon action of one sort or another depend all consequences in the way of realization of values, and of their prevention and depreciation. There is no genuine alternative between action and withdrawal from action. The only alternatives are between different methods of action. He would be a bold person who would deny that, were it possible, knowledge and thought offer a better method for directing action than do external authority, self-interest and the vested interest of a privileged class, reliance on imitation and precedent, or violent force and so on. Few would deny, I think, that *if* intelligence could be raised to the position of the controlling method of action, it would change social life to an extent not short of revolutionary. Few would deny that if and when intelligence were once installed in this rôle, the conservation and extension of its function would become an object of supreme consideration.

The basic question is, then, one of fact. Is it possible for intelligence informed by knowledge to be a fundamentally significant method of projecting and directing action, individual and collective? Certain objections and misunderstandings will be considered later. At this point we shall consider some reasons why the possibility is within the bounds of reasonable endeavor at the present time. The consideration of these reasons will also disclose the nature of intelligence conceived as method of action.

V

The development of the natural sciences since the seventeenth century has demonstrated the falsity of the idea that reason and thought apart from action can issue in valid knowledge. The primary bond of union of thought with existence or "reality" is action. These statements do not rest upon opinion but upon the observed fact that the progress of natural knowledge has been made constant and secure only by the adoption of the experimental method. Thought *suggests* a course and way of acting so as to effect a change of conditions. The execution of the procedure which is suggested effects consequences which enable the validity of the idea to be judged and which bring about its further development. In this way thought is converted into authentic knowledge. The process by its very nature is self-continuing. Ideas must be framed in a form which will indicate acts to be performed and the interpretation to be put upon their consequences. Here is the criterion which controls the operations of thinking and the development of ideas. Consideration of their applicability to action in the two ways just mentioned gives the criterion for selection and rejection among the multitude of suggestions and fancies which vegetate and come to birth in mind. Think in terms of action and in terms of *those* acts whose consequences will expand, revise, test, your ideas and theories. This is the first commandment of the experimental method. It is by observation of this commandment that thinking, inquiry, observation, and interpretation have been rendered fruitful in progressive knowledge of nature.

On the other hand, action, doing, when directed by ideas, brings new facts to light and thus ensures the progress of thought and the generation of new knowledge. Before and apart from the use of experimental method, new facts were merely stumbled upon. Their disclosure was a matter of accident. And what is even more important, they did not find their proper place in a larger system. They remained isolated or else they were forced by thought into some merely intellectual scheme and system. Facts which are discovered by the use of experimental observation, on the other hand, either fall naturally into place because the ideas instigating the experiment of which they are the fruit supply their natural context; or, if what is discovered is unexpected and inconsistent with those ideas, new ideas are suggested that lead to new experiments. In either case, they do not remain a surd and perplexity but they help define a problem for further inquiry.

This revolutionary change in thought and knowledge, this complete shift from aloofness from action over to adoption of action into the very structure and procedure of thought and knowledge, makes necessary a reconsideration of all beliefs and traditions based on the assumption that the gulf between knowledge and action is intrinsic and final. We can go further than this statement. As a matter of fact, in certain limited but important fields it is demonstrated that intelligence and action can be effectively wedded, and control of conditions brought about. In these fields, we have not the possibility but the accomplished actuality of knowledge being the authorized method of action.

Reference is here made, of course, to the field of inventions which have taken place as a direct product of the advance in natural knowledge that is due to the experimental method. The telephone, telegraph, radio, steam locomotive, electric light, dynamo, internal combustion engine, automobile, and airplane are, for example, so many exhibits testifying to the reality, already effected, of knowledge as instrumentality of action. Our entire machine age and its technology is the same testimony written large.

This situation of accomplished fact suggests, and in an emphatic way, the possibility of extension of the same union to the wider social field. If we can effect the use of intelligence as method of control in the physical and mechanical field, why should we not strive to develop it in the field of human relations? Moreover, the social effects of the limited and more technical control that has been effected do more than suggest the possibility of a wider and deeper moral application. They create an urgent need, a necessity, that it be done. The contrast which exists between insight, foresight, and direction in the physical and in the human territories has become a commonplace. It is almost equally a commonplace that because of this contrast, it is not yet decided whether the control that has been effected in the physical field is to be a blessing or a curse: whether, in other words, the machine and its technology are to be the servants or the masters of mankind. What is not so generally recognized is that the heart of the problem is whether the experimental method can be made as fundamental in social knowledge and action as it now is in physical. If it cannot, the split between mere drift in human affairs and mastery in material things is bound to widen, and possibly to result in the destruction of civilization.

Just what is the experimental method which has brought forth such fruit and such continued possibility of fruit-bearing in the physical sciences? If experiment means simply trying, there is nothing new about it. Life itself is an experiment; everything we undertake is experimental in one way or another. When the most assured dogmatist starts out to act in conformity with his dogma, he may have some private and subjective certainty as to the rightness and beneficence of his course. He may deem it absolutely warranted by the assured truths which he assumes that he possesses. But actually he is *trying* something. He cannot absolutely guarantee the consequences of what he does. His dogma will not guarantee them in fact. It will only blind his eyes to many bad results of his action and prevent his learning anything from what he does. The outsider, when he looks at what is going on in another country, say Russia or Italy, spontaneously speaks of them as experiments, as trials. Even though they may seem to be something else to some of those engaged in them, that is what they are. In a world where there is as much complexity and contingency as there is in our world, it is true both that action is necessary and that action must be experimental, a trying.

Experimental method, in the sense in which we have referred to it, is then something different from the bare fact of the omnipresence of uncertain trial in all action. The difference is that between experiment which is aware of what it is about and experiment which ignores conditions and consequences. Empirical action in the sense in which *empirical* is applied to the practice of a physician who is guided by custom, by accumulation of particular past experiences rather than by scientific insight, is experimental in a sense, but distinctly *not* that of experimental *method*.

Experimental method is the universal and inescapable fact of *experimentation become conscious of itself and so directing action by this consciousness.* It is opposed to dogmatism, to empiricism as the rule of custom, to authoritarianism, to personal egoism, etc. But also it has a positive content of its own.

In the first place, every experimentation which is not aware that it is a trial operates in a world of unknowns, of contingencies and uncertainties, without taking that fact into account. Or if it does take it into account it deals with it through magic—which includes for our present purpose every ritual and formula blindly adhered to. Experimental method takes honest account of the fact of contingency by consciously propounding and defining a *problem* as the base from which action proceeds. Experimental method converts the conditions which bring about uncertainty into terms of a definite question to be asked, a definite problem to be resolved. It recognizes that uncertainty is inevitable and then turns it to positive account. For it searches for data which will first enable us to pose a question, and then to think of a course of action which will help us find the answer to the question. Experimental method thus teaches us how to deal with doubt. We do not cover it up and deny its existence. We are to cultivate it. But we are not to cherish it, as ancient skeptics did, as an end in itself. It then tends to paralyze action. We are to cherish doubt as but the first stage in the development of a question so put that it will direct action to the discovery of facts which will answer the question.

In the second place, experimentation which is so conscious as to take proper account of itself operates on the basis of an idea. This idea is used as an *hypothesis*. That is, it is employed as directive of action for the sake of the consequences which action produces, and which when produced indicate how to proceed next. Experimental method is fatal to dogmatism because it shows that all ideas, conceptions, theories, however extensive and self-consistent and esthetically attractive they may be, are to be entertained provisionally until they have been tested by acting upon them. To state the fact in its full force, ideas prior to active test are intellectually significant only as guides and as plans of *possible actions*. The actions when undertaken produce consequences which test, expand, and modify the ideas previously tentatively entertained. The experimental method is thus opposed once and for all to all methods which claim to be sure-fire.

Persons of natural energy are urged on by their very energy to action. This urge to direct action, to doing something right away, is a chief psychological cause of inclination to dogmatic belief. Uncertainty is a hindrance; it defers overt action. Curiosity, inquiry, reflection, examination, all postpone it. So a person having strong bent toward doing things is impatient of thought. He tends to lay hold of any belief or theory which will justify him in going ahead full steam. Now the experimental method does not sickly over this determination to action by the pale cast of thought. It rather would utilize it, while giving it a new temper through enforcing upon it recognition of need for keeping track of the consequences of what is done, and modifying the further progress of action accordingly. It does not propose thought as a substitute for action, but rather the introduction of thought into action as its directive principle.

Finally, a marked trait of experimental method is its introduction of the principle of degree and measure. It puts probability in place of what claims to be the absolute, and endeavors to measure degrees of probability. It recognizes the extent to which different and alternative possibilities enter into action. In pursuing the chosen one, it does not slam the door in the face of others. It renders action more alert and wary. For before thought passes into action a number of alternative hypotheses are considered and practice is thus rendered flexible and readaptable when need for change of direction shows itself. Firmness is required in order that the consequences of action may be adequately instructive, but firmness is not allowed to become so rigid that it moves fatalistically to an uncriticized end.

VI

The meaning of experimental method may be further developed by considering certain objections and misunderstandings which are more or less current. Almost all of these have a common source. Old ideas that are deeply embedded have a kind of inertia and momentum of their own. They are not only difficult to displace by newer ideas, but they are employed to interpret new ideas even when the latter are intended to replace them. Most of the objections we are about to consider spring, ironically enough, from reading into the new conception of intelligence, reached by connecting it with action, the old conception of reason and intellect whose meaning was formed by keeping them separate from action. The new conception of intelligence is treated as if it were the old "intellect" with merely a new function added. Of course defects and contradictions are then found in it.

First, there is the radical misconception which assumes that the method makes action just as action an end in itself. The previous discussion should have rendered this mistake so obvious that it may briefly be disposed of. It is action informed by knowledge and guided by an operative idea or working hypothesis which is commended, and such action is instrumental to the disclosure of new facts for new observation and enjoyment, and to the evocation of more significant ideas. Both *knowing and acting* as such are ultimately instrumental to the protection, expansion, and installation of values to be directly experienced.

The second misunderstanding is of an opposite nature, though sometimes both are joined in the same person. The operational theory of knowledge and action holds, as we have seen, that ends and ideals must not be sought in the blue; that they are to be reached through inquiry into existing conditions taken both as obstacles and as potential means. This intellectual acknowledgment of the existent state of things is conceived by some critics to be a commendation of a policy of conformity and servile acceptance. This conclusion would follow naturally from the conception of thought as something isolated from action. But in experimental philosophy this intellectual acknowledgment is a preliminary stage in the formation of a method of action which will bring about *change* in the existing state of affairs. To form relevant and effective ideals we must first be acquainted with and take notice of actual conditions. Otherwise our ideals become vacuous or else filled with a content drawn from Utopia. Existent conditions do not determine the end and purpose. They determine the *problem* with which a purpose has to deal. In forming the purpose, there is room for all the imagination and all the adventure which any mind can bring to the situation. Indeed, there is a positive demand for imagination, and no limits are set to its flight except that its product be capable of application in action to bring about a changed state of affairs. Even this limitation permits objects of other flights to remain for private esthetic enjoyment. But it protects ideals in this aspect from being confused with ends that are valid to intelligence. Thus it prevents action from being itself so confused as to invite deception and insincerity.

The third point is so similar that it needs only brief mention. The experimental theory connects thought biologically with attempts at adaptation which are characteristic of all animal life. The statement of the theory was accompanied by pointing to the radical difference between the kind of adaptation which takes place through the medium of thought and that which takes place without thought through mere habituation. Yet the experimental theory is charged with teaching the doctrine of accommodation to whatever exists in any potent degree. Actually the experimental philosophy signifies (as was pointed out in its first statement) that genuine experimental action effects an adjustment *of* conditions, not *to* them: a remaking of existing conditions, not a mere remaking of self and mind to fit into them. Intelligent adaptation is always a *re*adjustment, a re-construction of what exists.

In the fourth place, as already indicated, the adoption of intelligence as the very heart of a philosophy of action does not exclude firmness of conviction nor daring. It rather affirms that convictions must be firm *enough* to evoke and justify action, while also they are to be held in a way which permits the individual to learn from his further experience. It implies that every sound conviction will be confirmed, in the degree of its soundness, by subsequent experience. It trusts to convictions which are firm because con-firmed in experience rather than those which are intense mainly because of immaturity. At the same time it recognizes that maturity often leads to the limitations of rigid fixation, and that inexperience and ignorance when animated by sincerity are often capable of thoughts and adventures of which a mind closed in by habit and indurated by past experiences is incapable.

Fifth, the philosophy is not one of opportunism. As opportunism is usually understood, it implies that only small situations are recognized and dealt with in thought and action, small in the sense of being rather narrowly limited in place and of short span in time. Experimentalism recognizes that extent, like depth, is a function of the situation dealt with. There exists a whole nest of situations varying in inclusiveness and scope. Continuity is a chief trait of situations which demand intelligent action. Consequences abide and are cumulative. Hypotheses of great comprehensiveness and long-time span are therefore imperatively needed. They form the larger policies and define the more enduring ends of conduct. All that is demanded by the logic of the experimental philosophy is that whether the situation be small or great, and the guiding idea of near-by or far-off application, the spirit of hypothesis and experiment enter into the procedure for managing it.

Sixth, the method is not identical with a sweet reasonableness in which sweetness in the sense of weak compromise is more evident than reasonableness. The kind of measure to be undertaken in any particular situation is a function of *that* situation. It cannot be derived from the general concept of method. Just because the experimental method has *not* been operative to any great extent in the past in social affairs, social situations are marked by conflicts of interest in which force, open and underhand, is used by those occupying privileged positions. The method of intelligence requires that we open our eyes instead of shutting them to these conflicts, for they are an inexorable part of the conditions to be acknowledged intellectually and dealt with practically. The method of action employed in such situations cannot, if it is the method of intelligence, be identical in detail with that which will be followed when intelligence has already obtained a greater foothold. For example, experience shows that the method of violent action has usually been so wasteful that the antecedent presumption is against it. But an experimental philosophy as such cannot absolutely prejudge this case any more than it can any other. As far as experience and reflection indicate that pacific measures are most likely to be effective, the philosophy is pacifist; where the reverse is indicated by the best available knowledge of actual conditions, it is revolutionary. All that the method intrinsically calls for is that neither extreme be made so absolute a doctrine that it obstructs inquiry and pushes the plan of action in advance into prejudged channels. Both absolute pacificism and absolute progress reached only through class struggle suffer from the same disease. Neither of them is consistent with experimentalism. Even those persons who hold with either of them usually have certain exceptional cases in reserve at the back of their minds.

Finally, it is not true that the method is intellectualistic or that it exaggerates the place of thought, inquiry, observation at the expense of emotion, desire, and impulse. This misunderstanding is perhaps the best illustration to be found of the effect of carrying over into experimental philosophy a conception of intellect framed on the basis of separation from action. Were there such a thing as intellect or reason all by itself, then a method based upon it would be fatally exposed to this objection. There is no doubt that careful discrimination and acute criticism, that clarification of ideas and integration of them into a coherent whole, follow from the experimental method. But what equally follows (but is overlooked by the objection) is that these exist only as they operate with and in the material which demands action. Since they have no existence by themselves but only *in* the material of the concrete situation, they are colored throughout by the quality of that material. If that calls out ardor and enthusiasm, repulsion and disgust, then thinking is impregnated with these emotions. The very idea of the method implies *interest* in the situation and its constituents, whether positive or negative, desire or aversion. All that the method demands of emotion is that it be not permitted to swamp and suppress thought and observation; or, stated positively, that emotion be employed to intensify and stimulate the intellectual as well as the overt phase of the action undertaken.

The idea that people have ever been emotionally indifferent in the degree in which they are intellectually aroused is contradicted by the facts of all productive intellectual activity. The contrary idea is probably due to traditional philosophies and psychologies that have cherished a conception of intellect as something outside the situation in which action is to occur, and to the correct inference that *such* an intellect would necessarily be "cold": intellectual and nothing but intellectual. Since intelligence as the method of action is what it is as the method, the how, *of* a particular scene of action, it will share in all the excitement involved in the active situation. It may be passionate to any degree—provided it be intelligent passion.

VII

If method could be separated from the subject-matter in which it operates, then experimental method would be neutral as respects any particular type and condition of social life and equally applicable in any and every one of them. As a matter of fact, a complete and adequate operation of the method is consistent only with certain types of society, because method and subject-matter stand in one-to-one correspondence with each other. A *truncated, one-sided* application of the method may be found, it is true, in any situation; it may be used even in behalf of anti-social measures. The children of darkness are often wiser than the children of light, and a predatory character may use the experimental method in a *limited* field more effectually than a would-be benevolent person in a wider field. But only when intelligence is not accepted as the *central* virtue can we stop short with a particular limited use of it. The choice of intelligence as the preferred method of action implies, like every choice, a definite *moral* outlook. The scope of this choice is so inclusive that the moral implication outlines, when followed out, an entire ethical and social philosophy. In our philosophy of education, its two main constituents, the relationships of the social and the individual and of knowledge and action, coalesce in this conclusion.

In the first place, the experimental method cannot be made an effective reality in its full adequacy except in a certain kind of society. A society which includes warring class interests will always fight against its application outside of a particular limited field. Sinister class interests flourish better in the dark. If the free play of intelligence were not intrinsically a foe of their schemes, they would not fear it as they do, and they would not attempt by continuous propaganda to palm off substitutes for it. The social implication of the philosophy of intelligence may be judged from the fact that its opposite is obscurantism, while obscurantism is the chief ally of social abuses, corruptions, and iniquities. The objective precondition of the complete and free use of the method of intelligence is a society in which class interests that recoil from social experimentation are abolished. It is incompatible with every social and political philosophy and activity and with every economic system which accepts the class organization and vested class interest of present society.

The positive side of this statement is that life based on experimental intelligence provides the only possible opportunity for *all* to develop rich and diversified experience, while also securing continuous coöperative give and take and intercommunication. The method cannot be fully established in life unless the right of every person to realization of his potential capacities is effectively recognized. For without this condition the full material for judgment of values in action will be absent. Every bar to free communication from one to another has precisely the same limiting effect. There are marked differences between the experimental method in physical and in human matters. But one phase of physical science is significant for our purposes. Science progresses because a discovery made by one inquirer is at once made available for all workers in the field. Without constant exchange and mutual reinforcement, the science of nature would still be in a rudimentary state. Free communication on one side signifies power to receive and to participate in values on the other side. The great problem of society is to combine a maximum of different values, achieved by giving free play to individual taste and capacity, with a minimum of friction and conflict. The experimental method solves this problem as no other method can.

The experimental method is the only one compatible with the democratic way of life, as we understand it. Every extension of intelligence as the method of action enlarges the area of common understanding. Understanding may not ensure complete agreement, but it gives the only sound basis for enduring agreement. In any case where there is a difference, it will conduce to agreement to differ, to mutual tolerance and sympathy, pending the time when more adequate knowledge and better methods of judging are at hand. It is impossible to estimate the full import of the method on the basis of present conditions. The present economic organization stimulates the use of experiment in one-sided ways restricted to technical fields: those of machinery in the service of profit. This economic organization will itself be modified by extension of the method. Every accomplished extension will extend the variety and scope of human experience; it will liberate and intensify the processes of coöperative exchange and sharing of values. The adequate installation of the method in life would result in such an identification of the method with the values which it ensures that its own value would then be a matter of sight and not, as now, of faith and idea.

It is possible to put the processes of social change and of education in opposition to one another, and then debate whether desirable social change would follow education, or whether radical social change must come before marked improvements in education can take place. We hold that the two are correlative and interactive. No social modification, slight or revolutionary, can endure except as it enters into the action of a people through their desires and purposes. This introduction and perpetuation are effected by education. But every improvement in the social structure and its operations releases the educative resources of mankind and gives them a better opportunity to enter into normal social processes so that the latter become themselves more truly educative.

The process of interaction is circular and never-ending. We plead for a better, a more just, a more open and straightforward, a more public, society, in which free and all-round communication and participation occur as a matter of course in order that education may be bettered. We plead for an improved and enlarged education in order that there may be brought into existence a society all of whose operations shall be more genuinely educative, conducive to the development of desire, judgment, and character. The desired education cannot occur within the four walls of a school shut off from life.

Education must itself assume an increasing responsibility for participation in projecting ideas of social change and taking part in their execution in order to be educative. The great problem of American education is the discovery of methods and techniques by which this more direct and vital participation may be brought about. We have conceived that the office of a philosophy of education at the present time is to indicate this pressing need and to sketch the lines on which alone, in our conception, it can be met. The method of experimental intelligence as the method of action cannot be established as a constant and operative habit of mind and character apart from education. But it cannot be established *within* education except as the activities of the latter are founded on a clear idea of the active social forces of the day, of what they are doing, of their effect, for good and harm, upon values, and except as this idea and ideal are acted upon to direct experimentation in the currents of social life that run outside the school and that condition the effect and determine the educational meaning of whatever the school does.

INDEX

Action, regulation of, by intelligence, 59ff., 66ff., 69f.; non-intelligent ways, 299. *See also* Knowledge and action
Adjusting "to" conditions, 67, 312
Administration, school, centralization of authority, 214ff.; democratic conception, 237ff.; discussed, 213-56 (Chap. VII); education of administrators, 282ff.; modeled after business, 227ff.; place of teachers, 213, 218ff., 237ff., 242; school and parents, 251ff.; stress on "efficiency," 209f., 220f. *See also* Board of Education; School
Adult education, continuing necessity, 123f., 130f.; defined, 131; discussed, 122-59 (Chap. IV); for the underprivileged, 144; in Delaware, 143, 157; in Massachusetts, 143; in ordinary life, 132ff.; intelligent citizenship, 130, 131f., 135f., 144f., 155f.; in Wisconsin, 143; new demands for, 122ff., organization of, 156ff.; professional *vs.* whole population, 130, 134; responsibility of the profession, 130, 131f., 133f. *See also* Adult learning
Adult learning, Thorndike on, 151
Advertising, educationally considered, 137f.
American Association of Adult Education, referred, to, 156, 158
American Association of University Women, referred to, 141
Antioch College, alternating plan, 247
Arnold, Matthew, quoted, 12
Art, as related to the economic, 297f.; as escape, 66. *See also* Esthetic capacities
Atomism in educational theory, 209f., 258, 260, 289f., 301f.

Attitudes, social, in school, 172-77; in teachers' colleges, 259ff., 266ff., 269f.
Authority, its waning power, 10f., 122f.

Board of Education, discussed, 215ff., 221ff., 253ff.
Bobbitt, Franklin, quoted, 226n., 227n.

Child Study groups, referred to, 143
Citizens, education of, 130, 131f., 135f., 144f., 155f., 160. *See also* Adult education
Clapp, Elsie, referred to, 243
Compartmentalization, in American life, 5f.; in school work, 5ff., 15ff., 25, 184f., 204
Competition, in life, 200; in school, 69, 201f.; once moral, 40f.
Conflicts in society, produced by modern industry, 55, 123f.; protected by compartmentalization, 6ff.; reduced by shared planning, 65; reflected in education, 20ff., 32, 199ff. *See also* Confusion of thought
Confusion of thought, brought by breakdown of authority, 122f.; brought by industrialization, 32, 35, 50, 53, 54ff., 123f.; in culture, 73; in education, 1-31 (Chap. I), 34ff.; in society, 32, 34ff., 65, 161, 172, 183f. *See also* Conflicts in society
Correspondence schools, 141
Counts, George S., quoted, 65, 244, 254, 254n., 255
Cubberly, Ellwood P., quoted, 215, 216, 218f., 224f.
Cultural lag, bad effect of, 49f., 59f., 63f.